BARKER PLAYS TWO

Howard Barker

# PLAYS TWO

THE CASTLE
GERTRUDE – THE CRY
ANIMALS IN PARADISE
13 OBJECTS

OBERON BOOKS
LONDON

First published in this collection in 2006
by Oberon Books Ltd
521 Caledonian Road, London N7 9RH
Tel: 020 7607 3637 / Fax: 020 7607 3629
e-mail: info@oberonbooks.com
www.oberonbooks.com

*The Castle* first published in Great Britain by John Calder
(Publishers) Limited in 1990

A catalogue record for this book is available from the British
Library.

ISBN: 1 84002 648 0

Cover image and design: Dan Steward

Printed in Great Britain by Antony Rowe Ltd, Chippenham.

# Contents

# THE CASTLE
## A Triumph

*What is Politics, but the absence*
*of Desire…?*

# Characters

STUCLEY, a Knight

BATTER, a Servant

KRAK, an Engineer

SKINNER, a Witch

ANN, a Changed Woman

NAILER, a Priest

CANT, a Villager

HUSH, a Villager

SPONGE, a Villager

HOLIDAY, a Builder

BRIAN, a Builder's Mate

POOL, a Circuit Judge

SOLDIERS

PRISONERS

WOMEN

# ACT ONE

## SCENE ONE

*A Hill. A MAN, wrapped against the rain, stares into a valley. A SECOND MAN enters. He stares at the first.*

BATTER: Thinking, this is a puddle, this is. This is a wet and bone-wrecking corner of Almighty negligence. Thinking, oh, these shifting sheets of dropping damp. Christ, I did wrong to, or Mohammed, is it? Oh, my sun, my date trees, you poor bugger, out of hot bricked yards and cool mosaics, YOU HAVE TO BE A GREAT HAIRY ENGLISH BASTARD TO WEAR THIS! OI!
*(He tears open his clothing, exposing his chest to the weather.)*
England, your great frozen paw, Oi!
*(The other has not moved.)*
You are looking on my meadow. On my meadow which –
*(He stares in disbelief.)*
NO CUNT HAS MOWN!
*(He turns to ANOTHER off.)*
Have you seen this!
*(STUCLEY enters, follows the direction of his finger.)*
STUCLEY: Oh, the faithless bastards…
BATTER: Fallow, every fucking thing!
STUCLEY: Oh, the disloyal bastards…
BATTER: Not one in cultivation!
STUCLEY: My first glimpse and –
BATTER: And the wood not coppiced!
STUCLEY: My first glimpse and –
BATTER: And the pond not cleared, and no bugger with the cattle!
STUCLEY: ALL BASTARD ROTTEN!
*(He turns to BATTER.)*
Ask them what they – my territory – what they –
BATTER: *(Running off.)* Hey!

STUCLEY: They have stripped me of every kind thought
by this. Lying in their mess and squirming in the hot
straw I imagine, while we suffered, I APOLOGIZE I FEEL SO
ASHAMED!
(*He shakes his head in despair.*)
All the good things I told you of this place and we clap
eyes on the dead opposite. I'm glad it's raining, good! Piss
rain you bastard sky, all I ever said is contradicted, good!
All the glowing eyes round camp fires is pure fuck now,
I'm lord of pigshit and made a proper fool of…

BATTER: (*Running, shouting.*) IT'S US! STUCLEY AND RETAINERS
AFTER SEVEN YEARS!

STUCLEY: You stick yourself in every sordid place, and run
your ribs against the stakes, chucking blood down by the
panful, and what do they do? They roost! They roost and
shit the good estate in your absence, Christ, we will break
their hearts for this! What are you staring at?

KRAK: I am looking at this hill, which is an arc of pure
limestone…

STUCLEY: So it is, it is, yes, oh, I am so full of good, why
does everything betray me? BECAUSE IT IS THE WAY OF
THE WORLD! GOOD! All tenderness is doomed to ridicule,
poetry is lies and mercy only fit for giggling over! Is my
wife dead? Must be, must be because I love her so, she's
dead, it stands to reason, WHERE IS SHE BURIED? What
was it, fever? Fever, merciful fever? No, she was banged to
death by bandits, CAN YOU FIND SOMEONE OR NOT?

BATTER: Some filth is coming, I don't know who, some
staggering filth, but I wouldn't know my mother after this
time, if Christ had gilded her.
(*A WOMAN enters.*)
Do you know us or not?

CANT: You're Batter.

BATTER: She knows me! And my face ploughed up with
scars!

CANT: Done much murder?

STUCLEY: DONE MUCH MURDER? DONE MUCH MURDER? I'M
YOUR LORD YOU WHITE RAG, YOU!

CANT: How beautiful you are, you great male things, I would
kiss you if you'd let me, or in the bush there something
better –

STUCLEY: WHAT?

CANT: Oh, come on, we've had old men here, who only
move by memory, not great stallion bits like yours, all –

STUCLEY: WHAT IS THIS!

CANT: My man's not come back so you do his business for
him – here –
(*She goes to lift her skirts. STUCLEY knocks her aside with a
staggering blow.*)

STUCLEY: I won't be fouled by you, mad bitch, what's
happened here, what! I slash your artery for you!
(*He draws a knife.*)
Down you, in the muck and nettle!
(*She screams.*)
MY TERRITORY!
(*He straddles her.*)

BATTER: Hey!
(*STUCLEY wounds her, she screams.*)

STUCLEY: My shame, you – LOOK WHAT YOU'VE MADE ME
DO! I've – I've –
(*He tosses the knife away, wipes his hand.*)
To come home and hear vile stuff of that sort is – when I
am so clean for my lover is – no homecoming, is it?

KRAK: So much emotion is, I think, perfectly
comprehensible, given the exertion of travelling, and all
your exaggerated hopes. Some anti-climax is only to be
expected.

STUCLEY: Yes.
(*He shrugs.*)
Yes.

KRAK: The only requirement is the restoration of a little
order, the rudiments of organization established, and so
on. The garden is a little overgrown, and minds gone
wild through lack of discipline. Chaos is only apparent
in my experience, like gravel shaken in water abhors the
turbulence, and soon asserts itself in perfect order. As for

the absence of hospitality, that does not offend me either,
but I should like a desk at some stage.

(*Pause. BATTER stares at him.*)

BATTER: Well, I'll be fucked.

(*Pause.*)

No, I will be. He raddles my brains, he does. He pits his
long, dark fingers in my ears and stirs them up. GIVE ME
MY BRAINS BACK, YOU!

(*He laughs, prods CANT with his boot.*)

Get up. Buzz down the valley and tell the oh-so-honest
English Stucley's back with one mad retainer and a wog
who can draw perfect circles with shut eyes. Run!

(*He chases her off.*)

STUCLEY: Wait!

(*He looks to KRAK.*)

I run to my wife's bedroom. Catch her unprepared and all
confusion. Oh, my lord, etcetera, half her plaits undone!
Oh, my lord and all –

(*He chases off.*)

Wait!

(*Pause. KRAK is about to follow, when a WOMAN appears.*)

ANN: My belly's a fist. Went clench on seeing you, went rock.
And womb a tumour. All my soft, rigid. What are you
doing on my hill?

KRAK: (*Turning.*) Looking. In so far as the mist permits.

ANN: It always rains like this for strangers. Drapes itself in
a fine drench, not liking to be spied on. A woman, this
country, not arid like your place. Not brazen. Were you
captured and brought home to carry trays?

(*He looks at her.*)

My husband has turned skinny and beautiful. Was a fat
puppy when he left. Why was he not slaughtered like the
others? Stood around him, did they, taking arrows meant
for him? The sole survivor of some mincing scrap? NO ONE
REQUIRES YOU BACK, TELL HIM.

(*KRAK bows.*)

KRAK: You are the lady of this place, perhaps I might
introduce –

ANN: No. Manners are vile and servants worse. Get off my
hill.
(*He starts to go.*)
THIS WAS AN ORDINARY AFTERNOON AND NOW YOU'RE
HERE!
(*He goes. A SECOND WOMAN enters.*)

SKINNER: Stab him!

ANN: What –

SKINNER: Now! Stab him!

ANN: What –

SKINNER: I will!

ANN: Wait!

SKINNER: Wait, why wait!

ANN: You can't – we haven't – WE HAVEN'T DISCUSSED THIS –

SKINNER: Fuck, he's running!

ANN: Catch him, then –

SKINNER: Can't, can't now, hey! Come and be stabbed!
(*Pause.*)
He's gone into a thicket.
(*Pause.*)

ANN: I hope that wasn't – I do hope that wasn't – THE
MOMENT AFTER WHICH – the fulcrum of disaster – I hope
not.

SKINNER: Miss one moment, twice as hard next time. Miss
the next time, ten times as hard the next.

ANN: All right –

SKINNER: Block the trickle before it's a stream, block the
stream before it's a river –

ANN: ALL RIGHT, I SAID. Kill him later. What is he, anyway,
a quaint slave to cook weird Turkish afters. The damp will
do him if we don't.

SKINNER: You called him beautiful. Your husband. Beautiful,
you said.

ANN: He was. The bone has made an appearance.
(*Pause.*)
Well, he is. HE IS.

SKINNER: You won't –

ANN: I called him beautiful, I saw his face and it –

SKINNER: Go all cream and butter for his paddle, tell me –

ANN: Simple description of his face –

SKINNER: I WON'T ALLOW IT.

    (*Pause.*)

ANN: You go so ugly, in a second, at the bid of thought, so ugly.

SKINNER: I love you. That's what makes me ugly.

ANN: And your eyes shrink to points, and your mouth collapses…

    (*They embrace. CANT enters.*)

CANT: Bugger cut me with a dagger, look!

    (*She exposes a breast.*)

ANN: Where are they?

CANT: In the big 'ouse, going barmy. Stucley's chucked the loom out, picked it up and dropped it in the shit 'eap. Batter's slicin' old men 'ho used to carry 'im round on their backs. Lovely, 'e works the point under their skin an' twists it. They wanna know 'ho made all the babies.

ANN: Nobody told them?

CANT: Too fuckin' true, nobody told 'em. So Stucley goes to the church for consolation and finds it locked an' pigeons shittin' up the belfry, 'e goes screamin' mad and puts 'is foot through all the winders. Only the wog stays still, kneels in the parlour cooking something 'e calls coffee. Look, my tit's bleedin'!

ANN: Tell him I'm here. On the hill, tell him.

CANT: Why ain't she 'ere, 'e says, plaited and fragrant? Plaited an' fragrant! Bugger!

ANN: Tell him. He'll come.

CANT: I'll see what mood 'e's in. An' fuck you if 'e's wavin' daggers, I won't say nothin'.

    (*She goes to leave, stops.*)

Are they stayin'?

    (*Pause.*)

I'm only askin'. If they're stayin'?

    (*Pause, she goes out.*)

SKINNER: First there was the bailiff, and we broke the bailiff. And then there was God, and we broke God. And lastly there was cock, and we broke that, too. Freed the ground, freed religion, freed the body. And went up this hill, standing together naked like the old female pack, growing to eat and not to market, friends to cattle who we milked but never slaughtered, joining the strips and dancing in the commons, the three days' labour that we gave to priests gave instead to the hungry, turned the tithe barn into a hospital and FOUND CUNT BEAUTIFUL that we had hidden and suffered shame for, its lovely shapelessness, its colour all miraculous, what they had made dirty or worshipped out of ignorance, do we now –

ANN: No –

SKINNER: Just deliver it –

ANN: No –

SKINNER: Our bodies and our labour up to their groping fingers?

ANN: No.

(*Pause.*)

SKINNER: I helped your births. And your conceptions. Sat by the bedroom, at the door, while you took the man's thing in you, shuddering with disgust and trying hard to see it only as the mating of dumb cattle –

ANN: It was –

SKINNER: Yes, and I managed. I did manage. And washed you, and parted your hair. I never knew such intimacy, did you? Tell me, all this unity! –

ANN: Never –

SKINNER: And my husband's bones are kicked around the hills of Asia. Husband. The suffocating thing in darkness. Oh, good for wars in foreign places, let them stab away for Christ or Mohammed! And I prayed to everything not one of them would crawl back to this valley, but I was not a good enough witch, was I?

ANN: No…

SKINNER: They crossed the world, missed floods and avalanches –

ANN: Loose planks on bridges –

SKINNER: Snake bites –

ANN: Falling trees and plague villages –

SKINNER: Angry parents of raped daughters –

ANN: Barmy tribesmen –

SKINNER: And rancid whores whose cunts dripped instant death, how did they? Europe is a million miles long, isn't it, how did they pick their way back here, AN ANT COULD PASS THROUGH A BONFIRE EASIER!

(*ANN laughs. SKINNER looks at her.*)

How?

(*Pause.*)

ANN: Why are you looking at me like that?

SKINNER: How, then?

ANN: I suppose because –

SKINNER: You drew him.

(*Pause.*)

ANN: What?

SKINNER: Drew him. With your underneath.

(*Pause.*)

ANN: I do think – if we –

SKINNER: DOWN THERE CALLED TO HIM ACROSS THE SPACES!

ANN: Look –

SKINNER: I HATE GOD AND NATURE, THEY MADE US VIOLABLE AS BITCHES!

(*ANN clasps her, as she sobs with anger. STUCLEY enters, holding a white garment. Pause.*)

STUCLEY: Put this on, please.

(*They look at him.*)

I found it in the bottom of a trunk. Do wear it, please. Change in the bushes, as you like this place so much.

(*He looks at SKINNER.*)

And you, Skinner's widow, clear off.

SKINNER: Don't be the wife to him, don't –

STUCLEY: Get out.

ANN: (*To SKINNER.*) Go on. Trust me. Go on.

(*SKINNER withdraws. STUCLEY still holds out the garment.*)

STUCLEY: Trust you? Why?

(*He looks at her.*)

You look so –

(*Pause.*)

Trust you? Why?

(*Pause.*)

Imagine what I – if you would condescend to – what I
– the riot of my feelings when I look at –

(*Pause.*)

Trust you to do what exactly?

(*Pause.*)

In seven years I have aged twenty. And you, if anything,
have grown younger, so we who were never boy and girl
exactly have now met in some middling maturity, I have
seen your face on tent roofs, don't laugh at me, will you?

(*Pause.*)

ANN: No.

STUCLEY: That is a ploughman's hag and you – what is it,
exactly?

(*Pause.*)

I found the church bunged up with cow and bird dung, the
place we married in, really, what –

(*Pause.*)

So I prayed in the nettles.

(*Pause.*)

Very devout picture of young English warrior returning
to his domain etcetera get your needle out and make a
tapestry why don't you? Or don't you do that any more?

(*Pause.*)

Christ knows what goes on here, you must explain to me
over the hot milk at bedtime, everything changes and
dreams are bollocks but you can't help dreaming, even
knowing a dream is –

(*Pause.*)

It is quite amusing coming back to this I was saying to the
Arab every hundred yards I have this little paradise and he
went mmm and mmm he knew the sardonic bastard, they
are not romantic like us are they, Muslims, and they're
right! Please put this on because I –

ANN: No.

(*Pause.*)

STUCLEY: This wedding thing, you were sixteen years my
senior and a widow and I trembled, didn't I, and you said,

do not feel you must do anything, but may I kiss you I have always loved your mouth WHY WON'T YOU PUT IT ON. (*Pause.*)

So there we were thinking – it is not a desert, actually, it is full of fields and orchards the Holy Land – and some said tell my old lady I was killed and married Arab women or Jewesses, some of them. Fewer were killed than you might think, much fewer, after all we left with fifty and it was tempting, obviously, but I thought she – wrongly it appears – she –

(*Pause.*)

Have children in two continents, most of them. Not me, though. Not in one, alas.

(*Pause.*)

I thought the time had come to – it was meant to be two years, not seven, but you know – or perhaps you don't – how wars go – coming back was worse than anything – what we did in Hungary I would not horrify you with – they got more barmy by the hour. Not me, though. I thought she'll take my bleeding feet in her warm place, she'll lay me down in clean sheets and work warm oils into my skin and food, we'll spend whole days at – but everything is contrary, must be, mustn't it, I who jumped in every pond of murder kept this one thing pure in my head, pictured you half-naked on an English night, your skin which was translucent from one angle and deep-furrowed from another, your odour even which I caught once in the middle of a scrap, do you believe that, even smells are stored, I'm sorry I chucked your loom out of the window, amazing strength comes out of temper, it's half a ton that thing if it's – trust me, what does that mean?

ANN: You've not changed. Thinner, but the same. For all the marching and the stabbing. Whereas quietly, here I have.

STUCLEY: (*Tossing the garment aside.*) Fuck the garment! Get to bed with me and we'll stir up long forgotten feelings, go down deep to floors of fornication we've not –

ANN: It isn't possible –

STUCLEY: IT IS, YOU LIE DOWN AND YOU PART YOURSELF. (*Pause.*)

> They say coarse things, by habit almost. Not me, though, I
> tried to keep my language wholesome and – not difficult if
> you have faith –

ANN: You shouldn't have –

STUCLEY: I shouldn't have? What? What shouldn't I?

ANN: Have struggled to be pure.

STUCLEY: No struggle! If you have faith!

ANN: Have kept the perfect husband for me –

STUCLEY: WHY NOT, BECAUSE YOU WERE NOT EQUAL?

> (*Pause.*)

ANN: No.

> (*Pause. He is suspended between hysteria and disbelief.*)

STUCLEY: I think when God says – CRUSH THIS BASTARD
– I wish there was a priest here, but there isn't so I offer
you my version, you hark to my theology – He really is
the most THOROUGHGOING OF ALL DEITIES, no wonder
we all bow down to Him, His grasp of pain and pressure is
so exquisite and all comprehending, what human torturer,
what miserable nail-wrenching amateur in pain could pit
his malevolence against the celestial wit and come out on
top, no man I assure you could conceive of so many alleys
by which to turn a brain. As if I had not swallowed every
vileness conceivable and still stand on two feet, He chooses
to hamstring me not by your death – that I had always
reckoned possible, that I expected hourly to be splashed in
my face, but no, He has me from her own mouth hear my
lady has acquiesced in the riot of her cunt! And I have just
fought the Holy War on His behalf! Oh, Lord and Master
of Cruelty, who has no shred of mercy for thy servants, I
worship Thee.

> (*He kneels, lowering his head to the ground.*)

There is no arguing with genius like this, I threw the
dagger away, it's in the bushes somewhere or I might have
slit you open, but He takes care of everything. He does, oh,
praise Thee, praise Thee, now tell me she has children by
the very interlopers who greeted me as I climbed my very
own steps.

ANN: Yes.

STUCLEY: Yes! Yes! I know the source of our religion! It is
that He in His savagery is both excessive and remorseless
and to our shrieks both deaf and blind! I could be a bishop.
I missed my chance, slicing black men on the banks of the
Jordan, silly, that's for sloggers and boys obsessed with
weapons, no, the bishops have got their tongues in God's
arse and lick up the absolute, that's for me, PASS A BIT OF
PURPLE SOMEBODY! How many bastards, then?

ANN: One and three died.

STUCLEY: And you past forty! Such fertility, the Lord
denying even His own ordinances to make me squirm, she
will be pupping in her dotage if it hurts me, and I spent
enough juice in you to father forty regiments and not one
bred, further evidence, if evidence you needed of His
mighty genius, bow, bow, Thou who dost not miss a trick!
(*He bumps his head on the ground.*)
Bow, bow…
(*He stops, laughing.*)
Could be furious. Not me though.
(*He gets up.*)
I met somebody who put a lock on it. His lady's thing.
Padlocked it! Really, the barbarism! And got a lance
through him at Acre and fell into the sea, and sank down to
the floor of the blue waters, man and single key. Well, you
couldn't have two keys, could you!
(*He laughs.*)
You have to laugh, I do, I have great recourse to laughter,
of the demonic variety, I could kill you and no one would
bat an eyelid.
(*Pause.*)

ANN: Don't stay.

STUCLEY: Don't stay?

ANN: No. Be welcome, and pass through.

STUCLEY: One night and then –

ANN: Yes.

STUCLEY: What – in the stable, kip down and –

ANN: Not in the stable.

STUCLEY: Not in the stable? You mean I might –

ANN: Don't, please, become sarcastic, it –

STUCLEY: Inside the house, perhaps, we might just –

ANN: Useless sarcasm, it –

STUCLEY: Under the stairs, and creep away at first light –

ANN: Undermines your honour –

STUCLEY: WHAT HONOUR YOU DISHEVELLED AND
IMPERTINENT SLAG.

(*Pause.*)

You see, you make me lose my temper, you make me
abusive, why not stay, it is my home.

ANN: Not now.

STUCLEY: Not now, why not?

ANN: There have been changes.

STUCLEY: I begin to see, but where do you propose we –

ANN: Go on.

STUCLEY: To where?

ANN: The horizon.

STUCLEY: I own the horizon.

ANN: Cross it, then.

(*Pause.*)

I'm cruel, but I do it to be simple. To cut off hopes cleanly.
No tearing wounds, I'm sorry if your dreams are spoiled
but –

STUCLEY: It is perfectly kind of you –

ANN: Not kind –

STUCLEY: Yes, perfectly kind and typically considerate of
you, I do appreciate the instinct but –

ANN: Not kind, I say –

STUCLEY: YES! Down on your knees, now –

ANN: What –

STUCLEY: On your knees, now –

ANN: Are you going to be –

STUCLEY: Down, now –

ANN: Childish and –

STUCLEY: Yes, I WAS YOUR CHILD, WASN'T I?

(*Pause. He suddenly weeps. She watches him, then goes to him. He
embraces her, then thrusts her away.*)

PENITENCE FOR ADULTERY!

(*He sees a figure off, calls.*)

HOI! Tell me what's gone on, they've abolished the apology!

(*An OLD MAN enters.*)

They do their sin with such clear eyes! Are you a thief, or been up in my bedroom? The more innocent you look, the more sunk in treachery, it stands to reason! Do you know me?

HUSH: Yes –

STUCLEY: Oh, good, I'm known, GET DOWN THEN! It is going to take – this restoration of authority – a lot of time and bruising, I can see!

ANN: Don't make him bend.

STUCLEY: Why not, old bugger!

ANN: We're done with bending here.

STUCLEY: (*Forcing him to the ground.*) Done with it? It's nature!

HUSH: Forgive me, forgive me!

STUCLEY: Forgive, what for?

HUSH: Whatever offends you –

STUCLEY: Good! Oh, good! The first wise words since I set foot in my domain! He is not grey for nothing, he has scuttled through his eighty years with sorry on his lips, spewed sorry out for each and every occasion, good! I appreciate you, cunning licker of brute crevices, insinuator of beds and confidences. Kiss my hands and tell me what you did against me. The more extravagant, the more credence I attach to it, promise you.

HUSH: I did not praise you in your absence.

STUCLEY: Oh, that's nothing, you mean you abused me, surely?

HUSH: Abused you, yes.

STUCLEY: Excellent, go on.

ANN: This is disgusting.

STUCLEY: Disgusting? No, he longs for his confession!

HUSH: I did not tend your meadows or your stock –

STUCLEY: You mean you stole them off me?

HUSH: Stole them, yes. I did not pray for your safe return –

STUCLEY: Oh, shit this for a confession, this is the Valley of
    Wickedness, say you prayed for my slow-dying torture –

HUSH: Yes!

STUCLEY: Daily prayed the devil I would rot –

HUSH: Yes!

STUCLEY: Turned my house into a brothel, my bedroom,
    whooped in it –

HUSH: Yes –

STUCLEY: Go on, I am confessing for you, you do it!

HUSH: Adultery and fornication –

STUCLEY: On who? On her?

HUSH: On everyone!

ANN: I won't witness this –

STUCLEY: (*Grabbing her wrist.*) Must witness it!
    (*To HUSH.*) Stuck children on her, did you?

HUSH: Yes?

STUCLEY: No, in your words!

HUSH: I lay on her and others naked and did put my seed in
    them and –

STUCLEY: Oh, rubbish, it's beyond belief. I hate bad lies,
    lies that fall apart, there's no entertainment in them. Get on
    your cracking pins, you tottering old bugger...
    (*ANN helps HUSH to his feet.*)

HUSH: Thank you.

STUCLEY: Thank me, why?

HUSH: Because the worst thing in age is the respect. The
    smile of condescension, and the hush with which the
    most banal opinion is received. The old know nothing.
    Fling them down. They made the world and they need
    punishing.

STUCLEY: Good, I've no regrets if half your bones are out of
    joint.

HUSH: Me neither.

STUCLEY: I cherish nothing, cherishing's out, and what was
    soft in me has liquified into a poison puddle. Not to be
    fooled. That's my dream now, THANK YOU, UNIVERSE!
    (*Pause.*)
    Educated me. Educated me...

(*He goes out.*)

ANN: Tell him nothing.

HUSH: I won't.

ANN: Not even thank you or good morning.

HUSH: No.

ANN: He'll kill you if he knows you fathered children on me. Some vile Turkish torture. Do you want that?

HUSH: No.

ANN: Good. Half the children in this valley are off you.

HUSH: As many as that?

ANN: Yes, so keep your mouth shut.

HUSH: Promise you.

(*He starts to go out.*)

ANN: Why do you love your life so much?

(*He stops.*)

So much that even dignity gets spewed, and truth kicked into blubber, and will itself as pliable as a string of gut? You have no appetite but life itself, I mean breathing and continuing.

(*He shrugs.*)

There can't be a man alive with more children and less interest in the world they grow up in.

HUSH: I never sought my family…

ANN: No. You were led to the female and then turned back in the field again…

(*He turns to go.*)

IF YOU ACHIEVE IMMORTALITY I SHALL BE FURIOUS.

# SCENE TWO

*Another day. BATTER carries a desk on his back. He is followed by an OLD MAN carrying paraphernalia.*

BATTER: Down here, you quivering old bum, you walnut bollock, and careful with the precious instruments!

(*He lowers the tools.*)

This is the impedimenta of science, which in collusion with his genius will wring transformation out the dozing landscape. And he is mine, in all his rareness, mine, as if I'd birthed him, yes, DON'T LOOK AT ME LIKE THAT, I am his second mother! Through me, brute flesh and knuckle, he has existence, who might be just another husk of wogland, sons of Arabia blowing in the sand, I saved him, I, who was running head to foot with Arab gore, kicked back the door and saw him, and he stared into my eye, my eyes which were – THE ONLY BLUE – the rest being hot gore, and into my only blues his only browns stared pleadingly...imagine it...

SPONGE: I can...

BATTER: You can...you can imagine nothing... This was the middle of Jerusalem where every bastard male or female I trod by was split and opened up to inquisitive old daylight. I SPARED NO ONE. Well, we had been outside in rain and snow for seven months, there is snow in deserts...

SPONGE: I can imagine...

BATTER: No one who was not there can imagine anything. Never say 'I can imagine' again. It's a lie, nobody can. And he stared into the little lights of what must have been – my kindness – and I stopped, the dagger in my hand tipped this way...and that...slippery in my fist. I pondered. AFTER EIGHTEEN STAIRCASES OF MURDER ...and of course, because I pondered, the genius was safe. Funny. Funny that I pondered when this was the very bugger who designed the fort; the pen was in his fingers for some lethal innovation. HOW MANY MORE DEAD WOULD THAT HAVE COST?

SPONGE: I can't imagine...

BATTER: Not that I care about death, not even my own. In little avenues and parks they fret on death who have so rigorously hid from life –
(*KRAK comes in.*)
Have you done murder, genius?
(*He goes to him, holds his hands.*)
Not with those hands, no, but that is SHIT HYPOCRISY –
(*KRAK withdraws from him.*)
It is, because the line from a to b – you see, I have education, too – the linear trapezoid para – fucking – llelogram is FIVE HUNDRED CORPSES LONG! No offence to mathematics, no offence.

(*Cries off. STUCLEY enters dragging a MAN by the neck.*)

STUCLEY: Found him! Found him! My incumbent priest
who did the wedlock whilst squirming at his celibacy! True
or false?

NAILER: (*His neck wrenched.*) True!

STUCLEY: The knob beneath the vestment twirling at my
vows! It's all here, everything we left is like old ruins
underneath the grass! Are we making too much noise? I
know you have to concentrate.

(*KRAK is leaning on the desk, staring across the valley.*)

This man married me, and when I was away, condoned
my bitch's filth! I do believe, I do believe this, that human
beings left without severity would roll back the ages and be
hopping, croaking frogs, clustering thick on the female with
the coming of the Spring, and sunk in mud for winter...!

KRAK: The castle is not a house.

(*They look at him.*)

The castle is not a house.

NAILER: No lord's land, we said, and no common land, we
said, but every man who lives shall go as he pleases, and
we threw the fences down and made a bad word of fence,
we called fence blasphemy, the only word we deemed so,
all the rest we freed, the words for women's and men's
parts we liberated –

BATTER: (*To KRAK.*) Come again?

NAILER: And freeing the words we also freed the –

BATTER: Not you.

(*NAILER stops. Pause.*)

STUCLEY: What is the castle, then?

(*KRAK does not respond. STUCLEY turns to BATTER.*)

Lock this in God's house and make him wash it spotless
and set-up God's furniture again.

NAILER: (*Pulled out.*) God has no furniture.

STUCLEY: No, but the church has!

(*NAILER and BATTER go out.*)

I tell you, the world's here as we left it, just sunk a bit, like
the Roman pavement, you scuff it up, you spit, and there's
the sun shining out the mosaic, an old god never properly

obscured, Mithras waiting for his hour. So with vicars who
have gone barmy, there is the old tithe gatherer beneath
some weed of fancy patter I bet you…
(*Pause.*)
Go on…
(*KRAK holds out a large paper.*)
Has he made a drawing for me?
(*He smiles.*)
He has…
(*He looks at KRAK, beaming.*)
The Great Amazer!
(*He takes it, looks at it.*)
Which way up is it?
(*He turns it round and round.*)
I genuflect before the hieroglyphs but what –
KRAK: No place is not watched by another place.
(*STUCLEY nods.*)
The heights are actually depths.
STUCLEY: Yup.
KRAK: The weak points are actually strong points.
STUCLEY: Yup.
KRAK: The entrances are exits.
STUCLEY: Yes!
KRAK: The doors lead into pits.
STUCLEY: Go on!
KRAK: It resembles a defence but is really an attack.
STUCLEY: Yes –
KRAK: It cannot be destroyed –
STUCLEY: Mmm –
KRAK: Therefore it is a threat –
STUCLEY: Mmm –
KRAK: It will make enemies where there are none –
STUCLEY: You're losing me –
KRAK: It makes war necessary –
(*STUCLEY looks at him.*)
It is the best thing I have ever done.
(*STUCLEY's long stare is interrupted by a racket of construction
as a massive framework for a spandrel descends slowly to the floor.*

*On the construction, BUILDERS and the master, HOLIDAY.*
*STUCLEY goes out.)*

HOLIDAY: Oh, Christ, oh, bleeding hell, somebody!

WORKMAN: (*Calling to someone above.*) Steady, Brian!

HOLIDAY: I never should, I never should, should I? Expose
    myself to – are we safe? Are we down yet?

WORKMAN: Cast off, Brian!

HOLIDAY: (*Whose eyes are shut.*) I am in the wrong trade, can
    I open my eyes, are we –

WORKMAN: Down, Harry!

HOLIDAY: Down, are we?

    (*He opens his eyes.*)

    Oh, lovely earth, immobile, stationary thing!

    (*He kisses it.*)

    Do you sympathize with my condition? I exaggerate of
    course, I exaggerate to win the pity of my workmen. It is
    a good thing to advertize your weakness, it obliges them
    to demonstrate their manliness. Are you afraid of heights?
    When I am up I am horrified in case I slip between the
    boards, and when I'm down afraid some hammer will be
    dropped and plop through my cranium. I have an eggshell
    skull and yet I am a builder, that is one of life's perversities.
    In thirty years I have built two castles and an abbey and
    this tilt to my head is permanent, I have one eye always
    on the sky which may at any moment hold my extinction
    in some falling implement, what is wrong with the women
    round here, I am actually fond of women, when I did the
    abbey had some decent conversation with the nuns but
    this –

    (*Enter SKINNER, draped in flowers.*)

SKINNER: OLD HILL SAYS NO.

HOLIDAY: Does it, never 'eard it –

SKINNER: ROCK WEEPS AND STONE PROTESTS –

HOLIDAY: (*Calling off.*) Brian, I will 'ave that templet for the
    blind arch when you're ready –

SKINNER: (*Turning to KRAK.*) Weren't you loved? Some bit
    of you not nourished? Why are all your things hard things,
    compasses, nibs and protractors, the little armoury of your

drawing board, have you looked at a flower, go on, take one, the superior geometry of the –
(*He ignores her.*)
WHY DON'T YOU LOOK AT A FLOWER!

HOLIDAY: (*Shouting up.*) No, I won't come up there, I 'ave just been up there –

SKINNER: (*Turning back to HOLIDAY.*) The flower – five petals – each petal identical – LOOK AT THE FLOWER, WILL YOU, IT'S GOT TRUTH IN IT – all right, don't look at it, why should I save you, why should I educate you –

HOLIDAY: (*Still addressing his foreman.*) All right, do it your way –

SKINNER: Educate you, oh yes, educate him, look at him –

HOLIDAY: I said –

SKINNER: My breath, my knowledge, really, do you believe I'd – what – on this –

HOLIDAY: I said do it –

SKINNER: Waste my precious – on you – all my struggle through the dark, through clinging – really, on you – does he actually –

HOLIDAY: I'M SORRY, BRIAN, 'OW CAN I FUCKING CONCENTRATE!

SKINNER: SAVE YOU, YOU ARE NOT FIT!
(*Pause. He looks at her.*)
No, no, no time for it. Educate you and they pile up bricks, love to educate you but – oh, love to, but – look, the footings in already, go back where you came from, quick, this will not be finished, your coat is on the hook, run without stopping even though it hurts your hanging guts, run, I tell you, I know, I am the witch, quick.
(*Pause. He stares at her.*)
Quick…
(*BATTER comes in, looks at her. She turns her head to him contemptuously, then flings up her skirts and shows her arse. She walks off.*)

BATTER: Supposed to be a woman. A woman, calls itself.

HOLIDAY: Never saw a nun do that –

BATTER: No, well, you wouldn't –

HOLIDAY: Not in all the –

BATTER: A nun wouldn't, would she? Not a normal nun –

HOLIDAY: Barmy –

BATTER: Barmy, yes –

HOLIDAY: They 'ad their moods, they 'ad their comings-over as all women do, but – are these towers really going to be ninety foot above the curtain? I don't complain, every slab is food and drink to me, but ninety foot? Who are you – it's a quiet country what I see of it – no, the woman's touched, surely?

BATTER: (*Contemplatively.*) Skinner's arse…

HOLIDAY: What?

BATTER: He told me how he lay upon that arse, and she kept stiff as rock, neither moaning nor moving, but rock. So when the bishop asked for soldiers he was first forward, to get shot of her with Christ's permission. And found a girl under the olives, who moved with him and praised him. Well, he assumed so, they had not a word in common. And he kept on, the difference in women, the difference in women! But she outlasts him. There is no justice, is there? (*He turns to KRAK.*)
Is there? No justice?

BRIAN: (*Entering.*) Michael wants you about the quoins.

HOLIDAY: I will see Michael –

BRIAN: The courses for the quoins, 'e says –

HOLIDAY: Thank you Brian –

BRIAN: Don't tally with the specifications –

HOLIDAY: I will attend to Michael! I will explain to Michael 'ow many courses there are to the quoins –

BRIAN: Okay.

HOLIDAY: I will simplify the already simple drawing which his eyes are crossing over, but don't 'urry me! When you 'urry, you forget, and when you forget, that is the moment the dropped chisel is hastening to its rendezvous with the distracted 'ead. I will join Michael, but at my own bidding, thank you.
(*BRIAN goes out.*)
This is all new to me. This passion for the circle. Leaving aside the embrasures and the lintels, there are no corners.

Are none of the walls straight? Perpendicular, yes, but straight?
(*KRAK ignores him.*)
Out of curiosity, what was wrong with square towers?
(*Pause.*)
Just change, is it? Just novelty?
(*Pause. He desists.*)
All right, I'm coming!
(*He goes out. BATTER watches KRAK.*)

KRAK: Dialogue is not a right, is it? When idiots waylay geniuses, where is the obligation?
(*Pause.*)
And words, like buckets, slop with meanings.
(*Pause.*)
To talk, what is that but the exchange of clumsy approximations, the false endeavour to share knowledge, the false endeavour to disseminate truths arrived at in seclusion?
(*Pause.*)
When the majority are, perceptibly, incapable of the simplest intellectual discipline, what is the virtue of incessant speech? The whole of life serves to remind us we exist among inert banality.
(*Pause.*)
I only state the obvious. The obvious being the starting point of architecture, as of any other science…

BATTER: Very good, but why so big? I don't think even Acre was this big, the citadel, was it? The walls of this you could accommodate the parish in, all to be paid for out of what, I wonder? You have your methods, I expect, but these bitches never cropped for surpluses, and kept the sheep for pets as far as I can see, the wool was hanging off the hedges, paid for out of what, I wonder?
(*Pause.*)
And when they throw open the shutters, where's the sky, they'll say, give us back our fucking sky, they will, won't they? All they'll clap eyes on is masonry and arrow slits, it will blot the old blue out and throw long shadows over them, always at the corner of their eye, kissing or clawing,

even in the bedroom looking in, and drunken arses falling
out of beer houses will search in vain for corners to piss in
not overlooked. Why?
(*Pause.*)
Or don't you spend words on me, perhaps I'm only,
what – inert banality? What's that, you bilingual fucker,
you have more words in a foreign tongue than I have in
English, but then I have the dagger, who speaks volumes
when it comes to it, INERT BANALITY I christen it!
(*He kisses the blade. Thunder and black.*)

## SCENE THREE

*In semi-darkness, the figure of BRIAN running from the building
works. He is followed by CANT, pursued by SKINNER. SKINNER
catches her.*

CANT: I DONE NOTHIN'!

SKINNER: You unravel us! What we knit together you
un-stitch!

CANT: I DONE NO WRONG, LET GO YOU!

SKINNER: I don't hurt you, do I? Don't struggle and I – you
are asking to be –
(*She brings CANT to the ground.*)
There, I do that because you –
(*She sees her own clothes are muddied.*)
Look at me – we slither in their mess – this was all bluebell
once – patience, though, I am listening to you, I am all ears
why you were in the foundations with a brickie –

CANT: Wasn't!

SKINNER: Oh, this is too painful for excuses!

CANT: Well, I wasn't – what you were thinking – wasn't
anyway –

SKINNER: No –

CANT: DEFINITELY NOT!

SKINNER: But while we're on the subject...
(*Pause.*)

CANT: I haven't – you know I haven't – ever really overcome
my – not ever conquered my weakness for –

(*Pause.*)

It was easy before the builders come, but there are dozens of these geezers and they – I gaze at their trousers, honestly I do, whilst thinking, enemy, enemy! I do gaze so, though hating myself, obviously…

ANN: (*Entering.*) What?

SKINNER: In the footing with a brickie –

CANT: ONLY TO KEEP THE RAIN OFF.

SKINNER: What? Off what?

ANN: With her it is just – it is a hunger – I don't see what –

SKINNER: Punish her, of course!

ANN: When she is like she is? What –

SKINNER: Yes!

CANT: I DON'T WANNA BE PUNISHED!

SKINNER: You give her the truth, and she rejects the truth –

CANT: Skinner, I don't want to be –

SKINNER: And rejecting the truth she wrecks herself, and wrecking herself she wrecks others, and wrecking others –

CANT: Skinner –

SKINNER: (*Turning on CANT.*) They occupy your mind with that! WE MADE OURSELVES WHEN WE DITCHED THAT!

ANN: You are too angry –

SKINNER: Angry? Me? What? Mustn't be angry, no, be good, Skinner, be tolerant, her feelings being somewhat coarse what do you expect of peasant women, farmworkers ever on their backs, legs open in the crops, LISTEN, we all bring to the world, inside our skulls, inside our bellies, Christ knows what lumber from our makers BUT. You do not lie down to the burden, you toss it off. The whine 'I am made like that' will not wash, will it? Correct me if I'm wrong, will it? We have done such things here and they come back and straddle us, where is the strength if we go up against the walls skirts up and occupied like that?

(*Pause.*)

I do think, I do think, to understand is not to condone, is it?

(*Pause.*)

I do feel so alone, do you feel that?

(*Pause.*)

It always rains here, which we loved once. I love you and I wish we could just love, but no, this is the test, all love is tested, or else it cannot know its power…

CANT: I'm sorry.

SKINNER: The words, the words go drip, drip, drip…

CANT: Said I'm sorry, didn't I!

(*ANN indicates she should go. CANT slips away.*)

SKINNER: Where there are builders, there are whores, and where there are whores, there are criminals, and after the criminals come the police, the great heap heaving, and what was peace and simple is dirt and struggle, and where there was a field to stand up straight in there is loud and frantic city. Stucley will make a city of this valley, what does he say to you?

ANN: Nothing.

SKINNER: No, nothing, and every day I expected to be stabbed or stifled, didn't you? What is this waiting for? You have been here ten minutes and not said you love me. I suspect you terribly without a shred of evidence, I shall spoil us with it. Is it because you were happy with him once? You see, I never was, never with a man, and you so fecund and me horribly childless –

ANN: Not horribly –

SKINNER: Not horribly, no –

ANN: I don't declare my feelings –

SKINNER: No, you don't –

ANN: Can't be forever declaring feelings, you declare yours, over and over, but –

SKINNER: Yes –

ANN: It is your way –

SKINNER: Ridiculous way –

ANN: I am not forthcoming with these statements you require, you have to trust –

SKINNER: Yes –

ANN: Signs, more.

(*Pause.*)

SKINNER: I do. I do trust signs.

(*Pause.*)

We do not make a thing of flesh, do we, the love of women is more – they could eat flesh from off your body, we – no, actually I could eat yours, I could! Tell me why you love me!

ANN: I don't see that I need, do I, need to –

SKINNER: Oh, come on, yes, you do need to, and I will tell why I love you, the more they bore into the hill the more we must talk love, the bond, fasten it tighter! You are very cold this evening, I am not imagining it, you'll say I'm imagining it, but –

ANN: Yes.

(*Pause.*)

SKINNER: What, then.

(*ANN does not reply.*)

They talk of a love-life, don't they? Do you know the phrase 'love-life', as if somehow this thing ran under or beside, as if you stepped from one life to the other, banality to love, love to banality, no, love is in the cooking and the washing and the milking, no matter what, the colour of the love stains everything, I say so anyway, being admittedly of a most peculiar disposition I WOULD RATHER YOU WERE DEAD THAN TOOK A STEP OR SHUFFLE BACK FROM ME. Dead, and I would do it. There I go, WHAT IS IT YOU LOOK SO DISTANT.

ANN: I think you are – obsessive.

(*Pause.*)

SKINNER: Obsessive, me? Obsessive?

(*Pause. She fights down something.*)

I nearly got angry then and nearly went – no – I will not – and – wait, the anger sinks –

(*Pause.*)

Like tipping water on the sand, the anger goes, the anger vanishes – into what? I've no idea, my entrails, I assume. I do piss anger in the night, my pot is angerfull.

(*Pause.*)

I am obsessive, why aren't you?

(*Pause.*)

Every stone they raise is aimed at us. And things we have not dreamed of yet will come from it. Poems, love and gardening will be – and where you turn your eyes will be – and even the little middle of your heart which you think is your safe and actual self will be – transformed by it. I don't know how but even the way you plait your hair will be determined by it and what we crop and even the colour of the babies, I do think it's odd, so odd, that when you resist you are obsessive but when you succumb you are not WHOSE OBSESSION IS THIS THING or did you mean my love, they are the same thing actually.

(*Pause.*)

They have a corridor of dungeons and somewhere are the occupants, they do not know yet and she fucked in there, not knowing it, of course, not being a witch could not imagine far enough, it is the pain of witches to see to the very end of things…

ANN: Yes.

SKINNER: What?

ANN: To all you say and yet – I think I must talk with my husband.

   (*Pause.*)

SKINNER: Talk –

ANN: Yes, he is not as you –

SKINNER: Your what?

ANN: He also has got feeling and –

SKINNER: Talk to your what –

ANN: I have a right to sense as well as you!

   (*Pause.*)

   Even Nailer has recanted. Kneeling is back and they have not put the keep up yet.

SKINNER: There is no talking between you and a man. No talking. Words, yes, the patter and the eyes on your belt –

ANN: How shall we win!

SKINNER: I do not know how we will win! It is not a failing not to know the end at the beginning. Our power comes out of our love. Love also is a weapon.

   (*Pause.*)

ANN: Yes.

   (*Pause.*)

SKINNER: The way you say yes…

(*Pause.*)

We lay under the stars, and in the comfort of the trees
swaying, the felled trees, swaying, swore everlasting love.
I will not accept that everlasting love, even as you swear
it, is a lie, a permissible lie, because you do not know
the unforeseen condition. It is still everlasting, there
could be forty thousand murderers or forty thousand
starving children, violence or pity threatening, it still takes
precedence.

(*She turns swiftly.*)

Who is there, exactly?

(*She addresses the shadows.*)

Are you interested in love? Give us your opinion. I am in
the grip of this eccentric view that sworn love is binding –

(*KRAK steps out of the shadows.*)

KRAK: Why not? If sworn hatred is.

(*They look at him. He goes to leave.*)

ANN: I wonder if you smile? I have never seen you.

SKINNER: Don't talk to him. Accuse him.

ANN: (*Ignoring her.*) Or laugh, for that matter. But most
laughter's false. I trust smiles better.

SKINNER: No, that's talking –

ANN: Have you no children? I somehow think you have not
looked in children's eyes –

SKINNER: DO YOU THINK HE LISTENS TO THAT
MAWKISHNESS?

(*Pause.*)

KRAK: Children? Dead or alive?

# SCENE FOUR

*Sound of whispered incantations and responses. Sections of building
are lowered. NAILER is seen kneeling on the ground. STUCLEY
enters, holding a Bible. NAILER stops his devotions.*

STUCLEY: Christ's cock.

NAILER: Yes…?

STUCLEY: IS NOWHERE MENTIONED!

(*He flings the Bible at him. NAILER ducks.*)

NAILER: No…

STUCLEY: Nor the cocks of his disciples.

NAILER: No…

STUCLEY: Peculiar.

NAILER: The gospels are scrupulous in their avoidance of anatomical and physiological description. We have, for example, no image of Christ's face, let alone his –

STUCLEY: He was a man, though, wasn't he? A man, or why else did he descend to move among us?

NAILER: He was a man, yes –

STUCLEY: He was a man and I have lost five years trying to recover his dominions, five years for someone with no cock!

NAILER: He had one –

STUCLEY: He did have –

NAILER: For he was circumcised –

STUCLEY: He was circumcised, I read that, the circumcision, yes –

NAILER: Thereafter little reference, I admit –

STUCLEY: None whatsoever –

NAILER: Quite –

STUCLEY: What happened to it, then?

(*Pause. NAILER shrugs.*)

NAILER: Chastity?

STUCLEY: There is one chastity and only one. The exclusiveness of desire, not willed, but forced by passion, that's chastity.

(*He walks a little.*)

No, this is a problem for the Church, you know it is. The deity made manifest knows neither pain nor ecstasy, what use is He?

NAILER: Be careful, please…

STUCLEY: Careful, why?

NAILER: You may be overheard.

STUCLEY: By whom?

NAILER: You may be oveheard, that's all –

STUCLEY: BY WHOM!

NAILER: By Him Who Hears All, obviously –

STUCLEY: Fuck the lunatic!

(*NAILER winces. Pause.*)

I lay in a tent outside Edessa, while you frolicked in the
English damp, while you licked the dew off widows' arses,
tossed on my cot bleeding from the gums, roaring at the
bowel and throat, the flux of Asia shagging me both ends,
and longing to know Him, to have some sense of Him,
to put my finger into Christ and feel His heat, and what
pained me, what agonized me I assure you, was not the
absence of a face but His castration, this Christ who never
suffered for the woman, who never felt the feeling which
MAKES NO SENSE.

(*Pause.*)

He can lend no comfort who has not been all the places
that we have.

(*Pause.*)

And then of course, I knew He had, and we'd been tricked.

(*Pause.*)

NAILER: Tricked...?

STUCLEY: I am of the opinion Christ slagged Magdalene.

(*Pause.*)

NAILER: There is no reference –

STUCLEY: No reference, no –

NAILER: Or any indication in the gospels that I –

STUCLEY: There wouldn't be, would there?

NAILER: But all the –

STUCLEY: NEUTERED – BISHOPS – RIPPED – IT – OUT.

(*NAILER stares at him.*)

You restore it.

NAILER: Me?

STUCLEY: Yes. Fetch a book.

NAILER: Now?

STUCLEY: Why not now?

(*He shouts off.*)

BOOK!

NAILER: It is not in character, as I understand Him, He
should have exploited His position with the woman to –

STUCLEY: Exploited? Why exploited? The thing's called
love.

NAILER: She had known sex, had traded flesh, but through
Christ's pity, came to the spiritual –

STUCLEY: Yes! And by His cock communicated that!
(*HUSH enters with a volume and ink.*)
Down there, kneel, quick!
(*NAILER takes the pen, kneels.*)
Christ finds the Magdalene – you write – He sees and
pities her – and pitying her, finds her beautiful – get this
down quick – put the illuminations on it afterwards or we'll
be all night –

NAILER: I wasn't doing the –

STUCLEY: The mob's dispersed – He raises her – He holds
her hands, her hands which have fondled knobs and
money, these hands all fresh from fornication He takes in
His…
(*Pause.*)

NAILER: Yes?

STUCLEY: Where were we?

NAILER: Mani habitat –

STUCLEY: Mani habitat?

NAILER: Her hands in His –

STUCLEY: No, put this in English!

NAILER: English?

STUCLEY: Yes, this is the Gospel of the Christ Erect!
(*He is inspired again.*)
And by His gentleness, touches her heart, like any maiden
rescued from the dragon gratitude stirs in her womb,
she becomes to Him the possibility of shared oblivion,
she sheds all sin, and He experiences the – irrational
manifestation of pity which is –
(*Pause. He looks at NAILER, scrawling.*)
Tumescence…
(*Pause.*)
Got that?

NAILER: Yes…

STUCLEY: Now, we are closer to a man we understand, for at
this moment of desire, Christ knows the common lot.
(*Pause.*)
And she is sterile.

NAILER: Sterile?

STUCLEY: Diseased beyond conception, yes. So that they find, in passion, also tragedy…

(*NAILER catches up, looks at STUCLEY.*)

What use is a Christ who has not suffered everything?

(*He wanders a little.*)

They say the Jews killed Christ, but that's nonsense, the Almighty did. Why, did you say?

NAILER: Yes…

STUCLEY: Because His son discovered comfort. 'Oh, Father, why hast thou forsaken me?' Because in the body of the Magdalene He found the single place in which the madness of his father's world might be subdued. Unforgivable transgression the Lunatic could not forgive…

(*Pause. STUCLEY is moved by his own perceptions.*)

You see, how once Christ is restored to cock, all contradictions are resolved…

NAILER: The Church of Christ the Lover…

STUCLEY: Yes, why not?

(*Pause. NAILER is inspired.*)

NAILER: Therefore – therefore – the missing symbol of communion is – is –

STUCLEY: What?

NAILER: Milk! Body, blood and semen!

STUCLEY: Oh, luscious bishop of the new born church!

(*He shouts.*)

Bring him his hat!

(*He turns to NAILER.*)

Put this out, then, from your box, up the little stairs and leaning over them, put out the agonized virility of Christ! Fetch him his hat!

HUSH: What hat?

STUCLEY: I don't care what hat, bring a hat!

(*To NAILER.*) Begin, today I bring you hope, all you who have no hope – that's everybody – today I bring you satisfaction, all you who have no satisfaction – that's everybody again – Christ is rescued from His enemies! Make out there's been a thousand year conspiracy – what's that?

43

HUSH: (*Carrying a tool bag.*) Couldn't find a hat, but this –
(*He holds it upside down, shrugs.*)

STUCLEY: Yes – Yes! Place it on him, crown him!
(*NAILER looks uncomfortable. HUSH puts the bag on NAILER's head.*)

Oh, yes, oh, look at that! The dignity, the patter, and the aged mush! All creases, not of wisdom, but repented filth, but who knows that? I'd think to look at him, oh, terrible hours in the celibate cell! DON'T TELL ME I CAN'T ORDAIN YOU, that is taking your new enthusiasm to excess, I ordain you, I ordain you, first among episcopates of Christ the Lover, I ordain you, I ordain you, etcetera, look –
(*He dismisses HUSH with a gesture.*)

I must pay the builder and you have to help.
(*Pause.*)

NAILER: Help? I've no –

STUCLEY: He thinks I'm asking him to turn his pockets out! No, I mean invoke Christ the Lover round the estate. I mean increase the yield of the demesne and plant more acres. Plough the woods. I want a further hour off them, with Christ's encouragement, say Friday nights –

NAILER: They have already given up a day to the estate –

STUCLEY: You cannot have a castle and a forty hour week!
(*Pause.*)

Now I'm shouting. I'm shouting at God's rep! Genuflections, genuflections, I mean we cannot be defended without sacrifice. Don't they want to be safe?

NAILER: They gather on Fridays, it is the night the women talk –

STUCLEY: There has to be a stop to that. The excessive talking. Talking here is a disease. Say it offends the scriptures and will blight their wombs –

NAILER: They know full well it doesn't –

STUCLEY: LOOK, ARE YOU RECANTED OR NOT?
(*Pause.*)

NAILER: I only – beg to remind you – children they have had in bumper harvests here.
(*Pause.*)

STUCLEY: Yes. I am forever tripping over them.

NAILER: They also are a wealth.

STUCLEY: More's the pity I've no tin mine to stuff them in, but they can clear the heath –

(*ANN enters. He turns on her.*)

We have the keep up to your horror! For some reason I can't guess the mortar is not perished by your chanting, nor do the slates fall when you wave the sapling sticks.

(*He goes towards her.*)

As for windows, none, or fingernails in width. Stuff light. Stuff furnishings!

ANN: The cattle have been driven off the common.

STUCLEY: Yes. The common is too big.

ANN: Too big?

STUCLEY: To be misused like this. The common will be smaller and the rest given for sheep.

ANN: Sheep.

STUCLEY: You know, wool grows on them!

(*He laughs, then turns.*)

YOU DISCUSS THINGS LIKE A PROPER WIFE!

(*Pause.*)

Terrible impertinence.

(*HOLIDAY enters. STUCLEY swings on him.*)

Am I imagining, or is the rate of building falling off? I look out of my window and the same low, ragged outline –

HOLIDAY: Ragged?

STUCLEY: Outline in the sky, which does not double as I wish it would –

HOLIDAY: Double?

STUCLEY: Are you short-staffed or something? Of course not double but it's static –

HOLIDAY: It's not a marrow it's a castle –

STUCLEY: It's static, I swear it is –

HOLIDAY: I have one hundred labourers and they are shifting four courses every fortnight –

STUCLEY: Yes, you have all the answers, doesn't he, all the answers, and I have only got my eyes, why don't you look me in the eyes?

HOLIDAY: I do, but briefly –

STUCLEY: Briefly, like a liar –

HOLIDAY: No, I have a thing about –
STUCLEY: Me, too, even now your are –
HOLIDAY: Yes, I am scanning upwards for the –
STUCLEY: WELL, LOOK.

(*Pause. HOLIDAY stares him in the eyes.*)

HOLIDAY: There are – scaffolding up –

(*He points with a finger.*)

And someone – butter-fingers might – WHAT?

STUCLEY: (*Tearing off.*) Where's my genius? My engineer!
ANN: (*To HOLIDAY.*) Give up…
HOLIDAY: Wha'?
ANN: Give up.
HOLIDAY: She is most persuasive, I must say, with 'er
    monosyllables. If you must know, I would rather be
    erecting hospitals myself.
ANN: Do, then.
HOLIDAY: (*To BATTER, shuffling off.*) Monosyllabic wisdom.
ANN: Do!
HOLIDAY: (*Turning.*) For what? Gratitude? Mix with straw
    and eat it? Lovely gratitude, yum, yum!
ANN: First you do it, then you see. But first, you do it.
HOLIDAY: (*Shaking his head.*) See first.
ANN: You can't see first. Everyone wants to see first. See
    afterwards.

(*HOLIDAY goes out.*)

BATTER: (*Following.*) How the drowned man crossed the
    swamp…

(*Pause. She looks at NAILER, who is kneeling in prayer.*)

ANN: What are you doing?

(*NAILER mumbles.*)

Have you seen yourself?

(*Mumbles.*) Find you a mirror…

(*She delves in her pockets.*)

NAILER: All symbols can be ridiculed. On the one hand,
    authority is costume, but on the other –
ANN: Never mind the words, Reg, look at the –
NAILER: I don't need to –
ANN: Look –

(*She holds up a small mirror.*)

NAILER: Thank you, I am perfectly aware what –

ANN: LOOK!

> (*He looks.*)
> What's that?
> (*Pause.*)

NAILER: A mitre.

> (*Pause.*)

ANN: A mitre? Reg, you have got a bag on your –

NAILER: I am sick of your wisdom! Women's wisdom! Sick of it!

ANN: Now, don't be –

NAILER: Argument, opinion, and debate! The whispering until the candle toppled in the wax –

ANN: Reg –

NAILER: Long nights of dialogue –

ANN: Reg, there is a tool bag on your head.

> (*Pause. He regards her with contempt.*)

NAILER: Oh, you literal creature… It was tool bag…it is no longer a tool bag, it is a badge… IF YOU KNEW HOW I YEARNED FOR GOD!

ANN: Which god?

> (*Pause, then patiently.*)

NAILER: The God which puts a stop to argument. The God who says, 'Thus I ordain it!' The God who puts His finger on the sin.

ANN: Sin…?

NAILER: WHY NOT SIN?

> (*Pause. He gets up.*)
> And no more Reg.
> (*He looks at her, goes out. A wind howls over the stage.*)

## SCENE FIVE

*STUCLEY, KRAK, leaning on a wind.*

STUCLEY: There never was a wind like this before! You got a buffetting, but this…!

KRAK: It is the relationship between the air and the mass – the wind is trapped between the towers and accelerates to three times its velocity –

STUCLEY: He's changed the climate! What can't he do?
(*He takes him by the shoulders.*)
You Turk. You Jew. You pedant. Make it snow.
(*KRAK looks at him.*)
KRAK: You ask a great deal of a simple engineer –
STUCLEY: No, stuff your reservations, make it snow.
(*Pause.*)
Because you can, you ice-cold shifter of old worlds, you can…
(*Pause. Flakes of snow flurry over the stage. STUCLEY laughs, seizing the bewildered KRAK and lifting him bodily in the air.*)
I could chuck you into space and you would circle round my system like a star, twinkling at me from that secret eye!
(*He drops him.*)
Play snowballs with me! I did love boyhood more than anything! Play snowballs!
KRAK: (*Looking at the few flakes.*) There is scarcely –
STUCLEY: Chase me, then!
(*He turns to run. KRAK waits.*)
Oh, it is beneath his dignity…
(*Suddenly he flings himself on KRAK. They struggle. KRAK asserts his superior physical strength and forces STUCLEY to the ground. For a moment, he threatens his life. Then he releases him. STUCLEY gets to his feet, amazed.*)
What?
(*Pause.*)
What?
(*Pause.*)
Could have ruptured my throat!
(*He rubs the place.*)
I do hate men of intellect. The curtain of the intellect, the mathematics, the poetics, concealing what dog itch, I wonder.
(*Pause.*)
That hurt, that did…
(*Pause.*)
Old man…
KRAK: More arches.
STUCLEY: Where?

KRAK: The outer work. Double the arches. Double the ditch.
  (*He scrambles up, hurries out.*)
STUCLEY: Builder!
  (*He follows. Pause. SKINNER enters with CANT, hands
  reaching for the snow.*)
CANT: 's not settling…
SKINNER: Fuck!
CANT: Stoppin'…
SKINNER: Fuck and fuck!
CANT: Got some bits…
SKINNER: LOST MY CRAFT!
CANT: Don't say that, you got some –
SKINNER: Laid a carpet three feet deep here once!
CANT: Remember it…
  (*SKINNER covers her face. Pause.*)
  P'raps the brew was –
SKINNER: You did the brew…
CANT: Maybe the toads weren't fresh enough –
SKINNER: Not the toads…
CANT: Or sprawning – that was it! A sprawning toad shall
  not –
SKINNER: Not the toads! Shut up about the toads. The
  power's gone…
CANT: Not gone, just –
SKINNER: Gone!
  (*Pause.*)
CANT: I don't think you should – just because of –
  (*SKINNER kneels, her face covered.*)
  Skinner?
  (*Pause.*)
  Because one –
SKINNER: Leave me alone, will you? I thank you for your
  kindness, but –
  (*CANT withdraws. A heavy snowfall. SKINNER does not move.
  In the silence the sound of a metallic movement. Armoured figures
  appear from different directions. They congregate, are motionless.*)
BALDWIN: (*At last.*) The oath!
ROLAND: The oath!

REGINALD: The oath!

ALL: We do vowe no peace shall be on earth, no ear of wheat standen, no sheep with bowel in, no hutte unburn, no chylde with blood in, until such tyme we have our aims all maken wholehearte and compleate!

REGINALD: Baldwin!

BALDWIN: Here!

REGINALD: Reginald here!

BALDWIN: I see your armour, Reginald!

THEOBALD: Theobald here!

ROLAND: I see your badge!

 (*Pause.*)

 The flaming cow ran with its entrails hanging out –

BALDWIN: I cut the dog in half –

THEOBALD: One blow –

BALDWIN: The dog in the two halves went –

THEOBALD: The head this way –

ROLAND: Its entrails caught around a post –

REGINALD: Double-headed axe went –

ROLAND: Its entrails caught around a post –

BALDWIN: Two-handed sword went –

ROLAND: Pulled out the seven stomachs of the flaming cow –

THEOBALD: Village bell went –

BALDWIN: Cut the dog in half –

REGINALD: The head this way –

THEOBALD: Ding –

BALDWIN: Cut the boy in half –

REGINALD: Or girl was it –

THEOBALD: Ding –

BALDWIN: Eighty millimetre gun went –

THEOBALD: Ding –

ROLAND: The seven stomachs of the bowelless cow –

REGINALD: Tracer from the half-track went –

ROLAND: The cow now with no entrails went –

BALDWIN: The mounting of the Bofors went –

REGINALD: Into the rick, into the thatch –

BALDWIN: Spent cases rattled on the deck –

THEOBALD: Or girl was it –

ROLAND: The cow now with no entrails went –
THEOBALD: Bereft of entrails –
ROLAND: Stomachless –
BALDWIN: The boy in two halves through the village went –
THEOBALD: Ding –
REGINALD: Or girl was it –
BALDWIN: The flaming messenger of our approach –
ROLAND: Barked its –
THEOBALD: Bellowed its –
REGINALD: Screamed its –
THEOBALD: Crack division –
BALDWIN: Crack division –
REGINALD: Spent cases rattled on the deck –
THEOBALD: I fear naught, Baldwin!
BALDWIN: Fear naught!
ROLAND: Encrimsoned and imbrued!
REGINALD: Down came the thatch and in the pig squeal and
    the woman squeal and the man squeal and the –
THEOBALD: Fear naught, Reginald!
ROLAND: Defend the right!
REGINALD: Down came the thatch!
THEOBALD: Baldwin!
BALDWIN: I see your armour!
    (*Silence. HOLIDAY enters.*)
HOLIDAY: Yep?
    (*He looks around.*)
    Somebody ask for me?
    (*Pause.*)
SKINNER: The bricklayers are guilty, too.
HOLIDAY: Come again?
SKINNER: The bricklayers are guilty, too.
HOLIDAY: (*Turning away.*) No, someone asked for me...
SKINNER: (*As he goes.*) You mustn't look up all the time.
HOLIDAY: 'ullo, advice from every quarter –
SKINNER: Because it will not come from there.
    (*He stops.*)
HOLIDAY: What won't?
    (*She does not reply. He is about to go, then, looking around him.*)

I saw your arse...
(*Pause.*)
Excuse me, but I saw your arse – you showed your arse
and I – they say you don't like men – which is to do surely,
with – who you 'ad to do with, surely...
(*Pause.*)
Anyway, I saw your arse...
(*He turns, despairingly, to go.*)
SKINNER: All right.
HOLIDAY: (*Stops.*) What – you –
SKINNER: All right...
(*The walls rise to reveal the interior of a keep.*)

# ACT TWO

## SCENE ONE

*The hall, unfinished. KRAK, in a shaft of light.*

KRAK: He wants another wall, in case the first three walls
    are breached. The unknown enemy, the enemy who does
    not exist yet but who cannot fail to materialize, will batter
    down the first wall and leaving a carpet of twitching dead
    advance on the second wall, and scaling it, will see in front
    of them the third wall buttressed, ditched and palisaded,
    this wall I have told him will break their spirit but he aches
    for a fourth wall, a fourth wall against which the enemy
    who does not exist yet but who cannot fail to materialize
    will be crucified. As for the towers, despite their inordinate
    height he orders me increase them by another fifteen
    feet. A fifth wall I predict will be necessary, and a sixth
    essential, to protect the fifth, necessitating the erection
    of twelve flanking towers. The castle is by definition, not
    definitive…

BRIAN: (*Rushing.*) RON'S 'EAD! RON'S 'EAD!

STUCLEY: (*Flying in.*) THE BUILD – A! THE BUILD – A!

BRIAN: Took yer eyes off, Ron!

STUCLEY: His eggshell! Someone tapped it with a spoon!

BRIAN: Took 'is eyes off and down comes a brick!

BATTER: (*Smartly.*) Was not, idiot. Found him lying in the
    ditch, haunches naked and dew drops on his hairy arse.

STUCLEY: What!

BATTER: Trousers down and head bashed.

STUCLEY: What!

BATTER: Woman murder!

BRIAN: Trousers down and –

BATTER: Woman murder!

    (*They look at him.*)

    Well, what else, he was not pissing under scaffolding.

BRIAN: Ron would never –

BATTER: Ron would never, 'e knows. To piss would be to take your eyes off what's above, or soak your legs. No, this was woman murder, most undignified he looked –

STUCLEY: WHO WILL TRANSLATE MY BLUEPRINTS NOW!

(*ANN enters. STUCLEY turns on her.*)

Who did this, you! Oh, her mask of kindness goes all scornful at the thought – what, me?

(*He swings on BRIAN.*)

YOU DO THE JOB!

(*And to ANN.*) And such a crease of womanly dismay spreads down her jaw, and dignified long nose tips slightly with her arrogance – what, me? It stops nothing, this.

(*To BATTER.*) Find the killer who tried to hinder the inevitable!

(*As BATTER leaves, with BRIAN.*) Listen, I think morality is also bricks, the fifth wall is the wall of morals, did you think I could leave that untouched?

(*He turns to go, stops.*)

Gang meets at sunset by the camp! The password is –

(*He whispers in KRAK's ear.*)

DON'T TELL!

(*He goes to leave.*)

Gang meets at sunset and no girls!

(*He hurries out. Pause.*)

ANN: Gravity. Parabolas. Equations. The first man's dead. Gravity. Parabolas. Equations. Are you glad?

(*KRAK does not move.*)

Say yes. Because you are. That's why you're here. Grey head. Badger gnawed about the ears and eyes down, bitten old survivor of the slaughter, loosing off your wisdom when you think yourself alone, I know, I do know, grandfather of slain children, aping the adviser, aping the confidant, but actually, but actually, I do know badger-head, you want us dead. And not dead simply, but torn, parted, spiked on the oaks, limbs between the acorns, a real rucking of the favoured landscape, the peace when you came here made your heart knot with anger, I know, the castle is the magnet of extermination, it is not a house, is it, the castle is not a house...

(*Pause.*)

I am so drawn to you I feel sick.

(*Pause.*)

The man who suffers. The man who's lost. Success appalls me but pain I love. Your grey misery excites me. Can you stand a woman who talks of her cunt? I am all enlarged for you...

(*He stares at her.*)

Now you humiliate me. By silence. I am not humiliated.

(*Pause.*)

KRAK: They cut off my mother's head. She was senile and complaining. They dismembered my wife, whom I saw little of. And my daughter, with a glancing blow, spilled all her brains, as a clumsy man sends a drink flying off the table. And her I did not give all the attention that I might. I try to be truthful. I hate exaggeration. I hate the cultivated emotion.

(*Pause.*)

And you say, come under my skirt. Under my skirt, oblivion and compensation, shoot your anger in my bowel, CUNT ALSO IS A DUNGEON!

(*Pause.*)

ANN: Enthralling shout...

(*Pause, then he suddenly laughs.*)

And laugh, for that matter...

(*Pause, then he turns to leave.*)

I mean, don't tell me it is virgins that you want, the unmarked flesh, untrodden map of girlhood, the look of fear and unhinged legs of –

(*He returns, slaps her face into silence. Pause.*)

You have made my nose bleed...

# SCENE TWO

*The PROSECUTORS descending. A court assembling.*

NAILER: Thank you for coming.

POOL: Thank you for asking me.

NAILER: The rigours of travel.

POOL: Not to be undertaken lightly.

NAILER: No, indeed. Indeed, no. His trousers were down.

POOL: So I gather.

NAILER: I do think –

POOL: The absolute limit.

NAILER: And misuse of love.

POOL: Make that your angle.

NAILER: I will do.

POOL: The trust which resides in the moment of –

NAILER: Etcetera –

POOL: Most cruelly abused. Make that your angle.

NAILER: Thank you, I will.

POOL: Fucking bitches when your goolies are out…

NAILER: (*To the court.*) A man proffers union – albeit outside the contract of marriage – a man proffers union – albeit without the blessing of Almighty God – he offers it by tacit understanding, by signs, by words negotiates this most delicate and sacred of all –

SKINNER: (*From the dock.*) ANN!

NAILER: Lays down, abandons, puts aside all those defences which the male by nature transports in his demeanour, and in the pity of his nakedness –

SKINNER: ANN!

NAILER: Anticipating the exchange of tenderness, arms outstretched for the generosity of the feminine embrace –

SKINNER: WHERE ARE YOU, YOU BITCH – no, mustn't swear –

NAILER: A crime therefore, not against an individual – not against a single man most cruelly deceived –

SKINNER: Descend to swearing – better not –

NAILER: But against that universal trust, that universally upheld convention lying at the heart of all sexual relations marital and illicit –

SKINNER: Temper and so on, no, no, no, Skinner, stop it, it's the daylight got me going – beg pardon –

NAILER: And thereby threatening not only the security of that most intimate love which God endowed man with –

SKINNER: Daylight – got me going – sorry –

NAILER: For peace and for relief but –

SKINNER: I am not ill-tempered as a matter of fact, I don't
know where that idea's come from that I – and anyway
I know you hate it, loudness and shouting, you do, such
delicate emotions and I – THEY HAVE DONE AWFUL
THINGS TO ME DOWN THERE – do my best to be – to be
contained – that way you have, you – THERE IS A ROOM
DOWN THERE AND THEY DID TERRIBLE THINGS TO ME – I
mean my cunt which had been so – which we had made
so – THANKS TO YOU WAS DEAD – so it wasn't the abuse it
might have been, the abuse they would have liked it to be
had it been a living thing, were it the sacred and beautiful
thing we had found it out to be and – am I going on, I do
go on – are you – so thank you I hated it and the more
they hurt it the better I – I was actually gratified, believe it
or not, yes, gratified –

NAILER: But the very act of procreation itself, which is
collaborative, which is, for its success wholly dependent on –

SKINNER: They have this way you see, of relating the torture
to the offence – the things they say – you wouldn't – are
you in here, I can't see – put your hand up I can't – am
I being reasonable enough for you, not shouting am I,
actually I'm half dead – where are you sitting, I –
(*She looks around.*)
I call it daylight but it's relative – I WANT TO SEE YOUR
HAND – Can I have a stool or not?
(*A MAN goes to fetch it.*)
NOT ONE WITH A SPIKE IN THE MIDDLE! They think of
everything – they do – imaginations – you should see
the – INVENTION DOWN THERE – makes you gasp the
length of their hatred – the uncoiled length of hatred
– mustn't complain though – was I complaining – was I
– beg pardon – I have this – tone which – thanks to your
expertise is mollified a little –
(*The MAN returns with a stool.*)
WHAT DOES THAT DO, BITE YOUR ARSE?
(*She looks at it, on the ground.*)
Looks harmless, looks a harmless little stool, boring bit of
carpentry DON'T BELIEVE IT!
(*She goes towards it, extends her fingers gingerly.*)

Spring trap!

(*She leaps back.*)

Spring trap! Legs fly up and grip your head, seen stools like that before, didn't think I'd fall for that, did you, not really, didn't think I'd –

(*She sits on it, in utter exhaustion.*)

You have to kill them, don't you? Death they understand. Death is their god, not love. Because after he was dead they built nothing, for one day THEY BUILT NOTHING. And because all things decay, in actual fact for one day the castle went backwards! I mean – by virtue of erosion and the usual rot – there was less castle on Monday than on Sunday! And what did that? DEATH DID! I call it death, they call it murder, they call it battle, I call it slaughter etcetera, etcetera, the word is just a hole down which all things can drop – I mean, I put a stop to him.

(*Pause.*)

And he was quite a nice man, as far as they – there is a limit to those even of the best intentions – he talked of mutual pleasure – really, the banality! It really hurt my ears – after what we had – to talk of – MUTUAL PLEASURE – can you believe – the very words are…

(*She dries.*)

STUCLEY: We are up against it. We are, we really are, up against it.

(*He walks about.*)

Having hewn away two hills to make us safe, having knifed the landscape to preserve us we find – horror of horrors – THE WORST WITHIN.

(*Pause, he looks at all of them.*)

I find that a blow, I do, I who have reeled under so many blows find that – a blow. Who can you trust? TRUST!

(*He shrieks, the word is a thing butted at them.*)

I say in friendship, I say in comradeship, I say without malice YOU ARE ALL TRAITORS!

(*They deny it.*)

Thank you, thank you, you deny it, thank you, the vehemence I love it, thank you, lovely vehemence orchestrated and spontaneous THANK YOU BUT.

(*Pause.*)

Things being what they are I have no choice, times being
what they are I feel sure you understand in everybody's
interest it is crucial I regard you all as being actively
engaged in the planning of my murder – no, not really, not
really, silly, but as a basis for –

NAILER: Yes.

STUCLEY: He knows!

(*Pause.*)

I have changed my view of God. I no longer regard Him
as an evil deity, that was excessive, evil, no. He's mad. It is
only by recognizing God is mad that we can satisfactorily
explain the random nature of – you say, you are the
theologian.

NAILER: It appears to us He was not always mad –

STUCLEY: Not always, no –

NAILER: But became so, driven to insanity by the failure and
the contradiction of His works –

STUCLEY: I understand Him!

NAILER: The absurdity of attempting to reconcile the
simultaneous beauty and horror of the world is abolished
by the recognition of His –

STUCLEY: THEY ARE BUILDING A CASTLE OVER THE HILL
AND IT'S BIGGER THAN THIS.

(*Pause.*)

Given God is now a lunatic, I think, sadly, we are near to
the Apocalypse…

(*He turns.*)

Gatherings of more than three we cannot tolerate.

NAILER: The church –

STUCLEY: I exclude births, deaths and marriages! And
periodical searching of all homes I know you will not
wish to hinder, what have the innocent got to conceal, it
stands to reason all who complain have secrets, juries are
abolished they are not reliable, quaint relics of a more
secure time, I sleep alone in sheets grey with tossing, I
cannot keep a white sheet white, do you find this? Grey by
the morning. Does anyone find this? The launderers are
frantic.

BATTER: Yes.

STUCLEY: You do? What is it?

BATTER: I don't know…it could be…I don't know…

STUCLEY: Why grey, I wonder?

SKINNER: (*Stands suddenly.*) WHAT HAVE YOU DONE TO YOUR HAIR?

(*Pause.*)

It's plaited in a funny way, what have you – IT'S VILE.

(*Pause.*)

Well, no, it's not, it's pretty, vile and pretty at the same time, DID YOU TAKE HIM IN YOUR MOUTH, I MUST KNOW.

(*Pause.*)

If I know all I can struggle with it, I can wrestle it to death, but not the imagined thing, don't leave anything out, OF COURSE I AM ENTITLED TO A DESCRIPTION.

(*Pause.*)

This floor, laid over flowers we once lay on, this cruel floor will become the site of giggling picnics, clots of children wandering with music in their ears and not one will think, not one, A WOMAN WRITHED HERE ONCE. The problem is to divest yourself of temporality, is that what you do?

(*She looks at NAILER.*)

I gave up, and longed to die, and yet I did not die. That all life should be bound up in one randomly encountered individual defies the dumb will of the flesh clamouring for continuation, life would not have it! I hate you, do you know why, because you prove to me that nothing is, nothing at all is, THE THING WITHOUT WHICH NOTHING ELSE IS POSSIBLE.

(*Pause.*)

I am aching from my breasts to the bottom of my bowel, but that is just desire, poof! And deprivation, poof! Love and longing, poof to all of it! AM I TO BE HANGED OR DROWNED? If you haven't had love ripped out your belly, dragging half your organs with it, don't talk to me, you haven't lived! Only the suffering to pass the sentence, you, for example…

(*She indicates STUCLEY.*)

STUCLEY: Tie her to the body of her victim.
  (*Pause.*)
SKINNER: Tie her to –
STUCLEY: And turn her loose.
SKINNER: (*In horror.*) Now hold on, what –
POOL: The mercy of Almighty God be –
SKINNER: What about my execution –
POOL: Be upon you now and always –
SKINNER: MY HANGING...!
  (*A reverberating explosion. Running to and fro.*)

# SCENE THREE

STUCLEY: You heard that!
BATTER: Of course I fucking heard it...
  (*Another boom.*)
STUCLEY: ANOTHER ONE.
BATTER: All right, another one...
STUCLEY: Why?
BATTER: Can't think.
STUCLEY: What is it!
BATTER: Can't think, I said –
STUCLEY: Comes from the East, you know!
KRAK: Yes.
STUCLEY: What!
  (*Pause.*)
KRAK: A castle.
STUCLEY: What?
KRAK: There is one.
  (*Pause.*)
STUCLEY: There is one...
  (*A third boom.*)
KRAK: You knew, and I knew, there could not be only this
  one, but this one would breed others. And there is one.
  Called The Fortress.
STUCLEY: Bigger than this...
KRAK: Bigger. Three times the towers and polygonal. With
  ravelins beyond a double ditch, which I never thought of...
  (*STUCLEY stares for a moment in disbelief.*)

STUCLEY: Everything I fear, it comes to pass. Everything I imagine is vindicated. Awful talent I possess. DON'T I HAVE AN AWFUL TALENT?

BATTER: Yes…

STUCLEY: What's a ravelin?

KRAK: A ravelin is a two-faced salient beyond the outer-work –

STUCLEY: I want some –

KRAK: You want –

STUCLEY: Some ravelins, yes. Say a hundred.

KRAK: A hundred –

STUCLEY: Two hundred, then!

(*A fourth boom.*)

AND THAT NOISE, WHAT IS IT!

KRAK: The coming of the English desert…

(*Pause.*)

STUCLEY: Yes…

NAILER: Almighty! Almighty!

STUCLEY: Yes…

NAILER: Oh, Almighty, Oh, Almighty…!

STUCLEY: Extinction of the worthless, the obliteration of the melancholy crawl from the puddle to the puddle, from the puddle of the maternal belly to the puddle of the old man's involuntary bladder… Good…and they make such a fuss of murder… NOT ME, THOUGH!

(*He sweeps out, with the others. ANN appears. She is pregnant. She looks at KRAK.*)

KRAK: There is one. With three times the towers and polygonal. With ravelins beyond a double ditch, which I never thought of, why polygonal, to deflect what, I wonder, some young expert who sits all night with his protractors, some thin German with no woman, it is the better castle –

ANN: Better –

NAILER: And the keep low, why? And banked with earth. He sleeps alone, the opposing engineer…

ANN: We find a rock.

KRAK: Stink of death to English woods. Hips on the fences. Flies a noisy garment on the entrail in the bracken.

ANN: I have your child in here.

KRAK: The trooper boots the bud open and sends my –
(*Pause.*)
Said my, then…
(*Pause. He smiles.*)
Error.

ANN: It is you that needs to be born. I will be your midwife.
Through the darkness, down the black canal –

KRAK: WHAT ROCK?

ANN: Off the coast. A barren place with nothing to lure
murder for.

KRAK: No such place.

ANN: No wealth. Nothing to draw the conqueror.

KRAK: All places will be conquered.

ANN: Useless pinnacle of gale-lashed –

KRAK: NO SUCH THING.
(*Pause.*)
Hot pans of blazing sun, spiky rocks in frozen waters,
sheep-gnawed granites in Arctic hurricanes, all pretexts for
murder and screaming up the barren slopes –

ANN: ALL RIGHT, WISDOM! ALL RIGHT, LOGIC!
(*Pause.*)
I have a child in here, stone deaf to argument, floats
in water, all pessimism filtered, lucky infant spared
compelling reasons why it should acquiesce in death.
(*She turns to go.*)

KRAK: IS THERE ANY MAN YOU HAVE NOT COPULATED WITH?
(*She stops.*)
I wonder…
(*CANT runs across the stage, picks up a stone, chucks it at
something off.*)

CANT: 's comin'!
(*A second figure runs by.*)

BRIAN: S – T – E – N – C – H!
(*And another.*)

MAN: (*Laughing.*) Scarper!
(*They turn, stare, as SKINNER staggers in. The decayed body of
HOLIDAY is strapped to her front. She leans backwards from her
burden, a grotesque parody of pregnancy.*)

SKINNER: Wind's a bastard, running ahead. And yet these walls make eddies, and running from me sometimes meet me slap!

(*They stare at her.*)

Not dead. Been feverish, of course. And much morning sickness all times of day…

(*ANN turns away her head.*)

Lay in the bluebells, odd sight this, on my back, head turned to gasp great lungfuls of the scent and then could not get up, you'd know this, my gravity was somewhere else, legs like windmills, beetle on its back or pregnant female, you get used to it, nothing you can't get used to, FIRST HORROR.

(*Pause.*)

Fashion of the rotted male, exclusive garment, everybody's wearing it NOT TO COPY and his organ butts against mine, would you believe, you can live without others, SECOND HORROR! Why are you pregnant all the time, other women spent their fertility decades ago, but you – been at the herbs again?

(*ANN weeps with despair.*)

He is losing weight. If I lie still the crows take bits away, kind crows, my favourite bird they are so solitary or live in pairs not like rooks and I was fond of rooks once, no, the solitary bird is best, you have power over her, shut her up…

(*KRAK does not move.*)

He hates you. You do your hair like that, and yet he hates you. Does anyone remember what this place was once? They don't, they really don't, the children say the castle has been here a thousand years.

ANN: You should go.

(*Pause.*)

SKINNER: Go…

ANN: Yes. Not hang round here.

SKINNER: Go where? I live here.

ANN: No such thing as live here any more, go where you might find peace and rub the thing off you, where you won't be stoned.

(*Pause.*)

SKINNER: No.

ANN: Do you like to be stoned?

SKINNER: Yes.

(*Pause.*)

Yes to punishment. Yes to blows.

(*Pause.*)

ANN: What have I done to you?

(*SKINNER laughs.*)

SKINNER: She thinks – she has the neck – she has the gall – to think she brought me to – she has to think herself responsible!

(*She looks to KRAK.*)

Careful! She's after your suicide! Hanging off the battlements for love! The corpse erect! Through her thin smile the knowledge even in death she got you up!

(*Mimicking.*) Did I do this?

(*She turns to ANN.*)

This is my place, more stones the better and pisspans, pour on! You and your reproductive satisfactions, your breasts and your lactation, dresses forever soddened at the tit, IT DID GET ON MY WICK A BIT, envy of course, envy, envy, envy of course. I belong here. I am the castle also.

ANN: You do suck your hatreds. You do – suck – so. And he – also sucks his.

SKINNER: (*As a group of hooded prisoners enters.*) That way the dungeon!

ANN: Gulls at the sewer…

SKINNER: Bear left and wait, the torturer's at breakfast!

(*They shuffle.*)

ANN: Snails on the eyes of the dead…

SKINNER: Tax evaders on the first rung, work-shy on the second!

ANN: Suck pessimism, suck fear…!

SKINNER: Don't hang about, the last lot came up again. Only some bits were missing!

(*ANN hurries out. The gang shuffles further. BATTER appears, with a short stick.*)

There are eighty-seven stairs and the last two flights they
throw you off!

BATTER: All right, get along…

SKINNER: Hullo, Bob…

BATTER: Wotcha, darling…

SKINNER: Look well…

BATTER: Thank you…

(*To the gang.*) 'HO SAID TO STOP?

SKINNER: Cold again…

BATTER: English summer…

SKINNER: Fuckin' 'ell…

BATTER: (*As he passes.*) Take care…

SKINNER: Will do…

(*The prisoners and BATTER depart. SKINNER takes an
apple from her clothes and begins to eat it. KRAK, who has
been watching in perfect stillness, suddenly kneels at her feet.
SKINNER stops, mouth open, apple aloft.*)

What?

(*Pause.*)

What?

(*Pause.*)

What, you bugger, what?

KRAK: The Book of Cunt.

(*Pause.*)

SKINNER: What book is that?

KRAK: The Book of Cunt says all men can be saved.

(*Pause.*)

Not true.

(*Pause.*)

She pulled me down. I did not pull her. She pulled me. In
the shadow of the turret, in the apex of the angle with the
wall, in the slender crack of thirty-nine degrees, she, using
the ledge to fix her heels, levered her parts over me. Shoes
fell, drawers fell, drowned argument in her spreading
underneath…

(*Pause.*)

European woman with her passion for old men, wants to
drown their history in her bowel…!

(*Pause.*)

SKINNER: Scares you…

KRAK: My arse. My arse, she says…

(*Pause.*)

SKINNER: Yes…?

KRAK: Cunt you lend or rent, but arse you have to will…
true ring of marrriage…brown button of puckered
muscularity…the sacramental stillness born of hanging
between pain and ecstasy… IN SHIT I FIND PEACE IS IT!
(*He scrambles to his feet.*)
Don't tell them I came here –

SKINNER: Tell who…?

KRAK: Where's cunt's geometry? The thing has got no
angles! And no measure, neither width nor depth, how
can you trust what has no measurements? Don't tell them I
came here…

SKINNER: No…

KRAK: FIND PEACE IN SHIT, DO I?
(*He looks around, goes out. HUSH enters with a dish. He places
it at SKINNER's feet.*)

SKINNER: Wha's that?

HUSH: Lamb.

SKINNER: What?

HUSH: Stew.

SKINNER: What?
(*He starts to slip away.*)
It's an offence to feed me!
(*CANT enters with a dish, lays it down.*)
What –

CANT: Baked apple –

SKINNER: You –
(*She withdraws running low.*)

SKINNER: Oh, God, Oh, Nature, I AM GOING TO BE
WORSHIPPED.

# SCENE FOUR

*KRAK is sitting at his desk. STUCLEY appears.*

STUCLEY: Saw you.
(*KRAK looks up.*)
Giving your brain away
(*Pause.*)
Saw you.
(*Pause.*)
Whose brain do you think it is?
(*KRAK just looks.*)
Well, no. Cock's free but brains are property.
(*He walks a little, stops.*)
Deceit floats up, like fat on the tea cup. Like bones scuffed years after the murder, the knife, the stain, the knickers that refused to rot, I FOLLOWED YOU INTO THE THICKET, YES...!
(*Pause.*)
Symposium of military architects. Twigs cracked but did they look, twigs shattered but did they look? Crouching with diagrams you might have slammed the doors of Asia and they would not have budged. SUPREME CONCENTRATION OF TREASONABLE GENIUS. Are you listening or not?

KRAK: Drawn cunt.
(*Pause.*)

STUCLEY: What?

KRAK: In twenty-seven versions.

STUCLEY: The diagrams you traded with the Fortress were they approximate or comprehensive, did they include the order of defence, the sally ports, which entrances were blind and which led to the keep, HOW SAFE ARE WE AFTER THIS?
(*KRAK holds up his drawing.*)
The representation of that thing is not encouraged by the church.
(*Pause. He is looking at it.*)
It's wrong, surely, that –

(*Pause.*)

I have never looked at one, but that –

KRAK: Gave him all my drawings. And got all his. They are experimenting with a substance that can bring down walls without getting beneath them. Everything before this weapon will be obsolete. This, for example, is entirely redundant as a convining method of defence –

STUCLEY: What –

KRAK: Its vertical profile, which I took further than any other architect, renders it utterly vulnerable…

STUCLEY: What –

KRAK: It goes up, instead of down. Is high, not wide. Is circular and not oblique. Is useless, in effect and an invitation to –

STUCLEY: ONLY JUST FINISHED IT.

(*Pause.*)

KRAK: Yes…

(*He returns to his drawing.*)

STUCLEY: DON'T DRAW CUNT, I'M TALKING!

(*Pause.*)

This is a crisis, isn't it? Is it, or isn't it? You sit there – you have always been so – had this – manner of stillness – most becoming but also sinister – dignity but also malevolence – easy superiority of the captive intellect – IS THAT MY WIFE'S BITS – I wouldn't know them – what man would – I know, you see – I am aware – I do know everything – I do – I think you have done this all to spite me – correct me if I'm wrong –

KRAK: Spite –

STUCLEY: Spite me, yes –

KRAK: Spite? I do not think the word – unless my English fails me – is quite sufficient to contain the volume of the sentiment…

(*Pause.*)

STUCLEY: You blind draughtsman…all the madness in the immaculately ordered words…in the clean drawings…all the temper in the perfect curve…

(*He pretends to flinch.*)

MIND YOUR FACES! DUCK HIS GUTS! INTELLECTUAL BURSTS!

(*Pause.*)

Tumescent as the dick which splits, splashing the ceiling red with sheer barminess, ROBERT!

(*Pause.*)

But I'm not spited. If you do not feel spited no amount of spite can hurt you, Christ was the same, ROBERT!

(*Pause.*)

We burn people like this. Who give away our secrets. Burn them in a chair. Fry them, and the fat goes – human fat goes, spit…! Does – spit!

(*ANN enters.*)

No. Robert I want.

(*She looks at them.*)

Violence not abundance.

ANN: The ease of making children. The facility of numerousness. Plague, yes, but after the plague, the endless copulation of the immune. All these children, children everywhere and I thought, this one matters, alone of them this one matters because it came from love. But I thought wrongly. I thought wrongly.

(*Pause. She looks at KRAK.*)

There is nowhere except where you are. Correct. Thank you. If it happens somewhere, it will happen everywhere. There is nowhere except where you are. Thank you for truth.

(*Pause. She kneels, pulls out a knife.*)

Bring it down. All this.

(*She threatens her belly. Pause.*)

STUCLEY: You won't.

(*Pause.*)

You won't because you cannot. Your mind wants to, but you cannot, and you won't…

(*Pause. He holds out his hand for the knife. She plunges it into herself. A scream. The wall flies out. In a panic, SOLDIERS. Things falling.*)

# SCENE FIVE

*A haze of light.*

SOLDIER ONE: Raining women!

SOLDIER TWO: Mind yer 'eads!

SOLDIER ONE: Raining women!

NAILER: The temper of the Almighty, who gave you
abundance, imagine His temper! Standing before Him how
will you say I did destroy that which it was not mine to
dispense with –

SOLDIER TWO: Mind yer 'eads!
*(A fall.)*

NAILER: The spirits of your unborn children will rise up in
accusation saying –

SOLDIER TWO: AND ANOTHER!

NAILER: Oh, wickedness to so wantonly cast off the gift of
life –
*(A fall.)*

BATTER: These bitches will put paid to the race...

SOLDIER ONE: TO YER RIGHT!

NAILER: I cast thee out, saith the Lord, I cast thee from my
sight –

SOLDIER ONE: TO YER RIGHT!

SOLDIER TWO: ANOTHER!

NAILER: STOP IT! STOP IT OR ELSE...!
*(A fall.)*
Oh, contempt, contempt of life!

BATTER: *(Looking up.)* That's it, that's it for today...

SOLDIER TWO: No more for today...
*(The SOLDIERS wander off. CANT appears.)*

BATTER: *(To CANT.)* All right, get on with this...

NAILER: *(Rising to his feet.)* They must be locked away. All
women who are pregnant. Chained at wrist and ankle,
like cows in the stall. They bear our future in their innards
and they kill it. BY WHAT RIGHT! All women big about the
middle, lock up!
*(He hurries out. CANT straightens the limbs of the fallen.)*

BATTER: Not theirs, birth. Not theirs, is it?

CANT: Dunno.

BATTER: Theirs only, I mean. What's your opinion?

CANT: No opinion.

BATTER: Go on, I won't tell.

CANT: No opinion!

(*She carries on.*)

Death is not yours, either.

BATTER: Wha'?

CANT: Not yours only, is it? Not an opinion.

BATTER: Come again…

CANT: We birth 'em, and you kill 'em. Can't be right we deliver for your slaughter. Cow mothers. Not an opinion.

(*KRAK enters. He moves among the fallen.*)

KRAK: Warm women, cooling…

(*He stops by another.*)

Cooling women…

BATTER: Husbands want to kill 'em. Want to murder 'em, but they are murdered.. Not finding anything to take revenge on, go barmy, mutilate the flesh they simpered over once…

(*Pause.*)

KRAK: She undressed me…

(*They look at him.*)

I lay there thinking…what is she…what does she… undressed me and…

(*Pause.*)

What is the word?

BATTER: Fucked?

KRAK: Fucked!

(*He laughs, as never before.*)

Fucked!

(*Pause.*)

Went over me…the flesh…with such…inch by inch with such…

(*Pause.*)

What is the word?

CANT: Desire.

(*He stares at her, then throwing himself at her feet, tears open his shirt, exposing his flesh to her.*)

KRAK: Show me.

CANT: Wha'?

KRAK: That!

CANT: Show –

KRAK: Desire!

(*She hesitates.*)

BATTER: Go on…

(*She puts her hand out, touches him unwillingly, mechanically.*)

KRAK: Not it…

CANT: Trying but I –

KRAK: Not it!

CANT: Can't just go –

KRAK: NOT IT! NOT IT!

(*She runs out. KRAK shudders. STUCLEY enters, looks at him.*)

STUCLEY: Lost love…! Nothing, nothing like lost love…

(*He rests a hand on KRAK's bent head.*)

And she was of such sympathy, such womanly wisdom I could not bring myself, for all the damage she had done me, bring myself to take revenge, any man would, you say, yes, any man would! Not me, though…!

(*He draws KRAK's head to his side.*)

And you, dear brother in lost love, I UNDERSTAND. The very substance of the body wilts, like dummies who have lost their straw, we flop! Oh, I know, I know his filetting, I TOO WAS FILETTED. And all the valley sobs with grief, shh!

(*He cups his ear.*)

The howl of men bereaved…odd sound among the trees, oh, extraordinary brotherhood!

(*Pause.*)

The new walls will be so low they cannot jump off. Not fatally. They will roll down the slopes only and –

(*He stops, looking from one to another. They stare at him.*)

BATTER: (*At last.*) Come for a walk…

STUCLEY: A walk?

BATTER: Through the meadows. Through the trees.

STUCLEY: Rather not.

BATTER: Rather not…

(*He looks about him.*)

Just like Jerusalem, when we got in, the women were thick on the steps and clotting up the doors, you trod the rolling carpet of their flesh, oh, intoxication! Rather not, he says!

STUCLEY: (*Resisting.*) WHAT'S THIS WALK EXACTLY!

BATTER: And you were up there, first always, up the ladders –

STUCLEY: Was I? Dangerous…

BATTER: Dangerous, yes, England and –

STUCLEY: Saint George! YOU'RE PUSHING ME WHERE I DON'T WANT TO GO.

(*BATTER sweeps him up in his arms.*)

BATTER: And light! So light, do you find that?

(*The SOLDIERS make no move.*)

Light as a child…

(*He walks through them, and out. KRAK scrambles to his feet.*)

KRAK: (*To the soldiers.*) His last walk. His last walk.

(*They ignore him.*)

Listen, his last walk…!

(*He offers himself.*)

Cut the skull through, will you! The one with the axe? Slice it round the top and SSSSSSS the great stench of dead language SSSSSSS the great stench of dead elegance dead manners SSSSSSS articulation and explanation dead all dead YOU DON'T HOLD WOMEN PROPERLY IN BED.

(*An effect of rain and time.*)

## SCENE SIX

*SKINNER, festooned with the skeleton, outside the walls. BATTER enters, with NAILER. Pause.*

BATTER: The Church of Christ the Lover. Fuck it.

SKINNER: What?

BATTER: New church. Tell her.

NAILER: The Holy Congregation of the Wise Womb.

BATTER: All right?

(*Pause. She looks at them.*)

NAILER: Christ, abhorring the phallus, foreswore his
maleness, chose womanly ways. Scripture in abundance for
all this.

BATTER: All right?

SKINNER: I don't like wombs.

BATTER: You don't like –

SKINNER: Hate wombs.

(*Pause. BATTER looks to NAILER.*)

BATTER: She hates –

NAILER: I have been up sixteen hours assembling a
theological foundation for all –

BATTER: All right –

NAILER: NOT ALL RIGHT.

(*Pause.*)

We acknowledge the uniquely female relationship with
the origin of life, the irrational but superior consciousness
located in –

SKINNER: Sod wombs –

NAILER: Do listen, please.

(*Pause. He proceeds.*)

The special sensitivity of woman to the heart-beat of the
earth – Romans Eight, verses nine to –

SKINNER: He does go on –

NAILER: – seventeen, which hitherto has held no special
place in doctrine but which henceforward will be –

SKINNER: PALAVER OF DISSIMULATORS!

NAILER: The foundation of the edict LET THERE BE
WOMANLY TIMES!

(*Pause.*)

BATTER: Wha'd yer think?

(*Pause.*)

Well, do you wanna church or not?

(*Pause.*)

SKINNER: She was all womb. Tortured me with her
fecundity, her moisture, birthing, birthing, very public,
down among the harvest, crouches, yells, and slings it
round her neck, where did I leave my sickle, oh, blood on
her knees and afterbirth for supper, and me like the arid

purse of rattling coins, to her whim and feminine mood of the moon stuff danced my service, and then STABS IT, STABS IT, THE VANITY OF IT!

(*Pause.*)

No womb lover me. Witches' blight if I could manage it. I won't help you govern your State, bailiff made monarch by a stroke of the knife…

(*Pause.*)

BATTER: No…

(*Pause.*)

You govern it instead.

(*She quivers.*)

SKINNER: Now wait – now wait a minute – WAIT! Are you – DON'T TEASE ME…!

NAILER: He is in a positive lather of good faith –

SKINNER: Some limp joke or spiteful provocation –

NAILER: None, I –

SKINNER: (*Grabbing NAILER by the collar.*) WHAT…! WHAT…

NAILER: You – are – hurting – my – throat –

SKINNER: (*Releasing him.*) Some bastard – some twisted – scratch my brain – I can't – fingers at the old seat of suspicion – what's your – YES! YES!

(*Pause.*)

Wait a minute, wait, what's your – get me swelling, get me gloating, dangle it before her eyes – she blobs about the eyes, the eyes are vast and breath goes in and out, in-out, in-out, pant, pant, the bitch is hooked, the bitch is netted, running with the water of desire GIVE ME POWER WHAT FOR, look at me, all twitching with the appetite for –

(*Pause.*)

All right yes…

(*Pause. NAILER tosses down the castle keys. SKINNER looks at them, then with a lightning movement, snatches them off the ground.*)

EXECUTE THE EXECUTIONERS!

(*She leaps.*)

All my pain, all my violence, all my scars say – hear
my scars, you – SUFFERING TO BE PAID OUT, DEBTS
EXTRACTED, SETTLEMENT IN YELLS! Oh, she is not
dignified, she is not charitable, the act of kindness from
the victim to the murderer, grey eyes serene in pain
absorbed, agony knitted into cloths of wisdom WHO SAYS!
Reconciliation and oblivion, NO! GREAT UGLY STICK OF
TEMPER, RATHER
(*She turns on her heel.*)
Nobody say it's all because I'm barren! I have had
children, I have done my labour side by side, and felt
myself halved by her spasms, my floor fell out with hers
and yes, I haemhorraged
(*Pause. They stare at her. She goes to the wall, runs her hand over
the stone.*)
I can't be kind. How I have wanted to be kind. But lost all
feeling for it... Why wasn't I killed? The best thing is to
perish in the struggle...
(*She turns to BATTER and NAILER.*)
No.
(*She tosses the keys down.*)
I shall be too cruel...
KRAK: Got to.
SKINNER: Who says?
KRAK: Got to!
(*Pause. She looks around.*)
SKINNER: Out the shadows, who thinks the only perfect
circle is the cunt in birth...
(*KRAK emerges from a cleft in the wall.*)
KRAK: Demolition needs a drawing, too...
(*Pause.*)
SKINNER: Demolition? What's that?
(*A roar as jets streak low. Out of the silence, SKINNER strains in
recollection.*)
There was no government...does anyone remember...
there was none...there was none...there was none...!

GERTRUDE

The Cry

For the Fraction

# Characters

GERTRUDE, a Queen

CLAUDIUS, a Prince

CASCAN, Servant to Gertrude

HAMLET, an Heir

ISOLA, Mother of Claudius

RAGUSA, a Young Woman

ALBERT, a Duke of Mecklenburg

# 1

*The orchard at Elsinore. A king asleep on the ground.*

GERTRUDE: (*Entering.*) I should
Surely
I should
Me
CLAUDIUS: (*Entering.*) No
GERTRUDE: Me
Let me
CLAUDIUS: It must be me who
GERTRUDE: Why not me
CLAUDIUS: Me who
GERTRUDE: HE IS MY HUSBAND WHY NOT ME
(*Pause.*)
CLAUDIUS: Because he is your husband it must be me
GERTRUDE: Let me kill
Oh let me kill for you
(*Pause.*)
CLAUDIUS: I'm killing
Me
(*Pause.*)
GERTRUDE: KILL MY HUSBAND THEN KILL HIM FOR ME
(*A fractional pause.*)
CLAUDIUS: Strip
GERTRUDE: Strip?
CLAUDIUS: Naked
GERTRUDE: Strip naked yes
CLAUDIUS: Let me see the reason I am killing
GERTRUDE: (*Tearing off her clothes.*) Yes
Yes
CLAUDIUS: And if he stirs
If his eyes open in his agony
Show him the reason he is dying
Let him see what I have stolen
What was his
And what now belongs to me
THE THING

THE THING

LET THE DYING DOG'S EYES SWIM YOUR

(*Pause.*)

He's not a dog

(*He shrugs.*)

I called him a dog

GERTRUDE: Do it now

CLAUDIUS: If anyone's a dog

GERTRUDE: DO IT NOW

CLAUDIUS: It's me

(*GERTRUDE positions herself above the head of the sleeping man, tilted, provocative.*)

GERTRUDE: Poison him

(*CLAUDIUS goes to kiss GERTRUDE. She shuts her eyes, averts her face.*)

Poison him

(*CLAUDIUS takes the phial from his clothing. He kneels by the sleeping man. He pours the fluid into the man's ear. GERTRUDE seems to vomit in her ecstasy. Her cry mingles with the cry of the sleeping man who shudders.*)

Fuck me

Oh fuck me

(*CLAUDIUS and GERTRUDE couple above the dying man. All three utter, a music of extremes. A servant enters holding a garment, and attends.*)

# 2

CASCAN: All ecstasy makes ecstasy go running to a further place that is its penalty we know this how well we know this still we would not abolish ecstasy would we we would not say this ever-receding quality in ecstasy makes it unpalatable on the contrary we run behind it limping staggering I saw it there I saw it there

(*He laughs.*)

A haunting mirage on the rim of life

(*He extends the gown for GERTRUDE.*)

Eventually I can't help thinking eventually it lures us over a cliff so what why not a cliff is a cliff worse than a bed a

stinking bed inside a stinking hospital no give me the cliff
do put this on the cliff every time your nakedness is so
perfect hide it hide it keep it for the dark or these rare acts
Madame

(*GERTRUDE goes to CASCAN and is enclosed in the gown.*)
And what magnificence your cry a cry I am if I may say
so not only familiar with but something of a connoisseur
of its varieties this cry I heard beyond the orchard wall
and marvelled at its depth its resonance I do not honestly
expect to hear its like again what could give birth to such
a cry a dying husband an impatient lover supremely
beautiful

(*GERTRUDE weeps.*)
But unrepeatable surely

(*Her shoulders heave in her grief.*)
Yes

Yes

We are surely near to the cliff now oh so close to the cliff

GERTRUDE: (*Wailing.*) MY HUSBAND

CASCAN: Yes

GERTRUDE: MY HUSBAND

(*She lifts her hands helplessly.*)
OH HOW I LOVED MY HUSBAND

CASCAN: Yes

Yes

GERTRUDE: Little boy

Oh little boy

(*CASCAN and CLAUDIUS watch the suffering of
GERTRUDE. A pause.*)
I called him little boy

(*She recovers.*)
He was ten years older than

No

Twelve not ten

Twelve

Twelve years older than

If anyone was little it was me

LITTLE GIRL

That would have made more sense I think

(*She gathers up her garments.*)

A sweet love silly possibly some loves are silly others find them irritating can you see my shoe simplicity offends the world and we were very simple shoe blue shoe ALL MY SHOES ARE BLUE NOW YOU INSIST ON IT

(*She smiles at CLAUDIUS through her tears. He brings the missing shoe to her. Leaning on CASCAN with one arm, she lifts her foot. CLAUDIUS fits the shoe. She turn to him.*)

OH WERE YOU EVER STRONGER IN YOUR LIFE

CLAUDIUS: Never

GERTRUDE: STRONGER

DEEPER

TIGHTER THAN A BOW

CLAUDIUS: Never

Never

GERTRUDE: Me neither

I FLOODED TO MY KNEES

(*They hold a profound gaze. She pulls away and strides off, trembling, erect…*)

CLAUDIUS: (*Watching her departure.*) She cannot walk straight

She

Her knees

She's all

(*His hand has travelled to his mouth.*)

Oh the religion of it

The religion

CASCAN: (*Who has not watched.*) I'll call dinner

(*CLAUDIUS seems not to hear.*)

I'll call dinner

When he doesn't come I'll look for him

First in the stables

After the stables I'll come here

CLAUDIUS: Yes

(*CASCAN goes to leave, stops. He looks at the body on the ground.*)

CASCAN: He could not meet her it was sad the way he could not meet her at the table in the bed this wandering this travelling but never meeting her I wonder if it will be the

same with you she changes she is not identical even a
sunset might profoundly alter her a passing cloud perhaps

CLAUDIUS: I meet her

I meet her very well

(*CLAUDIUS goes out. CASCAN inclines his head in a bow. The
sound of a deep bell.*)

# 3

*HAMLET examines the face of his dead father, formally displayed.
He lets fall the cloth that covers the face.*

HAMLET: I expected to be more moved than this

(*Pause.*)

Cascades

Storms of

Torrents of emotion

Never mind these things will come later when I least
expect them in bed with a bitch or on a horse eyes full of
tears you're crying she will say you're crying the horse will
neigh yes horse yes bitch I am and I don't know why I'm
blind I'm choking silly ha ha forgive me ha I'll get off off
the bitch off the horse have you a handkerchief

(*He laughs briefly.*)

Horses don't have handkerchiefs but bitches might to
wipe their crevices that stinks I'll say that stinks of filthy
copulations am I to wipe my eyes with that yes wipe away
and fuck your finicky fastidious and

(*He laughs, shuddering.*)

WOMEN ARE SO COARSE

They are

They are coarse

More so then men

Vastly more

Vastly

I have noticed it

More coarse than men

THE POLITE ONES ARE THE WORST

Behind their downcast eyes these

SWARMING VOCABULARIES

(*Pause.*)

Yes

Yes

Certainly I'll cry later

(*GERTRUDE enters in mourning.*)

How did you kill my father I can't work it out there is no
mark on him

(*He looks at her. He laughs.*)

I'm crying later

(*He runs to her, clasps her.*)

Say you understand I'm crying later

GERTRUDE: Yes

Later if you wish

HAMLET: Later

GERTRUDE: Or if you don't wish not at all

(*Pause.*)

HAMLET: Not at all?

(*He seems to consider this.*)

Yes

I had not thought of that

The possibility of not crying

SO ENSLAVED ARE WE BY THESE CONVENTIONS I HAD NOT
FOR A SINGLE MOMENT CONTEMPLATED

(*He discovers a word.*)

Tearlessness

When

Tearlessness might be my way

With

Death

(*He looks at the ground.*)

Forgive my shocking manners

GERTRUDE: Yes

HAMLET: I hide in shocking

GERTRUDE: Yes

HAMLET: When all the time I think these people are not
shocked

GERTRUDE: No

HAMLET: It is so hard to shock them I am failing to shock
them look they

GERTRUDE: Yes

HAMLET: ARE UTTERLY UNMOVED

(*He laughs a little.*)

When eventually I cease these futile efforts I shall perhaps
have passed through the purgatory of adolescence

GERTRUDE: Yes

HAMLET: POSSIBLY

(*He looks at her.*)

Or is shocking a career?

A vocation?

A profession worthy of the finest minds?

I don't know

You look so beautiful today

Severe of course

Always severe

When I was a boy a smaller boy I thought why is my
mother so severe that face looks chiselled out of stone she
is in agony I thought a sort of agony I wish I knew what
agony I do know now I know the source of that severity

(*Pause.*)

GERTRUDE: You do?

HAMLET: Oh yes

GERTRUDE: You know it and you decline to tell?

HAMLET: WELL YES

I DO DECLINE

MY FATHER'S HERE

(*He pretends to an offence.*)

Dear me

Oh dear

Decorum please

Decorum

Now I am king the entire emphasis of government will be
upon decorum sitting still for example

HOW FEW PEOPLE CAN SIT STILL

(*Pause.*)

Only you

(*Pause.*)

Only you sit still
(*He examines her.*)
Knees together
Folded hands
An hour at a time while they
SHIFT
FIDGET
AND FLAP THEIR HANDS
How they must dream
I have often thought this
Of your still white body
How they must dream it jerking like a puppet under skilful hands
(*He contemplates GERTRUDE.*)
I'm mischievous today

GERTRUDE: You are

HAMLET: My father is to blame
Tomorrow
A different man me
Promise
Hamlet you will say
Stroking my hair
Hamlet
Squeezing my hand
What brought about this shocking alteration
SHOCKING AGAIN
THE WORD
THE IDEA
(*He shakes his head.*)
Last day of infancy this
THIS
DAY
THE
LAST
How else could I honour him?
(*He goes to leave.*)

GERTRUDE: Shame killed your father
(*HAMLET stops.*)
Examine him

Some terrible looking lingers in his eyes
(*HAMLET returns to his father, draws back the cloth and studies his face. Pause.*)

HAMLET: Yes

Yes I see what I had taken to be common agony is
(*He shrugs uncomfortably.*)
I have not seen that many dead
A beggar in December
Some executed felons
And an ancient aunt but he
(*He bites his lip.*)
It's horror certainly but
(*He seems to squirm.*)
You say
(*GERTRUDE is about to speak.*)
Shh
(*HAMLET moves his position.*)
I SEE AN AWFUL ACT FROM UPSIDE DOWN
(*GERTRUDE is about to speak. HAMLET puts a finger to his lips.*)
An act which made him wish his life away
Yes
Existence had become intolerable to him
(*He shakes his head as if in disbelief.*)
AND I THOUGHT IT MUST BE POISON
I DID
I DID THINK YOU HAD POISONED HIM
(*He laughs, and stops.*)
No man dies of poison who does not welcome it into his veins I know from poisoners
(*He looks up at last.*)
You
Choked
Him
With
A
View
(*He stares at her.*)

# 4

*Rooks and a graveyard.*

GERTRUDE: I met your eyes
    I said I would not and then I met your eyes
    Up came the laughter
    In a wave
    I knew it would engulf me so I turned
    My shoulders heaved as if hoisted by ropes
    I stuffed the handkerchief into my mouth and
    Marched
    My shoulders heaving and my eyes awash with tears
    Marched
    How well I march
    No one dares run after me
    SHE HAS TO BE ALONE HER GRIEF COMPELS HER
    Admire my skirt
    OR SHAME SOME MUTTERED
    My skirt says everything to those who can read skirts
    SOME MUTTERED EVEN SHE KNOWS SHAME
    (*She lifts the hem to the knee.*)
    The bitches with their little life
    The dry-arsed hags of loyalty
    I FEEL I AM AT SCHOOL
    (*She laughs.*)
    Oh
    With you I am at school
    (*She releases the hem. It falls.*)
    The uniform was not like this
CLAUDIUS: Nor your cunt either
GERTRUDE: Neither was my cunt now pretend to comfort
    me with that oily gravity of heroic relatives I'll walk a little
    Dab
    (*She puts the handkerchief to her eyes.*)
    And
    Shake my head
    (*She shakes as if grief stricken.*)
    How good am I?
    (*She laughs under her veil.*)

HOW GOOD I SEE YOUR COCK ADMIRES MY PERFORMANCE
Take him out
CLAUDIUS: Out?
GERTRUDE: Now
　　Out
　　I have to kiss him
CLAUDIUS: Out?
GERTRUDE: I'll stoop as if
CLAUDIUS: As if what?
GERTRUDE: I don't know why should a widow stoop to
　　grieve of course
　　(*She issues a loud sob, her hands to her face, and tips forward.*)
　　Oh give me him to kiss
CLAUDIUS: (*Adjusting his position.*) You are
　　You are
　　You are so
GERTRUDE: KISS
　　KISS
　　(*She takes him.*)
CLAUDIUS: Oh God help everyone
　　I love you Gertrude God help everyone
　　(*Suddenly he thrusts her away.*)
　　OFF
　　OFF
　　(*He swiftly turns his back, adjusting his clothing as an old woman
　　enters, in mourning, on a stick.*)
ISOLA: My son's face
　　I looked at him
　　Oh what a face
　　I looked and looked
GERTRUDE: (*Rising.*) I could not look
ISOLA: The face was not a king's face where is your king's
　　face I said you look a fool today
GERTRUDE: It was a strange expression certainly I hardly
　　recognized him
ISOLA: And you saw faces on him I expect he never made
　　for others
GERTRUDE: Possibly

ISOLA: Possibly she says he fucked with you I daresay he
fucked his own wife surely?

GERTRUDE: Frequently

ISOLA: There are faces come of fucking never seen on
ordinary occasions

GERTRUDE: It wasn't one of those

ISOLA: No?

GERTRUDE: Not a fucking face no though they can be quite
foolish can they not if one for a brief moment stands aside
from if one so to speak climbs out the pool of one's desires
dangling one's legs over the side the swimming face there
can look foolish can it not foolish or worse hateful do you
not find but this face was different this face was a face I felt
of crumpled pride as if some little god had smacked him
(*Pause. ISOLA looks at GERTRUDE.*)

ISOLA: Gertrude I lick your hand
I have been a bitch but Gertrude I lick your hand Gertrude
leave my son alone

GERTRUDE: I can't

ISOLA: LEAVE ME ONE BOY GERTRUDE

GERTRUDE: I CAN'T LEAVE HIM ALONE
(*She winces.*)
I like you
I have always liked you
But I cannot leave your son alone
(*The old woman turns to go. She stops.*)

ISOLA: I saw you as a child once on a wall
Sitting on your hands
Little socks
Your legs swinging

GERTRUDE: Yes

ISOLA: I passed by

GERTRUDE: Yes

ISOLA: And as I passed your eyes met mine

GERTRUDE: Yes

ISOLA: Terrible eyes Gertrude

GERTRUDE: Yes

ISOLA: Terrible eyes and these legs swinging

GERTRUDE: I knew

ISOLA: You knew my mischief

GERTRUDE: Yes

ISOLA: Those legs swinging I knew you knew those swinging legs

GERTRUDE: And it was you who looked away

ISOLA: I could not tolerate your gaze

GERTRUDE: A child

ISOLA: Humiliated me

GERTRUDE: A child

ISOLA: AND I WAS THE QUEEN

    (*She turns to GERTRUDE at last.*)

    You

    Who was already shameless

    Made me ashamed

    (*Pause.*)

    Those swinging legs

    (*She goes out.*)

CLAUDIUS: (*Calling after her.*) THEY STILL SWING

    THEY SWING TODAY

    (*He laughs.*)

    It's true

    You sit on your hands and you

    DO IT

    DO IT FOR ME NOW

    (*GERTRUDE turns away.*)

    Gertrude

    Do what I say

    (*She turns, looks at him.*)

    Even if you lack the inspiration if it is an empty gesture women do it all the time don't they they swallow their indignation in the interests of a brittle harmony gratify me poor women one might say gratify me the married ones especially through gritted teeth they mock desire all right tomorrow and there's no wall anyway say we'll play tomorrow little white socks say tomorrow say

    SAY GERTRUDE

    SAY

    (*A pause. Her looks softens. She kisses him on the cheek chastely.*)

GERTRUDE: She went to a house your mother
    A poor house
    Nearly every day
    A poor man lived there with a crippled wife
    Not only crippled also blind
    And she cried out
    Not your mother
    The woman who was blind
    OH
    OH
    I SO WANTED TO KNOW WHAT MADE THAT CRY SO
    OH
    AS IF THE EARTH WERE TORN BY GREAT HANDS
    OH
    (*Pause.*)
    Her ecstasy
    Her horror
    I don't know which and when she died they ceased your
    mother and the poor man
    (*Pause.*)
    She took herself to a Dutch musician
    A bald man with too many teeth
    I KNOW HER HISTORY OH HER HISTORY
    (*She shakes her head.*)
    MY CRY IS NEVER FALSE
    (*She glares at CLAUDIUS.*)
    You know that
    You know it's never false and if it falters if it dies I won't
    pretend it Claudius I will not lie however wonderful my
    lying is
CLAUDIUS: Yes
    (*She turns.*)
GERTRUDE: They are watching us
    Like starved birds on a gutter
    Heads on one side
    They sense the clay depths of our uttering and hate us for it
    Take my arm now
    (*Pause.*)

CLAUDIUS: I must have it
  (*GERTRUDE turns to him.*)
  The cry Gertrude
  I must drag that cry from you again if it weighs fifty bells
  or one thousand carcasses I must
  IT KILLS GOD
  (*CASCAN appears in mourning and attends discreetly.*
  *CLAUDIUS alters, and addresses the servant.*)
  And that is our ambition surely to mutiny is mundane a
  mischief which contains a perverse flattery no killing killing
  God is our
  (*Pause. He goes to CASCAN.*)
  Obviously He rises again
  Always He rises
  I am not naïve
  ALWAYS THIS RISING AND HIS FACE MORE TERRIBLE EACH
  TIME
  (*Pause.*)
  Tell them we are coming tell them the Queen was
  overcome by grief and sought relief among the graves her
  sensitivity etcetera her delicacy etcetera let them look upon
  her stricken face her shrunken mouth is surely evidence of
  her despair it is more thin that newspaper more dry than
  newspaper yet all men know yet all men know yet all men
  off you go
  (*CASCAN bows and departs. GERTRUDE and CLAUDIUS*
  *ache, then turn and walk slowly after him.*)

# 5

*A dinner. HAMLET, RAGUSA and ISOLA attend. GERTRUDE*
*enters.*

HAMLET: The skirt's too short
  (*GERTRUDE stops.*)
  However excellent your legs might be
ISOLA: Shut up
HAMLET: The skirt's
ISOLA: Shut up

HAMLET: Too short
   How long has he been dead my father seven weeks and
ISOLA: Shut up you are a bore and a prude
HAMLET: Make a fool of yourself if you want to
ISOLA: THERE IS ONLY ONE FOOL HERE AND THAT IS YOU
   (*Pause.*)
HAMLET: Make a fool of yourself and actually your legs are
   not perfect
ISOLA: WHAT'S PERFECTION GOT TO DO WITH IT IT'S SEX IT'S
   SEX SHE'S GOT
   (*RAGUSA laughs. HAMLET stops.*)
   You are a bore and a prude
   (*Pause.*)
   I hate the word sex I really do I hate the word
   I tried to shut it out of my vocabulary but frankly it's
   impossible charm allure sensuality what little words what
   poor and little words oh God Gertrude
   (*GERTRUDE goes to ISOLA and kisses her cheek.*)
   Oh God Gertrude the sex in you
   (*Pause.*)
HAMLET: Surely what's erotic is the skirt?
ISOLA: IT'S HER
HAMLET: Being short and so on?
ISOLA: IT'S HER THAT HAS THE SEX AND YOU ARE
   (*She shakes her head.*)
   He thinks the skirt is sex
   (*RAGUSA laughs.*)
   He thinks a short skirt's sex
   Oh dear
   Oh dear
HAMLET: What a peculiar and disgusting grandmother you
   are
   I look at my friends and whilst they may revile their
   parents they discover in the parents of their parents a
   refuge from humiliating criticism they can confide they
   can confess I find this lack in my own life acutely painful it
   drives me into sordid acts of intimacy I inevitably regret
   (*He glares at RAGUSA.*)
   But one must talk with someone

ONE MUST SHOUT ONE'S PAIN INTO A JAR IF ONE HAS NO
GRANDMOTHER
(*Pause.*)
I'm waspish today
(*Pause.*)
I'm waspish and still a little infantile I had intended to
dispense with it I promised I promised in the presence of
my father's body never again would I be infantile but here
I am a little still I think a little infantile
(*He hangs his head. GERTRUDE kisses him.*)
GERTRUDE: Hardly at all
HAMLET: Hardly at all thank you
(*Pause.*)
Your skirt
(*He gestures vaguely.*)
Your sex
Your skirt and your sex
EMBARRASS ME
(*He writhes away from GERTRUDE.*)
ISOLA: You are a prig
(*RAGUSA laughs, incredulous.*)
And a prude
(*And laughs.*)
And a moralist
(*RAGUSA shakes her head with delight.*)
And you hide inside your indignation like a baby in a pen
SHAKE YOUR BARS WHO'S LISTENING
STAMP YOUR FEET WHO'S LISTENING
Your mother is magnificent
Too magnificent for you as she was too magnificent for
your father
Yes
Yes
He was my son and not yet two months in his grave but
still I say it she was too magnificent for him
MAGNIFICENT IS GERTRUDE
All the same she gave birth to a prig
That's God
God must have His little laughter

> A PRIG
>
> A PRUDE
>
> AND A MORALIST
>
> Kiss me
>
> Kiss your grandmother

HAMLET: No

ISOLA: (*To RAGUSA.*) You see

> He is a prig
>
> A prude
>
> And a

GERTRUDE: Shh

> Shh now

RAGUSA: I love this

> I love the way you speak your minds where I come from
> nobody does it's all politeness obviously the feelings are
> the same but oh we just go round and round it's a maze it's
> not conversation
>
> (*HAMLET looks coldly at RAGUSA.*)

HAMLET: Manners are a maze

> Beautiful is the maze of manners

RAGUSA: Is it

> I don't think so
>
> (*CASCAN enters and bows.*)

HAMLET: Ask him

CASCAN: Dinner is

HAMLET: How beautiful the maze is

> (*Pause.*)

CASCAN: Dinner is

HAMLET: He treads the maze

> He treads it in all weathers
>
> Storms of piss and floods of ordure steaming summers of
> soiled nakedness still he

CASCAN: SERVED ON THE LAWN TODAY

HAMLET: Still he

CASCAN: Ladies and Gentlemen

> (*Pause.*)

HAMLET: Treads the maze of manners

> I admire him

CASCAN: I cannot think why the Lord Hamlet should find in me anything to stimulate his admiration

HAMLET: You see?

CASCAN: The routine functions of a servant are hardly designed to satisfy the appetites and aspirations of a prince so subtle and refined as the Lord Hamlet is

HAMLET: You see?

THE MAZE

(*Pause.*)

And yet I think he fucks my mother

(*Pause, then HAMLET smothers his head in his hands.*)

I'M INFANTILE

I'M INFANTILE

Grandma

Grandma

(*He extends a pathetic hand. The old woman goes to him, takes him and leads him out. A pause.*)

RAGUSA: Hamlet

(*She falters.*)

Hamlet is

(*She shrugs in her embarrassment.*)

I profoundly dislike Hamlet

GERTRUDE: Yes

And yet nothing he says is wholly ridiculous is it not even the proposition he has just uttered some of his wildest accusations however random and malevolent if we are prepared to contemplate them seem less preposterous than at first appeared the shock of an accusation so often conceals its insidious attraction

(*She laughs.*)

NOW MR CASCAN IS MORE EMBARRASSED THAN YOU ARE

I am abstract

ALWAYS ABSTRACT

Go down to the lawn Mr Cascan has known me since I was a child and sat in white socks on old walls

CASCAN: Swinging her legs

GERTRUDE: Swinging my legs on walls

(*GERTRUDE smiles.*)

Play with Hamlet and if he spills his food ignore him he
does it to offend and eating with his mouth open it's all
Oh
You know my son
(*RAGUSA is about to go out when HAMLET bursts in again. He
stands, his hand poised to command attention.*)
HAMLET: Entering a woman
(*He chews his tongue in his anxiety.*)
Being entered by a man
The going in
The coming in
Is
(*He pulls at his face.*)
There is love and there is the coming in the coming in and
the going in and this
(*He struggles.*)
This saves the love from death it is not before the love
(*He grapples.*)
There is love and if the love is terrible it runs out of
language and in this agony of language this dying of the
language the coming in alone can save the love from
dying with the language the love which otherwise would
howl of wordlessness like a starved dog nailed into a room
implores the coming in to save it I am saying the coming
in does not come first how can it come before the love
implores it how it how it's how
(*They stare at HAMLET, who gazes at the floor in his solitude.
His hands knead the air. He turns to go.*)
GERTRUDE: Yes
(*He stops, and then goes out.*)
Yes
(*In the silence, RAGUSA begins to laugh. Failing to smother
the laugh, her shoulders heave. CASCAN goes out to the lawns.
RAGUSA lets free the laugh, covering her face with her hands.
GERTRUDE observes her.*)
RAGUSA: It is impossible to love him
And
He

So

(*She wipes her eyes with her wrists.*)

I sometimes go to place my hand on him a gentle hand as if to say stop now a little peace please all this speaking it's not

AND HE SLAPS IT

SLAPS IT AWAY AS IF I PITIED HIM

Touch me I say

There are many ways to know another God gave us hands

God gave us eyes why all this speech

MY BRAIN HE SAYS MY BRAIN IS WHERE DESIRE IS

I think that's sad

(*GERTRUDE looks at RAGUSA.*)

GERTRUDE: Yes

(*Pause.*)

Yes

(*Pause.*)

Yes

(*Pause.*)

I'm pregnant

(*Pause.*)

I TELL YOU WHY DO I OF ALL THE PEOPLE I COULD TELL TELL YOU

I suppose because it is a slap this telling

It is a way of slapping you

(*Pause.*)

Forty-two years old and pregnant I know the day I know the place you do you know you do whole walls in me slid back whole dykes in me were swept away you know what I mean Ragusa it was

(*She stops. She laughs at RAGUSA's discomfort.*)

You know nothing whatsoever

Wooden in a skirt

Wooden in shoes

And all of your opinion comes from magazines

NEVER MIND I'M TELLING MY CONDITION AND TO YOU

I was so sick this morning

CONDITION

I retched
CONDITION
And retched
CONDITION I CALL IT
This cry came heaving out of me a great dark cry
Ragusa heavy as a spade
MY BEAUTIFUL CONDITION
(*RAGUSA stares, afraid.*)
You may go now
(*RAGUSA goes to hurry away.*)
And Hamlet is correct
Desire's
In
The
Brain
(*RAGUSA runs out, as CLAUDIUS enters. He looks at GERTRUDE.*)
You're late

CLAUDIUS: Am I?

GERTRUDE: AM I AM I HE SAYS AM I LATE
You know you're late
Please don't be late

CLAUDIUS: Forgive me

GERTRUDE: Whilst in itself a little lateness might seem insignificant it is like many things of seeming insignificance deeply significant when added to the rest like uncut nails like unwashed feet flaccid hand-shakes fidgeting in seats the impression of a man is all the bits

CLAUDIUS: Gertrude

GERTRUDE: Taken together

CLAUDIUS: My nails are not uncut Gertrude

GERTRUDE: Please

CLAUDIUS: And I wash my feet

GERTRUDE: Don't
Please

CLAUDIUS: Thoroughly wash my feet

GERTRUDE: Be
Sarcastic

CLAUDIUS: And I am very rarely late

GERTRUDE: You were late yesterday

CLAUDIUS: Yesterday?

Was I?

GERTRUDE: Not very late but late

CLAUDIUS: Hardly late at all I think

GERTRUDE: Hardly late a little late what does it matter how
late the lateness was you were late

CLAUDIUS: GERTRUDE I WILL SMACK YOUR FACE

(*Pause.*)

GERTRUDE: We are to be in everything immaculate

CLAUDIUS: Yes

GERTRUDE: We are not allowing those who hate us to
discover any crack or crevice to insinuate a criticism in

CLAUDIUS: No

GERTRUDE: They will lever us apart

CLAUDIUS: Yes

I have said I am sorry I was late

GERTRUDE: OH SMACK ME SMACK MY FACE

(*CLAUDIUS hesitates.*)

No don't

Don't

Don't

I cannot go down with a face all

Can I?

With a smack?

(*Pause. CLAUDIUS does not strike her.*)

Thank you for wearing a suit

(*Pause.*)

CLAUDIUS: Yes

Well I

GERTRUDE: How fine you are Claudius

CLAUDIUS: That was the reason I was late I

GERTRUDE: I adore you Claudius

CLAUDIUS: I left in casual clothes

GERTRUDE: Adore you

CLAUDIUS: Only halfway down the stairs did I recall what
you had said

To wear a suit

I hurried back
I ran darling
I ran to do your bidding
Shirts everywhere
Ties
Boots

GERTRUDE: Good
Good

CLAUDIUS: Flinging on and flinging off

GERTRUDE: Good
Good

CLAUDIUS: Darling I am your hound I am your dog
(*GERTRUDE smiles through her tears…his eyes travel over her.*)
That skirt

GERTRUDE: Yes

CLAUDIUS: It's

GERTRUDE: Yes

CLAUDIUS: It's
(*He thrills to her.*)

GERTRUDE: Whatever it is it is for you

CLAUDIUS: Fuck
Fuck with me

GERTRUDE: No

CLAUDIUS: QUICK

GERTRUDE: No
(*She holds him with a look.*)
Suffer it
(*She walks quickly from the room. CLAUDIUS is quite still, his gaze fixed on her departing form. CASCAN enters with a loaded and unwieldy tray. The sounds of laughter from the lawns.*)

CLAUDIUS: I haven't heard it
(*Pause. CASCAN stops.*)

CASCAN: Heard it?

CLAUDIUS: Have you heard it?
I haven't
Not for weeks
(*CASCAN looks bewildered.*)

CASCAN: Heard what my lord?

CLAUDIUS: THE CRY THE CRY OF COURSE

CASCAN: The cry?

CLAUDIUS: THE CRY OF GERTRUDE DO NOT BE OBTUSE
(*Pause.*)

CASCAN: How should I have heard it my lord if you have
not?
(*He makes a slight bow and goes to leave.*)

CLAUDIUS: I don't know
(*CASCAN hesitates.*)
How should you have heard it if I have not? All the same I
have not heard it
(*Pause.*)

CASCAN: I must serve the dinner

CLAUDIUS: You must serve it yes
(*CASCAN tries to leave for the lawn.*)
I HAVE TO HEAR THE CRY YOU KNOW THAT CASCAN DON'T
YOU THAT I HAVE TO HEAR THE CRY?

CASCAN: Yes
Yes
(*Pause.*)
Nevertheless I daresay you would not be gratified if my
lady stooped to imitate a thing so rare and reverenced as
this exclamation is?

CLAUDIUS: I would not be gratified no

CASCAN: Merely to perform what has been so spontaneous
an utterance would compromise the depths of her desire
and humiliate her perfect and pathetic nakedness I
daresay?

CLAUDIUS: It would
It would humiliate it yes
I REQUIRE THE REAL CRY CASCAN ALL MY LIFE I SOUGHT
IT SINCE I WAS A BOY AND PRIOR YES PRIOR TO BOYHOOD
IT IS THE CRY OF ALL AND EVERY MOVING THING AND ALL
THAT DOES NOT MOVE BONE BLOOD AND MINERAL
Why pathetic
Why pathetic nakedness?

CASCAN: All love is pathetic is it not my lord? From the
perspective of
(*He smiles.*)

From the perspective of the universal I was about to say
(*Pause.*)
I mean of course from my perspective
(*Pause. He declines his head.*)
The perspective of a celibate and solitary slave
CLAUDIUS: I don't know
(*Pause.*)
Yes
Yes it is pathetic possibly
(*Pause.*)
No
No
Yes
I don't know
I DON'T KNOW IF IT IS
(*CASCAN goes to leave.*)
The cry is more than the woman
(*CASCAN stops.*)
The woman is the instrument
But from the woman comes the cry
(*Pause. CASCAN bows slightly and retreats.*)
And men want kingdoms
Kingdoms
Counties
Forests
Walled estates with speckled deer parks fountains lakes of trout YOU MAY GO NOW lakes of trout and ponds of carp OFF YOU GO I don't require those melancholy proofs of masculinity HURRY CASCAN do I not if I possess the cry?
(*CASCAN has gone. CLAUDIUS is aware of his mother in the doorway.*)
CLAUDIUS: I'm sentimental
ISOLA: You're a fool
CLAUDIUS: So you say
ISOLA: I do say it
CLAUDIUS: You say it with such frequency it has entirely forfeited its effect
ISOLA: Shut up

CLAUDIUS: And I am not sentimental not sentimental at all
I don't know why I said that

ISOLA: Shut up I said

CLAUDIUS: To gratify you possibly
To pander to your prejudices

ISOLA: Claudius

CLAUDIUS: I was late for dinner and now I'm even later

ISOLA: Claudius
Gertrude does not love you

CLAUDIUS: (*Exasperated.*) Oh

ISOLA: CLAUDIUS MY SON GERTRUDE DOES NOT

CLAUDIUS: (*Violently.*) SO WHAT
SO WHAT
SO WHAT IF SHE LIES TO ME WITH EVERY BREATH

ISOLA: She does

CLAUDIUS: AND OOZING WITH MY FLUID FLINGS UP HER
LEGS FOR CRIMINALS TO PADDLE IN SO WHAT SO WHAT
(*ISOLA turns away.*)
SO WHAT IF SHE STOOPS TO SWALLOW DOGS
I do not want this conversation
OR TAKES SYPHILITIC SAILORS AT BOTH ENDS SO WHAT SO
WHAT
I do not want this conversation but you your face your
attitude not your attitude your face I really do resent that
face which ever since I was a child hung over me like the
brass disc of some nagging clock

ISOLA: YOU HAD MORE SENSE AT FIVE

CLAUDIUS: TICK TOCK

ISOLA: THAN YOU DO NOW CLAUDIUS

CLAUDIUS: TICK TOCK
I am concluding this conversation

ISOLA: Conclude it by all means

CLAUDIUS: The conversation is concluded

ISOLA: If you can call abuse a conversation

CLAUDIUS: (*Turning on his mother.*) I love the woman
I love
I love
I love the woman
Take my arm now take it let's oh let's be

TAKE MY ARM

(*ISOLA takes her son's arm. They are quite still. They look over the lawns.*)

ISOLA: I live for you my darling son

CLAUDIUS: I know

I do know that

(*A dinner gong is sounded. CLAUDIUS goes to obey its call. ISOLA holds him.*)

ISOLA: LET HER WAIT

OH LET THE BITCH WAIT

(*Pause. They hang back.*)

CLAUDIUS: (*Going to move.*) Now

ISOLA: NOT YET

Oh just look at the

(*CLAUDIUS goes to move.*)

NOT YET I SAID

(*CLAUDIUS is resentful but icily patient.*)

Look at the rage on that savage and frustrated face

CLAUDIUS: I am going

ISOLA: Did you ever see a darker and more vicious face it's like a wolf's it's like a bat's

CLAUDIUS: GOING I SAID

ISOLA: (*As the gong is beaten ill-temperedly.*) A STOAT

A LYNX

(*As CLAUDIUS abandons her and hurries out.*)

A CROW

A SHIT-BEAKED RAVEN

OH GO

OH GO

# 6

*GERTRUDE enters a room. She lifts her skirt above the knee for ISOLA, showing new stockings.*

ISOLA: They're nice

They're nice and your legs are a dream

A dream Gertrude I always thought so

(*Pause.*)

I said to my boy my poor dead boy I don't like Gertrude as
you know but with legs like those my liking's neither here
nor there is it no mother he said neither here nor there
(*Pause.*)
They're wrinkled Gertrude
(*Pause.*)
On the knee
(*GERTRUDE looks down at her knees.*)
I didn't like you then
GERTRUDE: I did not like you
ISOLA: We did not like each other but
(*As GERTRUDE tugs the stocking.*)
No
No
That's it
We didn't then but now we do you'll kill men with those
legs Gertrude those legs inside those stockings so what if
you're forty-two you'll kill
GERTRUDE: I will
ISOLA: Darling you will
And
Pregnant
As
You
Are
Gertrude
MEN CAN'T KEEP STILL
(*GERTRUDE laughs.*)
They can't
They can't
That friend of Hamlet
Albert Someone Albert Duke of Somewhere
GERTRUDE: Mecklenburg
ISOLA: HIS EYES
HIS HANDS
(*GERTRUDE laughs again.*)
FLUTTER GOES THE DUKE OF MECKLENBURG
(*They both laugh.*)
Give him your arse to kiss

(*They cease laughing.*)
Your lifted skirt
(*Pause.*)
Your gaze on the distance like a tethered mare
(*Pause.*)
Voices from another room
(*Pause.*)
Between your buttocks his uneven breath
(*Pause.*)
You turn
(*Pause.*)
He looks up from his knees
(*Pause.*)
At last he rises and his face is wet
(*Pause.*)
Terrible stare
TERRIBLE STARE
(*Pause. GERTRUDE is fixed by ISOLA.*)
Albert Duke of
DUKE OF WHERE?
(*Pause. GERTRUDE moves a little. She examines ISOLA.*)
GERTRUDE: Yes but I love a man
ISOLA: You love a man that's very nice but
GERTRUDE: I love your son
ISOLA: That's very nice but
GERTRUDE: NOT ANY MAN BUT YOUR OWN
ISOLA: GERTRUDE YOU ARE FORTY-TWO
    (*Pause.*)
    And forty-two's not twenty-two
    (*Pause.*)
    It is not twenty-two Gertrude is it?
    (*Pause. GERTRUDE is shaken.*)
GERTRUDE: How strange you are for a mother and not any
    mother but the mother of my lover
ISOLA: The mother of your lover yes but just as forty-two's
    not twenty-two so sixty-two is not
GERTRUDE: (*Bemused.*) You are corrupting me
    (*ISOLA stifles a gasp.*)
    I love your son and you

(*She lifts her hands in disbelief.*)
You are
You are corrupting me
ISOLA: Those stockings have a fault in them
(*They exchange a deep stare.*)
Gertrude
The knees
Those stockings wrinkle at the knees
(*ISOLA urges with a new tone.*)
Gertrude you thrive on men men are your ecstasy I was
the same I know you watched me fuck through infant eyes
I do not criticize you Gertrude I lavish you I
GERTRUDE: (*Hoisting her skirt and going to unhitch her stocking.*)
CHANGE THESE
ISOLA: I applaud your hunger I applaud your greed
GERTRUDE: (*Calling again.*) NEW STOCKINGS
HOW CAN I BE A PROSTITUTE IN THESE
ISOLA: Who said anything about prostitutes?
GERTRUDE: (*As CASCAN enters.*) CLEAN STOCKINGS
CASCAN: (*With a rapid bow.*) Madam
ISOLA: You said prostitute not me
(*CASCAN walks out again.*)
GERTRUDE: A PROSTITUTE WITH WRINKLED STOCKINGS
WILL NEVER
(*She tears at the suspenders.*)
Now I've laddered them
NEVER SUCCEED
So what
So what if they are laddered?
(*She rips at them in her irritation.*)
ISOLA: Pleasure is not prostitution Gertrude
GERTRUDE: (*Unhitching them.*) Laddered
Laddered
AND HIGHER HEELS I'M STOOPING IN SHOP DOORWAYS
ISOLA: You're funny
You're funny but I put it down to your condition
GERTRUDE: CASCAN
(*She kicks off her shoes.*)

BLUE SHOES

(*She glares at ISOLA.*)

Bare legs surely bare legs in blue shoes the stockings are superfluous?

(*ISOLA shrugs, tight-lipped. GERTRUDE seems calm.*)

I think when you urged prostitution upon me

ISOLA: Darling I never

GERTRUDE: Shh

ISOLA: I never did

GERTRUDE: You little knew my instinct and my inclination

(*CASCAN enters with blue shoes.*)

for the

(*Pause.*)

What?

What is it? Prostitution?

ISOLA: A profession I suppose

GERTRUDE: A profession thank you COAT

(*CASCAN places the shoes on the floor and goes out.*

*GERTRUDE, bare-legged, steps into the shoes.*)

He'll bring the wrong coat won't he?

NOT ANY COAT

ISOLA: (*Apprehensive.*) Oh dear

GERTRUDE: PROSTITUTE'S COAT

ISOLA: Oh dear oh dear

CASCAN: (*Entering, puzzled.*) Prostitute's coat? What sort of coat is

GERTRUDE: A COAT SUCH AS A PROSTITUTE WOULD WEAR

(*CASCAN is alarmed and swallows hard. His eyes briefly meet ISOLA's. She shrugs faintly.*)

Long

So it's hidden

(*CASCAN nods, looking at the floor.*)

The belly

So the belly's hidden and the hair

(*He nods again.*)

And belted

To draw a line at violation

So whilst I'm owned in one part I'm not owned everywhere

(*He nods again. He starts to go out.*)
And thin
To hint at poverty
(*CASCAN goes out. An awkward pause during which
GERTRUDE stares wildly at ISOLA, who cannot look back.*)
ISOLA: I'm your ally Gertrude
I'm your
I'm your
(*She shrugs feebly. CASCAN enters with a thin, long raincoat.
GERTRUDE puts it over herself and tightens the belt.*)
GERTRUDE: You see they were already in my wardrobe
The shoes
The coat
The instruments of my vocation
ALREADY THERE
(*She emits a small laugh, and turns to leave. She stops. Skilfully
she reaches under her coat. She lifts a leg, and produces from her
garments her pants.*)
Shan't need those
(*She tosses them to a figure who swiftly enters and stops.
GERTRUDE marches out.*)
ISOLA: IT'S ALL RIGHT
IT'S ALL RIGHT
IT'S ALL RIGHT
SHE'S FUNNY SOMETIMES
IT'S ALL RIGHT

# 7

*The Duke of Mecklenburg alone, holding GERTRUDE's underwear
exactly as he had received it. HAMLET enters. He looks. He walks.
He stops. He looks. He prepares to speak. He does not speak. He plays
with utterance.*

HAMLET: She's mad
(*Pause.*)
And like the mad embarrassing I'll take those what a
louche and perverse hospitality you must be thinking in
Mecklenburg such things could never or do you want them

say if you do for all I know you might revere the soiled and
sordid fragments of another's

SAY ALBERT IF YOU WANT THEM I PERFECTLY UNDERSTAND
THE

(*Pause.*)

I don't understand

(*Pause.*)

I do not understand at all why you are clutching those
ridiculous

(*He shrugs.*)

As if

(*ALBERT raises GERTRUDE's pants to his lips and kisses
them. HAMLET is still and watches, his brows knitted.*)

As if

(*ALBERT watches HAMLET.*)

As if

(*Pause. They stare.*)

At some point Albert I should like to talk of love

(*Pause.*)

So few ever speak of it

(*Pause.*)

And this in spite of OR BECAUSE YES POSSIBLY BECAUSE
SOME TERRIBLE EQUATION MIGHT ACCOUNT FOR IT the
relentless intimacy of our state the more they fuck the less
they contemplate

ALBERT: I love your mother and if she's mad good

(*A pause. HAMLET is exasperated, but patient.*)

HAMLET: Love

Love

Love my mother?

ALBERT: Help me to sleep with her

HAMLET: Love

Love my mother

ALBERT: Hamlet

HAMLET: Love her

ALBERT: OTHERS DO

(*Pause.*)

The way she stands

The way she clothes herself

OBVIOUSLY THEY DO
(*Pause.*)
I'm in such a state of
I'M IN SUCH A STATE
HAMLET: Yes
Yes you are
And if that isn't love I don't know what love is certainly I
will intercede for you I will say the Duke of Mecklenburg
has been observed inhaling some discarded laundry which
bears an intimate relation with you mother
ALBERT: Shut up
HAMLET: With your fundament at least and this is love
ALBERT: Shut up I said
HAMLET: What other word so rarely quoted and refined
could adequately describe
ALBERT: Hamlet
HAMLET: His torment
ALBERT: Hamlet
HAMLET: It's love it really is it's
ALBERT: You are diseased
(*Pause.*)
You hate life and you are diseased and however shrewd
and ruthless you are in your provocations still you are
diseased
YES I AM ABSURD
ABSURD AND KISS YOUR MOTHER'S PLACE
ABSURD
ABSURD
(*He runs out. HAMLET is still. GERTRUDE enters and kisses
HAMLET on the cheek.*)
HAMLET: I'm saying less
(*Pause.*)
Suffering more and
(*CLAUDIUS enters.*)
Saying less
(*He goes out.*)

# 8

*CLAUDIUS sits, his eyes on GERTRUDE. She feels his gaze. They are uncomfortable for a long time. At last CASCAN enters. He sits. A pause, as he collects his thoughts.*

CASCAN: Paradoxically
(*He strokes his face, a gesture of tact and thoughtfulness.*)
And tragically
(*He places the tips of his fingers together.*)
It would appear to be characteristic of passionate love that whilst all the drawers and cupboards so to speak of privacy are flung open and the contents flung about the room in an ecstasy of revelation always an obscurity prevails a locked safe so to speak for which there is no key
(*Pause.*)
In a strange and sinister equation the more we tell the more the untold becomes agony and even that which was once said becomes unsayable
(*Pause.*)
Strange
And
Probably
Only
An
Aspect
Of
Our
Impenetrable
Solitude
CLAUDIUS: I've penetrated it I've penetrated her solitude and she mine sorry but we have we did and that sorry sorry
(*Pause. CASCAN is patient.*)
CASCAN: Lord Claudius can't speak of the one thing he most
CLAUDIUS: I love you Gertrude
CASCAN: He most requires to speak of
CLAUDIUS: Darling I love you
(*He lifts his hand in a gesture of apology.*)

CASCAN: This is a matter of the utmost delicacy but often it appears the delicate can best be stated by one who if not himself indelicate nevertheless might bring to the subject
(*He stops.*)
I mean I can say what others can't
(*He turns to GERTRUDE.*)
Three months apparently and you've made no cry
CLAUDIUS: She has but
CASCAN: You have but these cries whilst reassuring and affectionate lack
CLAUDIUS: Not affectionate
CASCAN: Whilst powerful and urgent
CLAUDIUS: NOT AFFECTIONATE THANK GOD WE ARE NOT MAN AND WIFE
CASCAN: No
CLAUDIUS: Not affectionate
GERTRUDE SOMETHING'S LOST
(*He squirms on the chair. He turns away.*)
GERTRUDE: (*Walking pensively, stopping.*) I am accused
CLAUDIUS: Not accused
GERTRUDE: Accused and I plead guilty
(*Pause.*)
Not of failing to love I do love
CLAUDIUS: Yes
GERTRUDE: You know the love
CLAUDIUS: I know it yes
GERTRUDE: THE HUNGER AND THE LOVE I FEEL FOR YOU
CLAUDIUS: Yes
GERTRUDE: So I'm not guilty on that score
CLAUDIUS: GUILT I NEVER
GERTRUDE: ON THE SCORE OF LOVE NOT GUILTY
CLAUDIUS: I NEVER SPOKE OF GUILT GERTRUDE
(*Pause.*)
You make me feel ashamed
(*He lifts his hands helplessly.*)
You make me feel
(*He gestures wildly.*)

BUT I HAVE TO SAY IT BECAUSE YES BECAUSE OF THE
AGONY I SUFFER OVER YOU

WILL SAY IT

WILL

(*Pause.*)

Or get it said by some other means

(*He covers his face with his hands. A pause. GERTRUDE is
infinitely cautious.*)

GERTRUDE: Yes

However

Yes

It's true

(*She bites her lip. She looks at CLAUDIUS.*)

But do you wish to know the consequences of the fact that
what you charge me with is true?

CLAUDIUS: (*Exasperated.*) It's not a charge Gertrude

GERTRUDE: IT IS

IT IS A CHARGE

AND THE CONFESSION OF IT WILL SHRINK YOU

CASCAN: I warned him

GERTRUDE: Yes

I warn him also

CASCAN: At the time of your husband's death I said

CLAUDIUS: Shut up

CASCAN: This will only

CLAUDIUS: Shut up Cascan

(*Pause.*)

Please

(*Pause.*)

Cascan

(*Pause.*)

I do know Gertrude I am not naïve

GERTRUDE: Never naïve

CLAUDIUS: Never naïve and I know now as I always knew
your body for all that it's revered by me is flesh and being
flesh is ground ground trodden ground to which I'm bound
a dirt poor labourer who tills and spills and fights and fails
in his possession Gertrude it is God I'm fighting when I
fight in you

GERTRUDE: Yes
 Then you already dread
CLAUDIUS: Yes
GERTRUDE: What I'm now telling you
CLAUDIUS: Yes
 But every dread
GERTRUDE: Is desperate for its satisfaction
CLAUDIUS: Yes
GERTRUDE: The cry's betrayal Claudius
 (*Pause.*)
CLAUDIUS: Betrayal?
GERTRUDE: Betrayal
 And it comes from nowhere else
 (*A stillness overcomes CLAUDIUS. He lays his hands on his knees. ALBERT enters and waits, observing GERTRUDE. ISOLA enters as if from a walk.*)

# 9

ISOLA: You were funny
 (*She goes to kiss GERTRUDE on the cheek.*)
 All that about prostitutes
 (*She kisses her.*)
 I took you seriously
GERTRUDE: People should
ISOLA: People should?
GERTRUDE: Take Gertrude seriously
ISOLA: Oh she is third person Gertrude is she?
GERTRUDE: Gertrude is
ISOLA: She is and I don't criticize
 (*She looks at CLAUDIUS.*)
 SON I'M TERRIFIED FOR YOU
 (*Pause. CLAUDIUS lifts his eyes slowly to his mother.*)
 Son
 Son
 God knows I'm trying but you will have to save yourself
 (*She turns back to GERTRUDE.*)
 (*Referring to ALBERT.*) He's here again
 (*She nods her head in a conspiratorial way.*)

That Duke

That

Where's he from

That boy

He

GERTRUDE: Gertrude's boy?

(*Pause.*)

ISOLA: Yes

(*Pause.*)

Him

(*GERTRUDE turns to ALBERT.*)

GERTRUDE: Mecklenburg

ISOLA: Isn't it peculiar I cannot and I was educated to a high
degree I cannot say that word

GERTRUDE: Mecklenburg

ISOLA: Yes

You can say it but not me

I want to say oh anything but that

Middleburg

Magdeburg

But Mecklenburg

OH I SAID IT THEN

(*Her laughter is solitary and brief. She turns to CLAUDIUS
who ignores her. She leaves, distraught. In the subsequent silence,
CLAUDIUS rises to his feet.*)

GERTRUDE: Speak with Gertrude

(*Pause.*)

CLAUDIUS: Yes

(*He lifts his eyes to her at last.*)

Yes

(*And goes. ALBERT laughs.*)

ALBERT: Why do you speak of yourself as Gertrude is it
a form of etiquette the Danish court is so quaint in its
manners so archaic Hamlet says he wishes it were more
so and intends to bring back all those penalties that have
fallen out of use regarding for example bowing bowing we
have entirely abolished I can't remember when I last saw
anybody bow in Mecklenburg

(*He falters. Pause.*)

GERTRUDE: You must take her from behind
   (*A pause. ALBERT is dry-mouthed.*)
ALBERT: Yes?
GERTRUDE: If you want Gertrude
   (*He is able to nod.*)
   She is pregnant but you must do it from behind
ALBERT: Yes
GERTRUDE: And cover her mouth with your hand
   (*He nods.*)
   Do not kiss her
   (*He shakes his head.*)
   Do you understand?
ALBERT: Yes
GERTRUDE: And if she
   (*She shudders.*)
   If Gertrude
   (*To ALBERT's amazement GERTRUDE forces her fist into her
   mouth. Her body heaves. Her stifled cries come one upon another.
   A the end of her ecstasy GERTRUDE staggers from the room.
   CASCAN follows her, discreetly. ALBERT is paralyzed. He calls
   after them.*)
ALBERT: WHERE?
   WHERE?

# 10

*RAGUSA enters a park.*

ALBERT: (*Looking at last.*) Don't follow me
RAGUSA: I don't follow you Albert
ALBERT: Very well do not contrive to place yourself where
   you know I am likely to appear
RAGUSA: It needs no contriving Albert since you are always
   in the same place
ALBERT: And is Albert not at liberty to stand in this place-or
   another if he so desires?
RAGUSA: (*Puzzled.*) Albert?
ALBERT: How free is Albert?
RAGUSA: What's this Albert?

ALBERT: He regrets profoundly that he kissed you the kiss
    was spontaneous and inconsequential nothing should be
    predicated on a kiss of such small significance Ragusa
    (*He detects a third party.*)
    Oh look who's here be casual please
    Stand further
    Look as if
    Oh dear oh dear
    (*HAMLET enters. He smiles oddly.*)
HAMLET: Under the tree
    (*Pause. ALBERT looks pale.*)
    The elm
    (*Pause.*)
    If trees could speak oh what a history
    I'M SAYING LESS
    (*He goes out. ALBERT squirms.*)
RAGUSA: Albert pack your bags
ALBERT: (*Observing a distant figure.*) She's here
RAGUSA: Or don't pack them
    Don't stay to pack your bags I'll send them on
ALBERT: (*Distracted.*) Pack my bags?
RAGUSA: A dozen suits what's that to you the trains leave on
    the hour
ALBERT: Trains? For where?
RAGUSA: For Mecklenburg
ALBERT: Mecklenburg?
    LOOK SHE'S HERE
RAGUSA: Albert
ALBERT: UNDER THE TREE
    (*He starts to go to his rendezvous. RAGUSA tries to detain him.*)
    RAGUSA I DO NOT KNOW YOU
    (*Pause.*)
    I do know you
    Obviously I do know you I know you and I like you but
    TRAINS WHAT TRAINS
    (*They stare at one another. ALBERT is earnest.*)
    Ragusa
    The Queen is beautiful and forty-three
    Pregnant

Beautiful

And

Forty-three

PREGNANT BY ANOTHER MAN HER HEELS GOUGE

LACERATIONS ALL THE LENGTH OF ME

It is very exciting very very exciting Ragusa

I am so excited

RAGUSA: Yes

ALBERT: Even the kisses in which I smothered you

RAGUSA: Yes

ALBERT: They too came out of Gertrude's nakedness

I was so proud Ragusa

RAGUSA: Yes

ALBERT: So proud and vulgar that within two hours of
seducing you

RAGUSA: Don't go on

ALBERT: Yes

RAGUSA: Don't go on

ALBERT: A HOUSEMAID AND A WOMAN ON A TRAM

BOTH UGLY

BUT WHAT WAS THEIR UGLINESS TO ME?

(*He laughs.*)

Forgive

Forgive

(*He turns away.*)

She's there

Gertrude under the tree

(*He hurries off. RAGUSA stares after him. CASCAN is
discovered at the perimeter.*)

CASCAN: Miss

(*He bows ever so slightly.*)

The Lord Hamlet is

(*He stops.*)

RAGUSA: Yes?

CASCAN: Shh

(*He turns his head as if to catch a sound on the wind.*)

RAGUSA: Hamlet is what?

CASCAN: SHH I SAID

(*He strains his hearing. There is no sound.*)

Forgive me he requests your presence for a few words only
a few words he emphasizes very few
(*RAGUSA leaves. CASCAN pulls his coat close and sits on the
ground.*)

# 11

*ISOLA enters. She watches CASCAN.*

ISOLA: Help an old woman at the end of her life
(*CASCAN looks up.*)
Help an old woman no angel but rarely spiteful kind to her
tenants no not always kind two sons one remaining some
secrets some banquets and a few trips to the war hospitals
help her
(*He does not reply.*)
I'll beg
(*Pause.*)
I've never liked you
(*Pause.*)
Never liked you so my begging will probably give you
satisfaction
(*Pause.*)
I AM BEGGING
(*Pause.*)
No I'm not I've never begged I don't know how to do it
show me and I'll do it yes I do I begged a man once don't
abandon me I said that's different though that's love
(*Pause. CASCAN is embarrassed.*)
Let's have a drink
(*CASCAN looks appalled.*)
Sometimes it's good to drink with people you despise
(*Pause.*)
I don't despise you
(*She is at the end of her tether.*)
I do
I do
Of course I do
(*She sinks.*)
I own estates say if you want them

Furniture

Horses

Pick and choose

I'll walk in rags

I'll die in fields

I'M BRIBING YOU BE BRIBED DAMN YOU

(*She is depleted. CASCAN is not cruel.*)

CASCAN: Loyalty

(*He shakes his head.*)

It's comical to you

(*He looks at ISOLA.*)

What a painful discovery this was for me who was taught

loyalty to see my masters placed no value on it

(*He stands and brushes down his coat.*)

All the same it continued to prevail in me

An instinct

An archaism possibly

(*Pause.*)

ISOLA: Cascan

She's bad

(*Pause.*)

CASCAN: Your opinion of the Queen

ISOLA: Not opinion Cascan

CASCAN: Your opinion even were it proved to be

ISOLA: BAD IN THE HEART

BAD IN THE MOUTH

CASCAN: Not opinion but incontrovertibly

ISOLA: BAD IN THE WOMB

CASCAN: A statement of the truth still never could diminish

ISOLA: AND IN THE CUNT BAD CASCAN

CASCAN: (*Closing his eyes.*) My devotion

IT'S

AN

ECSTASY

(*Pause. ISOLA is spent. She tries to lift herself off the ground and fails.*)

ISOLA: Help me up

(*Her hand claws the air.*)

Oh help me

(*CASCAN extends his hand and raises her.*)
My boy is dead
(*She starts to go.*)
My boy is dead
(*She addresses no one.*)
In a war yes such a wicked war the battlefield was in his
head
(*CLAUDIUS enters. ISOLA addresses him as if he were not
known to her.*)
Horror
Unearthly shouts
And bits of flesh
THEY FOUND HIM NAKED AND HIS TUNIC RIPPED TO
SHREDS AS IF SOME WOLF HAD RAVENED HIM THE
SOLDIERS SAID
Who would do such
Who would do such
(*She wanders out, watched by the two men.*)
CLAUDIUS: She was a whore in her own time
MOTHER
A whore in her own time yes
MOTHER
My brother for example
NAME HIS DAD
(*Pause.*)
MOTHER
(*He is distraught.*)
I haven't time
CASCAN: No
CLAUDIUS: Not strictly time I do have time time is not in
short supply SPACE
CASCAN: Yes
CLAUDIUS: SPACE TO ACCOMMODATE MY MOTHER'S AND
CASCAN: Your own
CLAUDIUS: MY MOTHER'S AND MY OWN
(*Pause.*)
Yes
CASCAN: Her anxieties on your behalf are perfectly
comprehensible but a parent no matter how devoted

must appreciate a certain precedence asserts itself in the
emotional attachments of a

CLAUDIUS: THE QUEEN'S QUIET CASCAN QUIET ISN'T SHE
My emotional attachments yes
QUIET AS THE GRAVE
Attachments
ATTACHMENTS ASK A SLAVE ABOUT ATTACHMENTS
CHAINS
MANACLES
LOOK A MAN ATTACHED
(*He holds up his wrists. He laughs strangely.*)
I could have you executed for that word
The poverty
The slander
Of that word
(*Pause.*)

CASCAN: I intended no offence

CLAUDIUS: To call my agony attachment I say is offence
I'll change the law
As from tomorrow the crime of understatement carries a
penalty of death

CASCAN: It was tactless of me I confess

CLAUDIUS: TACTLESS
There you go again
TACTLESS
IT CUT ME TO THE QUICK
(*Pause.*)

CASCAN: Yes
Yes

CLAUDIUS: Never mind
A reptile has a cold vocabulary

CASCAN: I am not a reptile my lord

CLAUDIUS: No

CASCAN: As for executing servants for their choice of words
I think

CLAUDIUS: (*His hand to his ear.*) Shh

CASCAN: The Queen might entertain her own opinion as to
the justice of

CLAUDIUS: SHE I SAID

(*He glares at CASCAN.*)
CASCAN: The wind
(*Pause.*)
CLAUDIUS: The wind yes
(*Pause.*)
I'm in such pain
I'm in such pain
(*He smothers his head in his hands and rocks from side to side. CASCAN observes him for a little while, then discreetly withdraws. CLAUDIUS howls.*)

# 12

*GERTRUDE enters. She watches CLAUDIUS a while.*

GERTRUDE: The boy must die
(*CLAUDIUS looks up.*)
My darling
My darling
The boy must die
CLAUDIUS: Yes
GERTRUDE: Kill the boy for rampaging in my belly
CLAUDIUS: Yes
GERTRUDE: For hammering the silence where my child lies
HE THRUST MY FACE AGAINST THE TREE THE SMELL OF
HIS FINGERS AND THE ROUGH BARK SCRATCHED LOOK
SCRATCHES ON ME
(*She shows her cheek.*)
And cut down the elm
Whatever its antiquity it must not shelter sheep now sheep
or shepherds either
IT SAW MY NAKED ARSE
COMPLACENT TREE
(*She mocks the elm.*)
Men come and go beneath my leaves the lovers grow
embittered their oaths are cast into infinity fine girls decay
and in my shade rotting men write poetry
SUFFICIENT WISDOM OF THE PASTORAL VARIETY
Call the woodmen
Let it sing in the grate

Let its flames illuminate our white limbs lifting
Bone on stone
Mouth
Floor
Bruising
(*CLAUDIUS is thoughtful.*)
CLAUDIUS: His fingers
The odour of his fingers you described
(*He struggles.*)
These fingers closed your mouth presumably or you could
not have smelled them?
(*Pause.*)
Consequently any cry you made
GERTRUDE: Claudius I did not cry
CLAUDIUS: Would have been smothered would it not?
GERTRUDE: I TELL YOU NO CRY CAME
(*He looks at her.*)
How infinitely and passionately
CLAUDIUS: Yes
GERTRUDE: FORENSIC
You are Claudius
CLAUDIUS: Yes
Yes
I could draw from memory the landscape of your
underneath
Volcanic
Oceanic
As it is
(*They exchange a look of pained desire.*)
Invite him
Tell him under your coat you are undressed
Say but for shoes you are
OH YOU KNOW THE STUFF TO MAKE A BOY GO ALL
GERTRUDE: I know it yes
(*Pause.*)
CLAUDIUS: GERTRUDE I COULD MURDER YOU MYSELF
(*They stare.*)

# 13

*HAMLET enters holding hands with RAGUSA.*

HAMLET: I'm saying less
> (*Pause.*)
> I'm saying less and the reason I am saying less is that
> speech falters speech flinches when horror lifts a fist to it
> (*Pause.*)
> The more horror the less speech I don't say I am the first
> to have appreciated this
> (*Pause.*)
> We're marrying
> (*Pause.*)
> Ragusa is not fit to be my consort she is scarcely literate

RAGUSA: I am literate

HAMLET: And my best friend has already
> (*His mouth goes stiff.*)
> My best friend having
> (*Stiffly.*)
> My mother then
> (*He shakes his head.*)
> WORDS HOPELESS HERE
> (*He shakes his head more violently.*)
> So I am marrying her notwithstanding or
> (*He laughs now.*)
> BECAUSE
> BECAUSE
> OF IT
> (*He looks at the floor.*)
> You must love the worst you see
> SAYING LESS
> (*He nods his head violently in affirmation.*)
> Oh yes
> Saying less
> (*Pause.*)

GERTRUDE: Do you love Ragusa?

HAMLET: No
> No

Absolutely not the word love has not once confirm this
please Ragusa not once passed my lips nor will it love I
hate it all manifestations of the thing called love fill me
with horror and contempt I could elaborate still further but
oh I could speak volumes on this subject but
(*Pause.*)
I'll write it
I'll write the Book of Love whilst having never oh not ever
loved
(*He bows his head.*)
Bless me
Bless me with your poisonous kiss
GERTRUDE: (*To RAGUSA.*) And you do you
HAMLET: BLESS
(*GERTRUDE concedes.*)
No
She does not love me either
She endorses my analysis
GERTRUDE: (*Frivolously.*) The perfect marriage obviously
HAMLET: (*Hurting himself.*) I SLAP MYSELF
I SLAP MYSELF
(*GERTRUDE is horrified.*)
RAGUSA: (*To GERTRUDE.*) You are poor-minded
HAMLET: (*Again.*) I SLAP MYSELF
RAGUSA: You are belittling and you
HAMLET: SLAP
SLAP
RAGUSA: HAVE NEVER LOVED FOR ALL YOUR COPULATIONS
HAMLET: SLAP
GERTRUDE: STOP THAT
RAGUSA: FILTH
FILTH
MAN IS BETTER THAN THIS SURELY
FILTH
(*A silence. RAGUSA takes HAMLET in her arms.*)
Blood
Oh you have hurt your lip
Blood
(*She holds a handkerchief to HAMLET's mouth.*)

HAMLET: (*Removing RAGUSA's hand.*) We are a sacrifice
    Loveless
    Dutiful
    And
    A
    Sacrifice
    (*He leads RAGUSA away. CLAUDIUS looks anxiously at GERTRUDE.*)

CLAUDIUS: Do not be

GERTRUDE: No

CLAUDIUS: I beg you Gertrude do not be

GERTRUDE: No

CLAUDIUS: Humiliated

GERTRUDE: No

CLAUDIUS: Or made to squirm with shame from some

GERTRUDE: No
    No

CLAUDIUS: Morally fastidious and finicky

GERTRUDE: Claudius

CLAUDIUS: Shame is our enemy shame alone will spoil us
    Gertrude

GERTRUDE: I AM NOT ASHAMED
    I SHALL NOT BE ASHAMED
    WHEN DID I KNOW SHAME
    NEVER
    AND NEVER WILL I KNOW IT
    (*He recoils.*)
    Do not doubt me Claudius
    (*Pause.*)

CLAUDIUS: Forgive me
    (*Pause.*)
    Forgive me Hamlet is
    I never speak with Hamlet
    Hamlet is
    Perhaps I should one day perhaps I
    (*He smiles thinly.*)
    Hamlet is your son
    (*GERTRUDE goes to CLAUDIUS. She touches his face with profound love. She walks off, and stops suddenly.*)

GERTRUDE: But not our son
(*She holds her belly.*)
NOT OUR SON
(*She strides out, undoing her coat as she goes. CASCAN enters.*)

# 14

CASCAN: I find as time goes by as I watch the world from
my frankly privileged position
(*He stops, he smiles disparagingly.*)
Forgive me I really must articulate sometimes the more
curious and paradoxical perceptions that occur to me the
rest I promise you I keep strictly to myself
(*Pause.*)
I find men odder than ever by men I mean the male the
male I have because of the unusual circumstances of my
life observed from a somewhat zoological perspective
(*He laughs a little.*)
I am a male myself of course
(*He shakes his head.*)
A male myself and therefore included in my disquisition
(*He laughs again.*)
We prefer the wounds of women to the women
(*He shakes his head.*)
Why is that?
(*GERTRUDE enters, doing up the belt of her coat, bare-legged in
shoes. CASCAN looks at her.*)
The Duke of Mecklenburg is on the train
(*Pause. GERTRUDE is shaken.*)
GERTRUDE: The train?
CASCAN: The train to Mecklenburg
(*He watches GERTRUDE and CLAUDIUS.*)
Bags servants dogs and some items of your underwear I
daresay
CLAUDIUS: WHO CARES WHAT YOU DARESAY
CASCAN: Between his fingers as the landscape
CLAUDIUS: WHO CARES I SAID
GERTRUDE: SHH

CASCAN: (*Undeterred.*) Slips away blue lakes and yellow
    harvesting no it's incontrovertible that whilst men scale the
    fences of desire it's only for the wounds they give they do
    not actually require to
    (*ALBERT enters, breathless with exertion. They stare at him,*
    *incredulously.*)

ALBERT: I did not mean a word I wrote in that letter

GERTRUDE: Letter?

ALBERT: NOT ONE WORD

GERTRUDE: Letter?

CASCAN: I had not yet delivered your grace's letter

ALBERT: GIVE ME THE LETTER
    (*CASCAN takes a letter from his pocket. ALBERT rips it across*
    *the middle.*)
    LIES
    COWARDLY LIES
    (*He smiles at GERTRUDE.*)
    I WAS ON A TRAIN
    Yes
    RUNNING FROM MY TRUTH I FLUNG LIES BEHIND ME
    (*He laughs.*)
    I pulled the communication cord
    Brakes
    Squeals
    Ranting officials
    And
    This spoils it slightly
    Jumping to the ground I twisted my foot
    (*GERTRUDE laughs. A pause. CASCAN leaves. CLAUDIUS*
    *looks at GERTRUDE and follows him.*)
    I've no wish to offend

GERTRUDE: Don't mind him

ALBERT: The Lord Claudius has never harmed me and

GERTRUDE: (*Smiling.*) Don't mind him
    (*A pause. ALBERT is lost for words. He looks at her, shaking his*
    *head.*)

ALBERT: And you are

GERTRUDE: Yes

ALBERT: You are

GERTRUDE: Naked

   Yes

   (*ALBERT closes his eyes. His hands go to his head, which he comforts.*)

ALBERT: I cannot describe the exquisite tension you keep me in I

   (*He aches.*)

   I almost think

   I do think

   (*He scoffs.*)

   I AM AFRAID TO SEE WHAT I SO WANT TO SEE

GERTRUDE: Wait then

ALBERT: WHAT I HAVE SEEN AND HAVE TO SEE AGAIN

GERTRUDE: Wait

ALBERT: I AM IN SUCH A TENDER ECSTASY I WOULD NOT CARE IF I WAS DEAD IF SOME SHOCK STOPPED MY HEART WHO CARES WHO CARES

   Say you understand say you know why I stand here and do not run like some mad dog to climb your flesh all mouth and tongue and fists and

   (*He aches.*)

   Say you understand

   (*He shakes his head.*)

GERTRUDE: I'll undo the coat

   (*ALBERT turns from her to avoid the sight. As GERTRUDE loosens the belt of her coat she gasps.*)

ALBERT: I WAIT

   I WAIT

   I WAIT

GERTRUDE: Idiot

ALBERT: Yes

GERTRUDE: Oh idiot I am your death

ALBERT: BE IT

   BE IT

   (*He turns violently.*)

   BE MY DEATH GERTRUDE

   (*GERTRUDE's fingers hesitate at the buttons.*)

GERTRUDE: Boy

ALBERT: Boy me

Boy me

STRIP YOU

GERTRUDE: Oh Boy

ALBERT: STRIP YOU I SAID

GERTRUDE: Oh Boy

ALBERT: STRIP

STRIP

STRIP

YOU

STRIP

YOU

GERTRUDE: Boy I

(*She gasps again.*)

ALBERT: STRIP

GERTRUDE: Love

You

(*ALBERT goes to seize GERTRUDE.*)

Claudius

(*GERTRUDE pulls her coat tight over her body as CLAUDIUS enters. ALBERT is stopped in mid-movement.*)

CLAUDIUS

CLAUDIUS

(*ALBERT stares at CLAUDIUS, who is likewise struck motionless. They stare, transfixed.*)

CLAUDIUS

(*In a brief moment, CLAUDIUS fails to murder ALBERT.*)

ALBERT: She

She

(*Seeing CLAUDIUS has not acted, he goes to GERTRUDE and taking her in his arms, kisses her longingly.*)

I don't mind death

I don't mind you see

(*He sinks to her knees and embraces her belly.*)

NEVER A BETTER MOMENT WILL OCCUR TO ME THAN THIS

(*CLAUDIUS sits. GERTRUDE's fingers idly stroke ALBERT's head.*)

Not if I lived to seven hundred

(*ALBERT sobs.*)

GERTRUDE: Get your train now

CASCAN: (*Entering with a timetable.*) There's one at midday
but it's not
(*He turns it round.*)
Oh yes it is
It is straight-through
But
(*He peers at the small print.*)
Lots of stops
(*He looks at ALBERT.*)
Probably that won't worry you
What might be experienced as frustration by most
travellers will pass unnoticed in that peculiar condition
of melancholy which engulfs you now this station
that station what's it to you let it crawl until the dawn
breaks over Mecklenburg and the conductor under the
misapprehension you're asleep is shaking your shoulder
we've arrived this is the terminus arrived strange word
when your mistress is your white and long-limbed mistress
is your pregnant and exquisite queen of forty-three is
arrived no that's the wrong word surely?
(*Pause. ALBERT climbs to his feet.*)

ALBERT: Say one word I'll live with you forever
(*GERTRUDE's gaze falters. ALBERT goes out. CASCAN
watches his departure.*)

CASCAN: What a fine departure the stupidest individuals I
have observed design perfect departures for themselves
whereas the sensitive are invariably embarrassing
(*Pause.*)
Pain ruins their vocabulary
(*GERTRUDE sobs.*)
Gestures which might well be efficacious seem to them
facile or false
(*She wails. CASCAN looks at her.*)
They can't win

CLAUDIUS: Do you love him?
(*GERTRUDE shakes her head.*)
GERTRUDE ARE YOU IN LOVE WITH

CASCAN: Please that is ridiculous
CLAUDIUS: Cascan I
CASCAN: SO UTTERLY
CLAUDIUS: CASCAN
CASCAN: RIDICULOUS

> (*He goes out. GERTRUDE is quite still, her eyes are closed. CLAUDIUS tries to speak.*)

CLAUDIUS: I would have killed Gertrude

> (*GERTRUDE shakes her head.*)

> Gertrude I would

> I would have killed but

> (*She shakes her head more fiercely.*)

> FORGIVE ME WHEN I LOOKED AT HIM I SAW MYSELF

> I saw that

> Oh

> That

> Time-smothering

> Self-abnegating

> World annihilating

> DISBELIEF

> YOUR NAKEDNESS WAS MORE INCREDIBLE TO HIM THAN IF GOD STOOD AND PRESSED THE FIRMAMENT AGAINST HIS LIPS

GERTRUDE: It is God is it not?

> It is God my nakedness?

CLAUDIUS: Yes

GERTRUDE: To you?

> It is to you is it?

CLAUDIUS: Yes

> Yes

GERTRUDE: AGAIN

CLAUDIUS: Yes

> Gertrude

> Yes

> (*They gaze into one another. They are relieved.*)

GERTRUDE: I did not want him dead what is it to me if he is dead his body climbed in mine so what he might have been a surgeon a surgeon examining me and when

I looked down at the ground I saw his stuff spill out of me
it did not cling whereas with you I draw it to my depths I
hoard you I am a fist Claudius a fist retaining you
(*They are enraptured. Then GERTRUDE frowns.*)
The cry however
The cry is not kind
Where there is kindness such as you described to me no
cry comes so do not say I have betrayed you do not punish
me I made an instrument out of my body but you did
not play the instrument instead of killing you were kind I
do not criticize but I must wash now I must put on plain
clothes these high heels and this nakedness seem suddenly
absurd
(*She sobs. CLAUDIUS goes to act but a gesture of
GERTRUDE's stops him.*)
I must be quiet now with my child
(*A pause. She departs. CLAUDIUS is silent for some moments.*)

CLAUDIUS: QUIET NOW
GERTRUDE QUIET NOW
WHAT IS GERTRUDE QUIET
(*CASCAN passes with a bowl of water and sponge, a towel over
his arm.*)
Where are you
(*CASCAN stops. CLAUDIUS is bewildered.*)
Did you over hear the Queen say she wanted to be
washed?

CASCAN: I never overhear my lord
(*Pause.*)

CLAUDIUS: No
It is an intuition with you is it not an intimacy
I think should be stopped
I WILL WASH THE QUEEN
(*CASCAN inclines his head. CLAUDIUS takes the bowl.*)
I will if anybody does
(*CLAUDIUS goes out.*)

# 15

*CASCAN meditates. RAGUSA enters.*

RAGUSA: You know everything
   (*Pause.*)
   Don't you?
   Everything?
   (*Pause.*)
CASCAN: Yes
RAGUSA: Advise me then I have such a terror I am doing
   wrong not to others to myself marriage is the greatest
   moment in a woman's life to be a bride the day of all days
   surely and I do not love I do not hate I sometimes pity but
   love oh love I am betrothed out of a what an impulse of
   defiance Hamlet calls it faith I don't know I don't know if I
   (*CASCAN makes a gesture of irritation.*)
   share that
CASCAN: Shh
RAGUSA: Faith
   (*Pause.*)
CASCAN: It's not
   (*Pause.*)
RAGUSA: (*Puzzled.*) What?
CASCAN: The greatest moment of a woman's life
RAGUSA: Is it not?
   (*Pause. CASCAN watches her.*)
CASCAN: There are two moments of greatness in a woman's
   life
   (*He watches RAGUSA.*)
   The day on which she gives birth
RAGUSA: Oh yes certainly
   (*Pause.*)
   And the other?
CASCAN: The day on which
   (*Pause.*)
   Out of a terrible hunger
   (*Pause.*)
   She lies to her husband

RAGUSA: Hunger?

CASCAN: For another man now miss be kind enough to note
that nothing I have said may be constructed as advice a
servant does not give advice albeit he knows everything
advice is cheap service is
(*He smiles.*)
not cheap

RAGUSA: No
Not cheap at all
But rare and oh I wish Hamlet had you for his oh Hamlet
should have you

CASCAN: I could not serve the Lord Hamlet

RAGUSA: No you are the Queen's and
(*She shrugs.*)

CASCAN: Great is the Queen Gertrude
Great is the Queen
(*Pause. RAGUSA goes to leave.*)
Her life is such a seeking and so beautiful is her pain
(*RAGUSA stops.*)
How could I not relieve her?
It is a passion in me and a faith

RAGUSA: Yes
(*She bites her lip, frowns.*)
And my life is poor
(*She sobs and runs out.*)
SO POOR MY LIFE

# 16

*GERTRUDE's cry. CASCAN hurries off.*

HAMLET: (*Entering.*) Disgusting
(*The cry.*)
Disgusting
(*The cry.*)
Disgusting
Disgusting
Disgusting
(*The cry.*)

DÉGOUTANT

DÉGOUTANT

ABSOLUMENT DÉGOUTANT

The woman I decline to employ a word like mother
biologically correct thought it might be the woman
(*The cry.*)

DÉGOUTANT

ABSOLUMENT DÉGOUTANT

Is forty-three and by the laws of nature if nature were not
so contaminated with disease should have shed her last egg
whole easters and christmases ago this faded and
(*The cry.*)

DÉGOUTANT JE DIS

should be seated in a rocking chair with black blankets
spread across her knees
(*An infant's cry. HAMLET is stock still. ISOLA hurries in.*)

ISOLA: It's alive
(*And hurtles out.*)

HAMLET: Deformed surely his lip disfigured by a sneer of
such a magnitude it stands before his vision like a wave so
when she goes to raise him to her shrivelled breasts she
sees

ISOLA: (*Hurrying back again with a mass of linen.*) It's perfect
and a girl
(*She hurries out again.*)

HAMLET: Her filth repudiated PERFECT IN WHAT SENSE
repudiated by the howling product of her delinquencies
PERFECT IS A DEAD MAN'S QUALITY
(*He laughs, he sniggers. CLAUDIUS enters.*)

CLAUDIUS: Your sister smiled

HAMLET: (*Turning.*) Smiled did she who would not smile to
have escaped the fetid dungeon of my mother's womb the
thing was rinsed in torrents of
I SHAN'T GO ON
Flooded with the filth of
I SHAN'T
(*He purses his lips.*)
I'm saying more you notice this was unavoidable if I were
not to develop incurable erosions of my bowel

I bled some mornings but since I was restored to ranting
this haemorrhage has stopped
I SHAN'T HOWEVER SAY MORE OF MY MOTHER'S STINKING
FUNDAMENT ALBEIT MUCH MORE COULD BE SAID
(*CLAUDIUS glares at HAMLET.*)
CLAUDIUS: I say it
HAMLET: You say it yes
CLAUDIUS: The more that could be said
HAMLET: Yes
CLAUDIUS: I say it
HAMLET: Yes
CLAUDIUS: I say it and I say it
HAMLET: You say it and say it yes
CLAUDIUS: I say it and I say it and I say it again
HAMLET: You do yes
(*Pause. Their eyes hang on one another's.*)
If God meant cunt to be religion I think He would not
have situated it between a woman's legs would He?
ISOLA: (*Entering in delight.*) She is ADORABLE
HAMLET: By piss and shit would He?
ISOLA: Adorable AND WITH MY EYES SO GERTRUDE SAYS
HAMLET: Hidden from the sight of men and yet further
smothered in a forest what could that intend
ISOLA: I am going to be silly so silly about this child I warn
you
HAMLET: But to confirm its sordid function
ISOLA: AND WHY SHOULDN'T I?
CLAUDIUS: Function?
ISOLA: My first grand-daughter isn't she?
CLAUDIUS: Function he says
FAITH COMES FROM SECRET PLACES AND IN THE DAZZLING
CATHEDRALS OF LIGHT IT DIES
(*For the first time he removes his eyes from HAMLET.*)
Show him his niece or his sister is it let him see the
function's functioning
(*HAMLET goes to leave with ISOLA.*)
SHE CRIES
Not the child the mother

She cries for me
(*HAMLET looks back.*)
IN MY MOUTH SHE SAYS
ANYWHERE
BUT ENTER ME
(*Choking his resentment, HAMLET leaves with ISOLA.*
*CASCAN, in an apron, is discovered.*)

CASCAN: Not wise

CLAUDIUS: He maddens me

CASCAN: Not wise I said

CLAUDIUS: LET HIM PLOT MY EXECUTION
LET YOU
LET ANYONE
(*Pause.*)

CASCAN: Your death would be regrettable

CLAUDIUS: Is that so?

CASCAN: Insofar as it would devastate my lady
(*Pause.*)
Sufficient reason I suggest to refrain from fuelling her son's resentment
(*CLAUDIUS looks critically at CASCAN.*)

CLAUDIUS: Her cries I thought peculiarly similar to those she utters in the act of love yet this was pain surely?

CASCAN: The Lord Hamlet

CLAUDIUS: Of course birth pain might be an ecstasy or conversely yes we must consider this it might be agony for her to love the agony which comes from a mortality she longs to shed and which

CASCAN: The Lord Hamlet

CLAUDIUS: I AM A STUDENT OF HER SOUNDS

CASCAN: IS KING HERE NOW
(*Pause.*)

CLAUDIUS: The king governs the kingdom
Gertrude governs me
To him the armies and the acres
My whole life's in her belly in my opinion a superior estate
(*CASCAN frowns.*)

CASCAN: Yes
Yes

But those who rule us hate one woman's womb even to lie
beyond their dispensation
(*CLAUDIUS looks puzzled.*)
The police
CLAUDIUS: The police?
CASCAN: Are posted even there
(*CLAUDIUS frowns.*)
How little my lord understands of the ambitions of the
moralists
(*With a resigned air, CASCAN goes to leave. He suddenly stops in
his tracks.*)
You must murder Hamlet
(*CASCAN squirms.*)
I have usurped my service
I have broken with my faith
Never did I state a solitary objection nor initiate a course of
action never recommended or uttered one word of dissent
A SERVANT MAY NOT URGE
(*Pause.*)
I preserve my mistress and that is my defence
(*CLAUDIUS is shaken.*)
CLAUDIUS: Hamlet is the Queen's son
CASCAN: The stronger his passion to torture her
CLAUDIUS: Torture her?
She is his mother
CASCAN: He will burn her at the stake
CLAUDIUS: Cascan
CASCAN: IT WILL DEMONSTRATE THE AUTHENTICITY OF HIS
CONVICTIONS
Oh
Oh you do not know the moralists you do not know
the python length of their ambition and how could you
innocent oh innocent are the immoralists I must wash your
tragic daughter
(*He goes to leave.*)
What is her name?
(*CLAUDIUS shrugs.*)
Oh
Lend her a name if only to identify her grave

CLAUDIUS: You choose

(*CASCAN sweeps out but is obliged to step back to make way for GERTRUDE who enters holding a pair of high-heeled shoes in one hand and with the other pulling a gown around her nakedness. CASCAN and CLAUDIUS watch as GERTRUDE drops the shoes to the floor and controlling her frailty, steps into them. She proceeds to remove a lipstick from her pocket and with infinite will, colours her mouth. CASCAN suffers. CLAUDIUS exults. With a triumphant gesture GERTRUDE tosses the lipstick far away.*)

GERTRUDE: MUTINY

(*She laughs.*)

I MUTINY

(*She staggers. She grasps. The child cries.*)

Drink me Claudius

Let my daughter queue

(*GERTRUDE opens her gown at the breast. CLAUDIUS goes to her, kneels, suckles her.*)

CASCAN: (*Discreetly turning away.*) I like Jane myself

I like the single syllable

As if a clock on a high tower chimed but only once

(*GERTRUDE shudders in her ecstasy, her hand cradling CLAUDIUS's head. RAGUSA, hurrying in, is staggered by the spectacle and fixed to the spot.*)

Do you like Jane Miss?

(*RAGUSA's hands flutter in her speechlessness.*)

My mother gave me such a foolish name I have never dared reveal it

(*She runs out.*)

Perhaps it satisfied her thinking how I'd squirm to speak it but I don't I don't speak it and now she's dead of course

(*CLAUDIUS ceases. GERTRUDE covers herself. The child bawls.*)

No one knows it now

(*GERTRUDE sits.*)

Unless

And this I deem unlikely

Some official in the registry has selected it from among the most preposterous to act as an admonishment to

thoughtless parents yes let's say Jane let's spare the child
one cause for resentment
(*HAMLET enters holding the bawling infant in his arms and
rocking it.*)

HAMLET: (*As if charmed.*) Sucking my finger
Yes
I am perhaps her brother but is it love I don't think so
myself
(*He laughs.*)
Ragusa has laid a complaint against you mother
AGAINST THE QUEEN
SILLY I SAID
But all the same it has to be investigated that is the law
the most humble and despised among the citizens can call
their betters to account
A LAWYER WON'T TAKE LONG TO THROW THAT OUT
Ow
She sucks like a calf
But is it love I don't think so myself
No
Infants are not sentimental what they require is blood
DID I SAY BLOOD
I must mean milk
(*HAMLET offers the baby to GERTRUDE, who makes no move
to take it.*)
Ragusa's complaint
SILLY GIRL SHE WILL BE RIDICULED IN COURT
Concerns the welfare of an infant
(*He offers the child to CASCAN instead. CASCAN takes it.*)
Which I suppose must be the business of the state as
warfare is as gardening is as is the painting of the frontier
posts
(*He laughs.*)
Are they not the inheritors of the earth and all our labour
is it not directed to the enhancement of existence for the
newly and the as yet un
THE NEWLY AND THE AS YET UN?
(*He frowns. He goes to GERTRUDE.*)

You have got lipstick on your teeth
(*He stares at her, turns swiftly and goes out. CASCAN yells at*
*CLAUDIUS.*)
CASCAN: KILL HIM
   KILL HIM
   KILL HIM
   QUICK
   HE'S ON HIS OWN
   HE'S UNACCOMPANIED
   KILL HIM
   KILL HIM
   KILL HIM
   QUICK
   (*CLAUDIUS looks from CASCAN to GERTRUDE, hesitant.*
   *CASCAN, boiling with impatience, races after HAMLET holding*
   *the child in his arms.*)

# 17

*ISOLA enters with the infant in her arms.*

ISOLA: Jane
   Oh
   Jane
   AUSPICIOUS THIS
   An hour old or is it less an hour in the world and
   I'M NOT CLAIRVOYANT BUT
   Jane
   Oh
   Jane
   TWICE DRENCHED IN BLOOD
   (*CLAUDIUS races from the room.*)
   That is auspicious darling
   I'M NOT CLAIRVOYANT BUT
   TWICE RINSED IN BLOOD
GERTRUDE: Shut up or I'll smack you
ISOLA: TWICE GERTRUDE
   TAKE HER FROM ME
   TWICE RINSED IN BLOOD

GERTRUDE: Whose?
    Whose blood?
ISOLA: TAKE HER
GERTRUDE: (*Refusing.*) WHOSE BLOOD I SAID
    (*Pause. ISOLA stares, shakes her head.*)
ISOLA: I saw him running
    Babe in arms
    And with his apron on
    Flapping
    Flapping apron
    And these shoes with the steel tips on
    Sliding
    Slipping
    Whereas Hamlet's shoes are soft
    Down steps
    And skids
    THE KID I SAID
    A miracle
    He never tripped
    These shoes with the steel tips on
    Clatter
    Clatter
    The noise
    A regiment
    But Hamlet's lost in thought
    He never flinched
    The servant grabs him round the neck
    THE KID I SAID
    With one arm round his neck he pulls him back
    One arm
    The other
    Well
    Jane's in that
    And tries to choke him
    All this in silence
    Yes
    The kid's asleep
    He could have dropped her

But he hung on
His face white as a sheet
He isn't strong
No
Hamlet's stronger
But also Hamlet has a knife
So strength's nothing to do with it
THE KID I SAID
And sticks it in
Once
Twice
The servant drops
Not drops
He doesn't drop he sinks
Holding the kid
He sinks
AND HAMLET JUST GOES ON
OH HAMLET
HAMLET JUST GOES ON
I think
Oh more than necessary
I really think
And all the time Jane is asleep
It isn't noisy
The servant
I never liked him
The servant doesn't speak
Or moan
Or
Anything
(*Pause.*)
The blood was
(*Pause.*)
Oh the blood
(*She shakes her head.*)
I washed it off
I washed it off the kid and put her in clean things
The path however

OH THAT AWFUL PATH
(*Pause. GERTRUDE is still.*)
GERTRUDE: My daughter please
(*ISOLA hands over the child. She hesitates.*)
ISOLA: He should have dropped her
It doesn't hurt to drop a baby
Even on its head
They're soft
You and I
We know babies don't we
But him I don't think he had ever touched one
(*She shrugs.*)
To kill someone you must have two hands free
(*Pause.*)
I would have thought
(*She goes out. The infant makes small and anxious sounds. Slowly, absently, GERTRUDE loosens her gown at the breast.*)

# 18

*She turns her back, and feeds. CLAUDIUS enters.*

CLAUDIUS: Forgive me
(*GERTRUDE neither moves nor speaks.*)
Forgive me
(*Pause.*)
Forgive me
(*Pause.*)
I DON'T KNOW WHAT FOR GERTRUDE BUT I APPEAR TO
NEED FORGIVING
(*She is silent and still.*)
Possibly I don't
(*Pause.*)
Possibly I don't require forgiving possibly I have merely
as so often in our history detected in your manner how
extraordinary this is in your ABSENCE OF A MANNER EVEN
that I have somehow by some slip some oversight some
negligible omission contrived to injure you
(*GERTRUDE turns and studies him.*)

GERTRUDE: I
CRY
YOUR
CRIME
(*Pause.*)
CLAUDIUS: Yes
Yes
I know you do
(*He frowns. He turns to go.*)
I'll poison him
GERTRUDE: POISON
POISON WHO
(*CLAUDIUS stops.*)
CLAUDIUS: The king your son I'll
GERTRUDE: POISON WHO
(*She appears horrified. They comprehend one another.*
*CLAUDIUS leaves. RAGUSA hurries in.*)
RAGUSA: THE CHILD'S REMOVED
GERTRUDE: Remove her
RAGUSA: The welfare of the child must be of paramount
consideration in all issues of
GERTRUDE: REMOVE HER THEN
RAGUSA: (*Stepping forward briskly and snatching the infant.*)
The unseemly haste with which you concede possession of
your daughter confirms our doubts as to your suitability for
parenthood
GERTRUDE: Her name is Jane
But that was in her first life
(*She turns to call CASCAN.*)
BRING ME MY
(*Pause.*)
He's dead
MY BLACKEST AND MOST
He's dead
MY WORST BLACK
Dead now
Dead now
(*Pause.*)

He sponged me
Oh yes
My servant sponged me
Lovingly
Between my legs
Between my breasts
(*RAGUSA stares in disgust. She turns to go.*)
I DON'T KNOW WHERE MY THINGS ARE
(*GERTRUDE half-laughs.*)
He did the wardrobe
I DON'T KNOW WHERE MY THINGS ARE AND I'M NOT
DRESSED
(*RAGUSA hastens away. The child cries bitterly.*)

# 19

*HAMLET enters, wearing CASCAN's clothes.*

HAMLET: The world is full of things I do not understand but
others understand them evidently for example shoes those
shoes have heels of such extravagant dimensions how can
you move except by dislocating your entire anatomy it is
as if you held your body in contempt as if you found your
shape unsatisfactory shoes are a consequence of nature
certainly of cold and winter but should shoes not enhance
the action of our limbs should they not encourage us to
act in sympathy with the body's functioning not trick us
into grotesque parody the world is full of things I do not
understand but others understand them evidently
(*He passes around GERTRUDE, studying.*)
By this perverse and extreme elevation of the heel your
posture is so tilted by the shift of gravity a stranger
unacquainted with our habits would howl with ridicule I
look at athletes how beautifully they move and always in
such harmony whereas women who have lived in these
they stagger on their swollen joints and damaged knees
the world is full of things I do not understand but others
understand them evidently
(*Pause.*)

Be barefoot now
(*His eyes meet hers. She is adamant.*)
REMOVE
THE
UNMATERNAL
CLUTTER
CLINGING
TO
YOUR
FEET
(*She stares, unmoved.*)
For
The
Morally
Offended
Amputation
Is
Always
The
Last
Resort
(*GERTRUDE is defiant. With a gesture of self-assertion she slips the gown from her shoulders and lets it fall to the floor. She is naked before HAMLET. His gaze does not falter.*)
The world is full of things I do not understand
(*He senses the presence of a third party.*)
But others understand them evidently
(*He turns to see CLAUDIUS, holding a glass of wine. The sight causes GERTRUDE to catch her breath. The sound alerts HAMLET, who looks to her again. His mind works. He looks back and forth. GERTRUDE gasps, her hand to her mouth.*)
I am the servant
Surely
Therefore
I
Should
Serve
The

Drink?

(*He goes to collect the glass, his hand extended.*)

CLAUDIUS: (*With a bow.*) The King is not the Servant

He

Merely

Wears

The

Clothes

HAMLET: I

Ape

His

Excellence

(*CLAUDIUS relinquishes the glass to HAMLET who goes to carry it to GERTRUDE.*)

CLAUDIUS: Gertrude

(*HAMLET stops.*)

Do

Not

Drink

(*Pause. HAMLET calculates.*)

HAMLET: Don't drink?

For whom then is the drink intended or is the drink

your own forgive me oh I have in an excess of manners

confiscated yours

(*He goes to restore the glass to CLAUDIUS, who does not take it.*)

Please

Your

Glass

Of

(*Pause.*)

YOUR

OWN

GLASS

(*Pause.*)

GERTRUDE: You drink it

You drink his glass

(*HAMLET looks over his shoulder at GERTRUDE.*)

HAMLET: I

Drink

His
Glass?
I
Hamlet
Drink
The
Glass
Of
Why
(*Pause.*)
GERTRUDE: I don't know

I DON'T KNOW WHY JUST DRINK THE
(*Her hands lift.*)
I don't know why
HAMLET: One would think

Oh

Silly but

(*He shakes his head.*)
So many things I do not understand but others understand
them evidently
WHAT IS IN THE GLASS THAT I SHOULD
(*Neither GERTRUDE nor CLAUDIUS speaks. On a sudden
impulse HAMLET lifts the glass to his lips and swallows
the contents. GERTRUDE shudders. Her cry heaves out as
HAMLET staggers. CLAUDIUS exults.*)
CLAUDIUS: Gertrude

Gertrude

(*Her cry heaves out again. She holds herself as if she were terrified
of her own disintegration.*)
Gertrude

KILLING GOD

(*He is transfixed by her ecstasy. HAMLET sinks to his knees,
the glass unbroken in his hand, his eyes on his mother. Again she
heaves out her cry.*)
GERTRUDE: I CAN'T

I CAN'T

(*Her hands move as if she were grappling an invisible opponent.*)
CLAUDIUS: Gertrude

GERTRUDE: OH STOP

OH STOP

(*Again her cry comes. She is doubled. Still CLAUDIUS observes her. HAMLET, by his final exertion, stands the glass on its foot, an action of perfect will. He dies. Only now does CLAUDIUS go to GERTRUDE. He wraps her in an embrace of exquisite tenderness. They remain thus, a trio of extinction as ISOLA enters pushing a pram. She stops, observing the scene, and on tiptoe is about to leave again when the child cries. She stops. CLAUDIUS and GERTRUDE end their embrace.*)

ISOLA: I heard this

I thought

I heard this

I thought

(*She shrugs with terror, embarrassment.*)

NEVER MIND WHAT I THOUGHT

(*She wants to move off.*)

CLAUDIUS: Don't go

ISOLA: I want to

CLAUDIUS: Don't go Mother

ISOLA: I WANT TO

I WANT TO THOUGH

(*She seems fixed to the spot.*)

Shops

Sugar

Loaf

Shops

Loaf

Gertrude

(*She falters as GERTRUDE walks unsteadily towards her and with a wail falls into her arms. ISOLA is stiff, horrified. GERTRUDE's tears cease. She removes herself. She gazes at the floor.*)

GERTRUDE: My bladder

My ovaries

My bowel

This rushing in them as a storm in gulleys washes washes

My kidneys

My belly
My womb
The rivers boiling through
Latin names now
Urethra
Vulva
Mammary
Surging as the blood goes flooding more blood than any
body can contain
The brain however
THE AGONY OF BRAIN
(*She stares at ISOLA.*)
Go shopping now you rightly have discerned your own
extinction chalked on the wall
Go shopping and in the market say I won't pay that
Preposterous price say for a kilo of
ANYTHING THAT WILL DELAY YOUR HOMECOMING
(*She looks at the pram.*)
How I love a pram a pram pushed and the dormant child
between great bags of groceries washing powder and the
bus queue bleach and the tram
(*Biting her lip with apprehension ISOLA swiftly departs with the
pram. GERTRUDE is still.*)
Strip my son now of his clothes his clothes that were not
his and stretch him naked somewhere
HOW BADLY HE REQUIRED THOSE CLOTHES
CLAUDIUS: Yes
GERTRUDE: But do not clean them
CLAUDIUS: Clean them?
No
GERTRUDE: NEVER TO BE CLEANED THOSE CLOTHES
(*Pause. CLAUDIUS is about to move to embrace GERTRUDE
but she stops him with a look.*)
The cry
The cry
CLAUDIUS: Bigger
GERTRUDE: Bigger
Yes
BIGGER THAN MY BODY CLAUDIUS

CLAUDIUS: Yes

GERTRUDE: (*Horrified.*) MY WALLS WERE FALLING

CLAUDIUS: Yes

GERTRUDE: MY LIMBS CLAUDIUS
>MY HEAD
>IN ALL DIRECTIONS

CLAUDIUS: Yes

GERTRUDE: I DID NOT THINK
>AT THE CRY'S END
>I COULD BE STILL INTACT

CLAUDIUS: Yes

GERTRUDE: CLAUDIUS

CLAUDIUS: (*Exulting.*) Yes
>(*She shakes her head, seeing he does not know her horror.*)
>And you were not fucked
>(*Pause.*)

GERTRUDE: Your eyes

CLAUDIUS: My eyes yes

GERTRUDE: I was eyed
>EYED WAS ENOUGH
>(*RAGUSA enters. She stares at the body of HAMLET. They seem unaware of her.*)
>DON'T ASK ME
>OH CLAUDIUS DO NOT ASK AGAIN
>(*She stares at him, a plea. He defies her. She walks out.*)

RAGUSA: (*Her eyes not shifting from HAMLET's body.*)
>Poor woman take her to bed
>(*CLAUDIUS is puzzled, but turns to go.*)
>I'll be there however
>(*He turns. She laughs shrilly.*)
>I'LL BE IN THE BED
>(*She looks at him.*)
>NO-LAW BECOMES LAW THEREFORE I MUST BE
>(*She makes a gesture.*)
>I
>I
>I
>(*She smiles.*)
>ALREADY YOU BETRAY HER

*(CLAUDIUS goes to take a step towards RAGUSA and stops.*
*She taunts him with a laugh, shaking her head.)*
ALREADY I AM IN THE BED
*(RAGUSA goes out. CLAUDIUS is thoughtful. He goes to*
*HAMLET's body. He starts to remove CASCAN's suit but stops.)*
CLAUDIUS: Oh poor unloved

Oh

Poor

And

Never

Loved

*(He tries to strip the jacket.)*

I'm crying

Yes

I'm crying

*(He tugs.)*

Me

*(He stops.)*

And why not why not me poison notwithstanding why not
me

*(He points.)*

THAT WAS YOUR WIFE

Oh

Poor

And

Never

Loved

YOUR WIDOW WANTS TO SHUDDER UNDER ME

*(He shakes his head.)*

That Cascan

That Cascan he

*(He returns to his task.)*

No wonder you paraded in his clothes like some champion
flourishing a trophy

HE WATCHED WITH SUCH

I resented it

We both did

You and me

With such

THIS COLD WATCHING AND
(*He stops to recollect.*)
He made me feel turned on a wheel and dirty as if some
oily rain fell on a mask a grinning thing a fairground
object brass or peeling paint my life and my desires HOW I
WISHED TO SAY THIS BUT I NEVER DID are REAL
Ha
Ha
THIS COLD WATCHING
(*GERTRUDE has returned and waits. She is impeccable,
funereal.*)
I have the jacket
(*He holds it out in one hand.*)
The trousers I

GERTRUDE: Shh

CLAUDIUS: Haven't yet

GERTRUDE: Shh I said
(*He climbs to his feet. They exchange a long look.*)
CLAUDIUS YOUR DEATH IS NEXT
(*Pause.*)
I shuddered when I knew it I SAY DEATH I MEAN SOME
WRITHING MURDER call it death
(*Pause.*)
Not today not imminently today is grief today is silent
walking and staring in the pool of memory terrible
reflections in the pool and self-disgust the womb a
shrunken thing in masonry the thighs all chalk and mouth
a cave of dust another day however

CLAUDIUS: Yes
(*Pause.*)

GERTRUDE: Oh do you know it yes you do you know it too
I shuddered when did you know how long have you
CONCEALED YOUR
(*She glares.*)
I COULD STRIKE YOU

CLAUDIUS: I love you

GERTRUDE: I COULD STRIKE YOU
(*She sways. A pause. Her hand rises and falls.*)
My darling

Get out of my sight
My darling
GET OUT OF MY SIGHT
(*CLAUDIUS leaves.*)

# 20

*ALBERT enters in mourning.*

ALBERT: I came at once
    (*GERTRUDE turns. ALBERT folds his hands in front of him
    and stares at the floor.*)
    And that wasn't soon enough for me
    THANK YOU DEATH
    THANK YOU DISEASE
    (*He bites his lip.*)
    Poor friend
    Poor friend but was he
    Sitting on the train I thought was Hamlet anybody's friend
    It isn't him I'm here for is it Gertrude I am here for you
GERTRUDE: Our pleasure in the Duke's return is inevitably
    diminished by the circumstances in which we
ALBERT: Tip Hamlet in the river and let the river wash him
    to the sea let cod pull Hamlet in a hundred pieces dead
    or alive he's nothing to me am I coarse so are my feelings
    when I look at you I dream your arse I dream your legs
    wide open and my tongue already aches with anticipation
    of the deep searching it will do
    (*RAGUSA enters in mourning.*)
    Ragusa
    (*He goes to her.*)
    Ragusa
    Poor Danes
    Poor Denmark
    And poor you
    (*They embrace formally.*)
RAGUSA: He had so many plans
ALBERT: A more fertile brain I never knew
    (*CLAUDIUS enters with ISOLA. ALBERT goes to them and
    kisses the hand of ISOLA.*)

Is it not true he had commissioned architects to rebuild
Elsinore in glass?

Why glass?

RAGUSA: It is transparent

ALBERT: Quite so

It is defined by its transparency

RAGUSA: (*Looking at CLAUDIUS.*) All acts of love he wanted
under public scrutiny

Lying

Darkness

Secrecy

Hamlet abhorred

ISOLA: It started off with curtains

(*They look at her.*)

Down came all the curtains

Then he had the workmen take the locks off all the doors

Then it was the doors

IT'S DRAUGHTY HAMLET I SAID

(*She chuckles fondly.*)

Better you freeze he said than love is spoiled by

(*She stops.*)

WHAT IS THAT WORD? HE USED IT ALL THE TIME

RAGUSA: Clan – destine

ISOLA: That's the word

CLANDESTINE

Better you freeze than love is

(*She stops.*)

Poor boy

Poor boy because it is

(*Pause. The infant Jane is heard to cry offstage. ISOLA hurries off
to attend. GERTRUDE takes the few steps to HAMLET's body.*)

GERTRUDE: A killed child on the floor and in the corridor
another famishes

AND YET I AM MATERNAL

RAGUSA: Go to her

GERTRUDE: No

Let her gnaw the air or suck the crust form grandmothers
whose plunging teats are black from holiday resorts

MATERNAL YES

It's stopped
It's stopped
(*The child is silent.*)
How necessary it flatters us to think we are and how
terrible it is that we are never necessary
(*To CLAUDIUS.*) KISS ME
LIFT MY VEIL AND KISS ME
RAGUSA: THIS IS MY HUSBAND'S FUNERAL
(*She seethes.*)
Please
Please
GERTRUDE: (*Deliberately.*) ALL RIGHT I'LL LIFT IT
(*She throws aside the veil and waits.*)
RAGUSA: Please
(*She looks to CLAUDIUS.*)
And please again
(*CLAUDIUS hesitates. ALBERT seizes the initiative and kisses
GERTRUDE on the mouth. He steps back. GERTRUDE looks
at him.*)
How it gratified me when I came here
The sheer saying
What liberty
The sheer saying
The thought straight to the mouth
And no queuing
No queuing up behind behind the teeth
OUT THOUGHT
OUT INJURY
(*RAGUSA laughs strangely.*)
AND GERTRUDE FEARS SHE IS NOT NECESSARY
Oh
Gertrude
Gertrude
Is
Whereas
Hamlet
(*She shakes her head pitifully.*)
Unnecessary Hamlet
IN THE DITCH WITH HIM

(*She goes to leave and stops.*)
We planned your execution
It was in his diary
And not in pencil
Ink
The judges had been nominated and the trial was fixed
A contract with the axeman
Spanish
Far from cheap
(*She goes out. A stillness. Suddenly ALBERT declares himself.*)
ALBERT: I'm not leaving
(*Pause.*)
I left before but I was young then
(*Pause.*)
A schoolboy
(*Pause.*)
Bundled on a train
(*Pause.*)
Books
Bags
Chucked after me
NEVER AGAIN
(*He looks to GERTRUDE.*)
I have an army on the frontier show me your arse
(*GERTRUDE looks mildly at ALBERT.*)
You know armies
(*He menaces her.*)
How they love to march
(*Pause.*)
And burn
And crucify
(*She does not remove her eyes from him.*)
Turn infants on their lances
Ravish
Trample
And halfway through some crime they cry I've seen it in
the East
(*Pause.*)
So show your arse

(*Pause.*)

Poor Denmark

(*Pause.*)

Show me it

(*GERTRUDE lifts her heavy black skirt, and poses for him.
ALBERT passes a hand over his face in his ordeal. For a long
time he contemplates the object of his passion.*)

GERTRUDE: My unburied son

ALBERT: I'll bury him

(*A pause of inspiration.*)

GERTRUDE: My unkilled lover

(*ALBERT hesitates. GERTRUDE gasps in an ecstasy. She lets
fall her skirt and runs to CLAUDIUS, taking him in an adoring
embrace and smothering him with kisses.*)

CLAUDIUS: The cry

GERTRUDE: Yes

CLAUDIUS: Waiting

GERTRUDE: Yes

(*CLAUDIUS studies her.*)

CLAUDIUS: Always I thought the cry was in you

But it's not

It's outside

It waits

It walks

Some long hound pacing the perimeter

Frost clinging to it

Clouds of breath

GERTRUDE: CALL IT

CALL IT

(*CLAUDIUS lingers, then tears away. GERTRUDE overcomes
her upheaval. With infinite calm, she straightens her disordered
clothes. ISOLA hurries in, a white wedding garment over her
arm.*)

# 21

ISOLA: Cast your mind back

(*She sniggers with pleasure.*)

Cast your mind back and say who thought of it

(*GERTRUDE removes her black jacket.*)

I DID

GERTRUDE: You did yes

ISOLA: That boy I said

That boy's a branch for you

(*ISOLA takes the jacket.*)

NOT SUCH A BOY NOW

NO BOY THE DUKE OF

I can say it

MECKLENBURG

If you need to you can say a word previous to this

I never needed to

Duchess of MECKLENBURG

See

See

(*GERTRUDE steps out of her full black skirt.*)

Gertrude I like you

I always did

We had our falling out but never could I bring myself to

AND THAT WAS ALL CLAUDIUS

THAT WAS MY BOY

I fretted

I thought you

(*Pause. She takes the skirt.*)

NEVER MIND WHAT I THOUGHT YOU

This is so discreet

(*She holds up the white dress.*)

At forty-three a bride should be

I say discreet

IT ISN'T THOUGH IS IT

(*She laughs and pretends to shake her head.*)

NOT TERRIBLY

(*She laughs. GERTRUDE leaves her holding the garment.*)

GERTRUDE: How delighted you are Isola

ISOLA: Delighted for you

(*Pause.*)

For you

(*In a moment of pity GERTRUDE draws ISOLA's face near to her own and kisses her.*)

That's nice
(*She almost sobs.*)
That's nice of you
GERTRUDE: Not for me at all
Silly
Not for me
ISOLA: For Denmark obviously I don't know politics the way
I used to do but Meckel
(*She stops.*)
Mickel
(*She shakes her head.*)
Can't say it Gertrude
GERTRUDE: Not Denmark
Nor Gertrude either
I ALSO AM MATERNAL AND I KNOW WHAT PLEASES YOU
(*ISOLA looks up at GERTRUDE.*)
ISOLA: Give him an island
Far out in the Cold Sea
He'll plant
He might put up with me
Digging
A
Bit
(*GERTRUDE looks pityingly at ISOLA. She takes the garment
and goes out with it.*)
I HOPE YOU'RE HAPPY
(*Pause.*)
TWICE HIS AGE SO WHAT I'VE BEEN
(*Pause.*)
Oh yes I've been
(*Pause.*)
In love with boys
(*She reflects.*)
I say LOVE
(*CLAUDIUS enters.*)
Forget her son forget her yes it can be done forgetting
impossible you say and then someone it could be years it
could be straightaway

(*CLAUDIUS goes to ISOLA and placing his hands round her neck throttles her. ISOLA sinks to the floor. CLAUDIUS lifts his hands free of her. GERTRUDE enters in the wedding gown, glove-tight on her.*)

CLAUDIUS: The lies

The ludicrous lies

I cannot hear another lie however lovingly intended you and I we never lied cruel it is the place of never-lying look at us however were two ever better made to thrive in such a landscape me wire you stone I cannot look at you such polished stone you are and the thin stuff drawn over you your arse of stone your breasts of stone and the thin stuff clinging

(*He fights collapse.*)

She would have

She

Ha

I PUT HER OUT HER MISERY ANOTHER CHARITABLE ACT

To die at my hands

I don't see how she could object to that far better surely than to see me

DIE AT YOURS

Incomprehensible to her

She would have

She

Ha

(*He shakes his head. GERTRUDE walks out.*)

COME BACK

(*Something is flung in, and slides over the floor. CLAUDIUS is still, sensing it, not seeing it. Pause.*)

CASCAN

He's dead

CASCAN

Silly

Silly

CASCAN

DEAD OR NOT YOU LOOK

(*Pause and silence.*)

I'll be Cascan

HIS BORROWED TONGUE

(*He mimics the manner of the servant.*)

How well I understand from my somewhat remote perspective

How often I observe the paradoxical

Characteristically the stratagems of those who

(*He crawls over the floor towards the flung bundle.*)

And these manoeuvres whilst

(*He lifts a corner of the wrapping. He recognizes the contents. He lets fall the wrapping. He turns, still on his knees, hands at his sides, motionless.*)

Ostensibly

(*Pause.*)

Antithesis

(*Pause.*)

Implicit

(*Pause.*)

Abstract

(*RAGUSA walks in and instantly wails, covering her face with her hands.*)

Contradictory

(*Pause.*)

Delusion

(*Pause.*)

Implicated

(*Pause. She howls on.*)

Marginal

(*His list competes with RAGUSA's despair.*)

Dislocate

(*They compete.*)

TRANSITIONAL

(*CLAUDIUS covers his ears.*)

TRANSITIONAL

ALL RIGHT

ALL RIGHT

(*She controls her wailing. Pause.*)

Ragusa

RAGUSA: I have so
>   Oh
>   So envied you your
>   YOU MAY NOT LIVE OUTSIDE AS YOU TWO DO
>   YOU MAY NOT
>   (*CLAUDIUS is quite still.*)
>   I held her under water
>   Easy
>   I HELD HER UNDER WATER NOT ALL OF HER THE HEAD
>   Funny
>   When I came here I said
>   Funny
>   THE SHEER SAYING OF THESE PEOPLE
>   THE SHEER DOING OF THEM
>   (*She half-laughs.*)
>   Admit it
>   I lie between you now
>   I divide your bed
>   (*CLAUDIUS does not move. RAGUSA runs to him. She slaps him. She kisses him. She slaps him. She runs from the room. CLAUDIUS hangs his head.*)

CLAUDIUS: Oh their poor crimes
>   (*He shakes his head. He retrieves the body of the child.*)
>   The little mischiefs which they heap at the feet of God
>   (*He kisses her. He places her tenderly in the arms of ISOLA.*)
>   No wonder He smiles
>   (*The cathedral bells announce the wedding of GERTRUDE and ALBERT.*)
>   Have you seen the smile of God
>   IT DRIPS COMPLACENCY AS A DOG'S JAW STREAMS SALIVA
>   ON THE RUMOUR OF ITS FOOD
>   Gertrude
>   Gertrude
>   (*GERTRUDE walks in, hatted, suited, gloved for her honeymoon. She sits. At last the bells cease.*)

GERTRUDE: Two weeks in a warm climate
>   Two weeks in a warm climate more is not possible the business of the government demands his swift return

Two weeks of too-red flowers
Two weeks of too-blue seas
And the villa secluded all nourishment brought to the
room
How else should a woman learn her husband's ways
Which side of the bed he claims and if he lays an arm
possessively across me shudders or is still
The scents at dusk
The casement creaking in warm airs
I'll sleep I'll sleep I'll sleep as simply as a child
And with his child inside me he declares we cannot leave
without an heir he sinks his mouth into my hair and
breathes me did you breathe me there the odours of me
I don't compare men men compare already your acts are
fainter than rinsed drawings
WASH ME MY YOUNG HUSBAND WASH ME SOAP THE DEAD
MAN OFF MY SKIN
(*Pause. She recovers.*)
And life with him
The making of a garden grey this garden everything
I plant grey we are northern are we not great is the grey
stone and the moss grey grey waves and me grey naked I'll
stoop even in frost boots on my feet grey socks
(*She seems to laugh.*)
And he shaving in a so-high window will glance from the
mirror to my arse
Grey garden
Grey garden
Ashes scattered on it
Scattered ashes of burned men
HE'LL RUSH TO FUCK
HE'LL RUSH TO FUCK
AND OUR SLIDING HEELS WILL TREAD YOU IN
(*Pause. She looks at the still form of CLAUDIUS, kneeling.*)
Why don't you
Why don't you
(*GERTRUDE slips off the chair and goes to him, to take his head
in her hands. As she does so, her great cry comes, not from herself,*

*but from the land. She is seized by it. CLAUDIUS is dead and*
*she struggles with the weight of his body. As she supports it against*
*her hips, ALBERT enters, in a travelling coat, and observes the*
*spectacle…)*

ALBERT: Come now

*(GERTRUDE emits a sob, a shudder. CLAUDIUS slips to her*
*feet.)*

Come now

*(GERTRUDE, sensing her condition, reaches into her pocket for*
*a small bag and removes a lipstick and powder from it, and holds*
*up a mirror.)*

Stay like that

GERTRUDE: But I'm

ALBERT: Like that

*(She turns a ruined face to him.)*

Adored like that

*(She concedes. She walks smartly to the door. He follows. He turns*
*to call an order.)*

BURN THESE

BURN AND SCATTER THESE

*(They go.)*

•

ANIMALS IN PARADISE

# Characters

NORRIS, a Danish Widow

TENNA, a Danish Woman

MACHINIST, a Danish Philosopher

FOURTEEN, his Student

TAXIS, a Swedish Prince

DARLING, a torturer

PRACTICE, Servant to his Mother

WENSDY, a Swedish Courtier

SATDY, a Swedish Courtier

FIRST LABOURER, Swedish

SECOND LABOURER, Swedish

JULY, a Swedish Soldier

CALLTOLD, King of the Danes

OBSTETRICIAN, Swedish

CHILD, of Taxis and Tenna

FIRST STUDENT, a Dane

SECOND STUDENT, a Dane

THIRD STUDENT, a Dane

Cyclists

Dying Soldiers

Students

# PART ONE: A TOWER

## 1: THE BEAUTY OF A BRUISE

*A woman digs a grave. Another watches.*

NORRIS: (*Digging.*) Have a baby
    (*Pause.*)
    Have one
    (*Pause.*)
    Have one you cow have a baby you whore have a baby
    (*Pause.*)
    Oh my tits she says
    Oh my belly
    Spoil my body having a baby?
    (*She throws down the spade.*)
    Have one you cow have a baby you whore have a baby
    (*She picks a bundle off the ground.*)
    Goodbye darling goodbye oh goodbye my darling
    (*She places the bundle in the grave.*)
TENNA: When it suits me I'll have a baby
    (*She picks up the spade.*)
    After the war a beautiful baby by a prince or a singer
    (*She flings earth in the grave.*)
    I've slept with princes
    I've slept with singers
    And if I'm a whore you're an idiot five you have buried
    five babies for what who's the cow who's the whore look at
    my body compare it with yours five babies buried and four
    boys killed in the war ha
    DON'T HIT ME
    (*The women glare at one another.*)
NORRIS: My ugly belly is the room of our race
    My leaking tits give solders their drink
    My big and bruised hands fix men by their hips
    Let them squirm
    Let them struggle

They don't quit until they have spilled until they have filled
me
ALL RIGHT GLASS TITS?
ALL RIGHT RAZOR ARSE?
(*Pause. NORRIS takes the spade from TENNA.*)
I don't hate you
No
I don't hate
You're dry and brittle everything jagged everything sharp
when they come off you they're slashed men tell me fuck
Tenna they say I'd rather fuck glass
I don't hate you
Thank you for filling my little grave razor arse
(*The women stare at one another.*)

# 2: A STONE EVENING

*A dying queen.*

TAXIS: Shh
    (*He tiptoes.*)
    Shh
    (*He advances warily.*)
    Always she liked the dark
    Her eyes
    Her eyes preferred it
    Shh
    And quiet
    Her legendary love of silence oh
    Dark
    And
    Silent
    Monarchy
    Shh
    Mother
    Mother dear
    I quit the battle half-way through the soldiers frowned
    to see me marching backwards we've won I said I knew
    we'd won five horses later I stand here still shaking and

the blood of redheads smothers me I grabbed a single
sandwich but forgot to eat it look it's here I will if you don't
mind
(*He bites the sandwich.*)
Eat it
(*He bites again.*)
I love you
(*And another.*)
So
(*He wipes his hands on his clothes.*)
Always this silence always this dark I said to my lieutenant
don't assume from so much darkness that the queen has
died always she kept the shutters closed always the blinds
were down as for the sentries read nothing from the colour
of their clothes they wear black for weddings they wear
black on holiday are you dying however are you dying I
love you so
(*The pale hand of the old queen lifts from the bed and falls.*)
Yes?
No?
ANOTHER SANDWICH
I wish I had a brother
Someone braver
Someone stronger
Someone altogether more accomplished and more versatile
than me an engine of masculinity my loneliness can you
imagine it the harsh and barren place that was my infancy
SANDWICH I SAID
Or a sister
Someone to kiss when rain fell in my heart I don't know
why I say this now is not the time to reproach you now of
all times when you are dying are you dying I love you so
(*The pale hand rises and falls.*)
Yes?
No?
(*A solitary figure appears out of the darkness carrying a plate. He
stands beside TAXIS. TAXIS takes the sandwich. He chews. The
servant remains attentive.*)
She lifts a hand the same hand each time and

(*TAXIS swallows. He puts the crust on the plate.*)
it seems to me this tells a story I feel sure she desires
(*He wipes his mouth.*)
with her last breath to communicate some urgent thing to
me
Unless I am mistaken she
PRACTICE: Yes
(*Pause.*)
TAXIS: She does?
She does wish to communicate some
PRACTICE: Yes
(*Pause.*)
TAXIS: You would know
You the loyal and possibly most intimate of all her retinue
you possess the knowledge to interpret the flutter of her
fingers oh I pray for such a servant whose very habits
represent my own a mirror even a parody of the royal
demeanour what what then she there it goes again see see
(*The queen's hand rises and falls.*)
PRACTICE: Kill
(*Pause.*)
Kill the fingers say
(*Pause. TAXIS is puzzled.*)
TAXIS: Kill? Who? I do kill killing I do every day I have the
killed's blood on me she hardly needs to say
(*The hand rises.*)
Look
Read
Translate
Surely you have mistaken what my mother
(*The hand falls.*)
PRACTICE: Kill again
TAXIS: (*Wildly.*) I DO I DO KILL
(*The servant turns to leave.*)
Don't go
(*The servant stops.*)
Don't go without permission when I wish you to I'll say
don't dare anticipate my orders
(*The servant bows.*)

Study
Kneel
Put on your spectacles
(*TAXIS thrusts the servant violently to the floor. The plate rolls.*)
My mother would not consume her faltering powers to
issue such unkind commands the dying wish to reconcile
the dying wish to bless they are poised on the threshold of
eternal peace are they not?
READ
READ
AND BE CORRECT
(*The queen's hand rises again. They gaze upon it. It falls. Pause.*)
Well?

PRACTICE: Forgive me
Kill she says
(*TAXIS is still. The servant trembles. A pause. TAXIS walks to
the windows. One by one he releases the blinds. Light floods in the
chamber.*)

## 3: WE ARE WHAT WE ARE

*The incessant ringing of bells. A philosopher is persecuted by cyclists.*

MACHINIST: I don't hear you
No
I hear nothing now
(*The cyclists persecute him.*)
It might be birds
It might be rivers
Or
Yes
The murmuring of an insatiable love
(*They increase the intensity of their bells.*)
Oh
This field of exquisite utterance
(*He mimics the act of listening. He laughs, coarsely.*)
Let me pass
The street is also mine

*(They bar his way. They ring with a rage. MACHINIST sways as if the pain would crush him. At last the cyclists ride away. He is left in silence. One cyclist cruises back again.)*

FOURTEEN: They complement you

MACHINIST: Do they

FOURTEEN: Yes

Their anger is only love

MACHINIST: Is it

FOURTEEN: A terrible and bruised love

MACHINIST: Bruised is it I am bruised also I am nearly deaf

FOURTEEN: Lead them

MACHINIST: I will lead them

I will lead them to the madhouse and slam the door

FOURTEEN: Master

Oh master

MACHINIST: Master yes not slave they will make slaves of every man who disagrees with them

FOURTEEN: They do not care who disagrees with them what drives them to this futile cruelty is that you keep silent your silence is the thing that makes them infantile say you disagree with them argue reason with them they will curse you possibly but

*(Pause. FOURTEEN feels foolish. He shrugs.)*

Oh I am so

*(He shakes his head.)*

I can't help it I am

*(He lifts his hands in a gesture of futility.)*

Simple and

*(He casts his eyes down.)*

I am embarrassed now because you have such contempt for innocence and everything I have said is

*(Pause.)*

Innocent

*(He prepares to cycle away. He pedals a little, stops.)*

It is very simple we are young and none of us wishes to die

*(MACHINIST shrugs.)*

MACHINIST: What have your wishes to do with the world? Possibly the world requires precisely that you should die?

Maybe your death however futile it may seem to you is
an aspect of things greater in their significance than your
ability to comprehend them? Maybe the sacrifice is greater
than the god in whose name the sacrifice is celebrated?
Who knows?

Not me certainly

Go away

Go away now

FOURTEEN: (*Wildly.*) Did you not make yourself a master?
Did you not seek the authority that comes with mastery?
Keep still I am talking to you did you not thrill to know we
drank your every word keep still I said keep still

(*MACHINIST ignores FOURTEEN and walks off.*)

Oh keep still

(*He sobs, now alone in the street. NORRIS enters, pushing infants
in a pram.*)

NORRIS: Stop snivelling find a woman tip her on her back

FOURTEEN: What for?

NORRIS: WHAT FOR

WHAT FOR

(*She snorts with contempt.*)

Babies

Babies

That's what for

WHAT FOR HE SAYS

Oh

THERE IS A WAR ON BABIES DIE GET BABIES THEREFORE

(*She goes off. FOURTEEN ponders. Then with a decision he
leaps on his cycle and pedals after NORRIS.*)

FOURTEEN: That's not logical…!

## 4: THE CLOUDS AND THEIR OPINIONS

*A fierce wind. A clifftop.*

TAXIS: How they hated her

The redheads

How they begged God to smother her to choke her with an
uncooked dinner to pox or plague her fifty priests prayed
day and night for their deliverance and she lived to ninety

Oh

I

Can

Hear

Their

Bells

(*Distantly the church bells of another country.*)

MOTHER YOUR BONES RING LOUDER

(*TAXIS shrieks with laughter as a coffin is borne on by six men. As they stop, cables descend from the sky and swing in the wind.*)

The storm will end the clouds will clear and from their spires and the attics of their universities they will see high in the air

HER

HER

UNBURIED HER

To stalk their sleep

To spoil their days

The infants at the kindergartens will say what's that dark tower on their cliff it fills us with horror

THE BLACK QUEEN SPOILS OUR LESSONS EVEN DEAD

They'll have to raise the walls and drape the coast in curtains

RAISE HER

RAISE MY MOTHER TO THE SKIES

(*Men hurry in and fix the cables to the coffin. It is winched high into the air and swings. TAXIS watches it enthralled. The wind drops. A crowd of courtiers enters. He looks at them at last.*)

Of course it isn't cheap

(*Pause.*)

I see you calculate

I see arithmetic swimming your eyes

This tower you are thinking will cause children in obscure villages to die

Yes

Oh yes

And men who might have been kind fathers so spoiled by labour they will blind their wives

I cost it at a million

(*He dares them with his gaze.*)
I'm no economist but I daresay it represents
(*He shrugs his shoulders.*)
Three hours extra labour from every man and they are
tired already they are undernourished from the war it is not
any tower it is staggeringly high and do we have the stone I
hear you say we have the quarries but the quarrymen were
conscripted for the navy how can we bring them home the
seas will be undefended and if not stone then brick but we
have no brick not even to repair bombed hospitals you see
I know I do know all the arguments nevertheless
(*He calls.*)
SPADE
The tower will rise at my feet and lift my mother to the
clouds at night she'll be illuminated how proud even the
poor will be how satisfied the dead
SPADE I SAID
(*A LABOURER hurries in. TAXIS takes a spade from him and
lifting it high, plunges it into the ground. He leaves it upright.
Reluctantly, the courtiers applaud. As the applause subsides, one
steps forward.*)
WENSDY: Some feel
Some wish
(*He struggles.*)
Some write
(*He rashly continues.*)
The war could stop now
(*TAXIS fixes him with a stare.*)
The war could die with your mother
(*Pause.*)
TAXIS: Name them
(*Pause.*)
Who feel
Who wish
Who write
(*WENSDY is trapped. He looks desperately to the other courtiers.
The LABOURER, who has watched this, goes to the spade and
jerks it out the ground. He looks at TAXIS, who regards him*)

*impassively. A dog barks distantly. The LABOURER turns on
WENSDY and kills him. No one moves.*)
Of course this tower could be wood
Wood we are not short of but possibly it is too high for
wood wood burns wood is not safe in gales on the other
hand wood is our wealth with wood we have conquered
the world I don't know I am in two minds or three
someone study someone put the case for wood and bring it
to me quickly
(*The courtiers bow and hurry away. The LABOURER remains.*)
I do not reward loyalty
(*The LABOURER bows.*)
If loyalty were rewarded who could trust the loyal? All
they did subsequently would be priced but thank you some
wished to see my brains on the grass not his
(*The LABOURER spits.*)
FIRST LABOURER: Peace
What would they do with it?
(*TAXIS shrugs. The LABOURER walks off.*)

## 5: A NIGHT WITHOUT TRAINS

*TENNA, naked and asleep over a table.*

MACHINIST: (*Entering.*) No trains
I'm late I'm late and you're asleep
No trains
I walked between the tracks no I didn't walk I ran I ran
between the tracks I was so afraid of disappointing you but
I have obviously I have disappointed you and to blame
the trains no to blame the war for stopping the trains silly
I'm late and I have disappointed you I apologize I've no
excuse
(*TENNA lifts her head, smiles wearily.*)
Bombs hit the station down came the glass a waterfall
the glass kept falling long after the bombs had ceased a
thousand tons somebody said you had to walk on it and
obviously you slipped you slid a lake in winter it was like a
winter lake but a vile smell
(*Pause.*)

And no trains
(*Pause.*)
Obviously
(*Pause.*)
I'll undress
(*Pause.*)
I'll undress shall I
(*He stops, a hand to his shirt.*)
Why did I tell you about the bombing of the station did I
really wish to tell you or was it because I sense your anger
and this mundane narrative was my way a silly way a futile
way of appeasing you?
(*He shakes his head.*)
Yes

Obviously

And now I'm angry I'm angry with myself I don't wish to
be naked and you don't wish me to be naked either it's all
oh I don't know

TENNA: Shh

MACHINIST: I blame myself

TENNA: Shh

MACHINIST: NAKED FOR WHAT IN ANY CASE

   I

   I

TENNA: Oh shh shh

MACHINIST: I

(*He sits with his head in his hands. Suddenly he jumps up.*)
No

No

I'm here for one reason one reason only do you want to
know the reason I'll tell you I'm here to fill your body with
my own to occupy your spaces to invade you claim your
territories rob you of your treasures devastate you burn
your cities wreck your farms yes all your order disordered
all your clean spoiled lie down stand up
(*He pulls TENNA violently.*)
turn over quick
(*She cries out sharply.*)
Yes

All this bombs and stations
TURN I SAID
(*TENNA protests but he is stronger.*)
Trains etcetera no
KEEP STILL OR I WILL STRANGLE YOU
(*TENNA is still.*)
Strangle you
(*Pause. The cyclists pass over the stage, ringing their bells.
MACHINIST seems drained. He picks up his chair and walks
with it. He places it far from TENNA, sits and stares into the
night.*)

TENNA: Strangle me
(*Pause.*)
Machinist
(*Pause.*)
Strangle me
(*He ignores her.*)

MACHINIST: They talk of peace but how terrified they
are for one thing what excuses would we have when
paradise failed to appear we could no longer ascribe our
wretchedness to the enemy we could not say we were
corrupted by the war peace would be painful the suicides
oh the suicides would soar
(*He laughs a small laugh.*)
I will strangle you
My darling one
We know I will tomorrow if not today…

## 6: THE THEORY OF TEMPERS

*A seashore. TENNA naked.*

NORRIS: (*Bearing a spade and a bundle.*) You look at the sea
too much
(*She drops the bundle and digs.*)
I knew a woman who looked at the sea
(*And digs.*)
She was thin
She had no tits

She had a razor for an arse
(*And digs.*)
I said all this gazing at the sea what are you a poet?
(*She lifts the bundle.*)
Get a baby I said
Babies cure poetry
(*She fills the grave. She pats the sand with the flat of the spade.*)
So she got a baby
She did
She listened to me
A darling it was
Great big arms
A full head of hair
A proper little warrior you could see
She drowned it
She drowned it and brought it to me
(*TENNA is still.*)
And the stars
That's as bad I knew a woman looked at the stars
TENNA: What are they like?
(*Pause.*)
NORRIS: Stars?
TENNA: Not stars
The ones over there
Over the sea
The ones we call the enemy
(*She walks to the edge of the sea.*)
NORRIS: They don't use knives and forks
(*TENNA looks at NORRIS.*)
That's the first thing
So what
Would you murder a stranger because he ate with a spoon?
(*Pause.*)
I might
I might kill a stranger for using a spoon
(*TENNA is puzzled. The women read one another's thoughts.*)
Oh
You
Silly

Bitch

You're crossing over

THEY WON'T WELCOME YOU

THEY EAT REDHEADS YOU RAZOR ARSE

(*NORRIS hurries down to the water's edge to seize TENNA in her arms. The women struggle. The cyclists go by, ignoring them. One circles, returns, throws down his cycle and hurries down the beach to intervene.*)

FOURTEEN: Stop

Stop

(*He waves his arms.*)

Stop

Please

Please stop it's so ugly

(*He is frustrated. The women fight on.*)

Isn't the world a sad enough place without you

It's

(*They twist and turn.*)

Whatever you are quarrelling about can almost certainly be reduced to a pair of propositions which

(*He covers his ears.*)

With the arbitration of an umpire

(*They fall in a heap.*)

Could be evaluated and

STOP

STOP

(*FOURTEEN begins to kick the bodies indiscriminately.*)

I'LL

NO WONDER WE HAVE WARS

NO WON – DER

(*He lands a heavy kick on NORRIS's arse. She falls flat. In the resulting silence, FOURTEEN chews his hand, horrified.*)

Sorry

Sorry I

(*TENNA climbs to her feet. FOURTEEN looks at her.*)

How beautiful you are white and smooth and hard as a shell you shine like the moon you

(*He gasps at TENNA's beauty. She slaps him. He is shocked. His shock amuses her. She kisses him. She turns and walks into the sea. He watches, amazed.*)

We

(*She keeps walking.*)

We could have a child

(*He is horrified.*)

WHY DON'T WE

(*She ignores him. FOURTEEN rushes to the edge of the water.*)

I've been conscripted into the army but I'm not going

(*He runs up and down the edge.*)

I refuse to go

COME BACK YOU ARE THE MOTHER OF MY CHILD

(*The sea rises. Waves crash. TENNA disappears.*)

HOW DARE YOU

HOW DARE YOU WHEN YOU ARE THE MOTHER OF MY CHILD

(*NORRIS sits up.*)

I CAN'T SWIM

I CAN'T SWIM

(*FOURTEEN wails. NORRIS pulls him onto the sand.*)

# 7: IT HELPS

*A whispering hall of beds and injured men.*

TAXIS: The smell

(*He walks with deliberate steps.*)

The smell of death the smell of maiming every monarch must become accustomed to it should hang about him thick like lilies it should cling not only to his clothes but to his skin

I BREATHE YOUR WOUNDS

(*He inhales. He struggles with the odour.*)

I think you must admire me I think you must find some space in your pain for me to enter in

MY MOTHER LOCKED HERSELF IN A ROOM

YES

WITH A MAP AND SCISSORS

The consequences of her actions did not permeate the
curtains
LET ALONE THE STENCH
The scissors she employed to cut out territory
Yes
(*He laughs.*)
And posted the bits to the army
CONQUER THIS
(*He laughs again.*)
YOU DID
OH YOU SO OFTEN DID
And nightmares too you brought back of killed things
Of me it will not be said
Taxis hung curtains between himself and death
WHO HAS THE WORST WOUND
WHO HAS THE MOST FOUL FLESH I'LL DRINK FROM IT
(*He walks between the beds.*)
You?
That's ugly
That even to look at makes me sick
Oh
(*He shuts his eyes.*)
Oh
You're worse
You
Are
A
Delirium
Of
Damage
I'll drink you
(*With a tremendous effort of will TAXIS laps the wound of the
soldier.*)
Oh
Oh
(*He gasps. PRACTICE is discovered walking down the aisle with
a tray and bottle of wine. TAXIS staggers to his feet and grabs the
glass, pours it down his throat, and fills it again. The wounded
praise their king in staccato sentences.*)

No more battle for you
No
Flowers now
Flowers cottages and lakes brimming with fish
(*They weakly cheer. TAXIS goes to leave. Something stops him.*)
I lied
I lie so easily but having lied the lie lodges in me a pebble
in my ribs can't breathe for pebbles
(*He returns a few steps.*)
The fish I cannot promise you because
And you know this
The war has spoiled the lakes with chemicals I think you
know this I can only say I WISH the lakes were heaving yes
I WISH they were
(*Some hands rise from the beds and fall.*)
Thank you therefore for applauding my untruth
WHAT GREATER COMPLIMENT CAN MEN PAY THEIR
MASTER?
My love to those who die
And long life to those who live
(*He is about to walk out when a box is delivered onto the stage.
It runs on castors. It stops. Protruding from the top of the box,
the redhead TENNA. Walking behind it, a woman. She bows
succinctly.*)

DARLING: This swam ashore
Naked
And
A
Terrorist
(*Pause. TAXIS goes to the box, leans on it, and examines
TENNA's face.*)
TAXIS: Blind terrorist
DARLING: She has eyes
They're narrow
TAXIS: Narrow?
DARLING: More like slits than eyes
TAXIS: Slits?
DARLING: Narrow slits and blue
TAXIS: (*Peering intently.*) Can't see for bruises

DARLING: I smacked her face

TAXIS: (*Triumphantly.*) I see the blue…!

(*He laughs.*)

Such a thin blue as if a frail monk dipped a pen in turquoise and drew

DARLING: I smacked her

TAXIS: A dithering line on parchment

DARLING: Kiss me

(*TAXIS kisses DARLING. He leaps away and addresses the injured.*)

TAXIS: A redhead

Gentlemen

Her brothers maimed you probably her father bombed your cows

And if she were to have children imagine how they will hurt ours

Oh

Intolerable

Prospect

Someone who has hands snap off her head

(*A silence. The injured stare into space.*)

As if a cork were levered from the neck of some rare champagne

(*He walks between the beds.*)

Pop

Froth

(*None of the soldiers speaks or meets the eyes of TAXIS.*)

You

(*TAXIS stops.*)

Your hands lie folded on the blanket white and strong

(*The soldier shakes his head. TAXIS moves along the lines.*)

Stumps

Pity

(*He perambulates.*)

Blind

(*He passes, turns back.*)

But that need not disqualify you

(*The blind soldier shakes his head. TAXIS moves on.*)

The very man
(*A soldier shakes his head vehemently.*)
Yes
Yes
The more you shrink the more certain I am
The privilege belongs to you
HAVE YOU NO ANGER YOU ARE LEGLESS AND A SCREAM TO
CONTEMPLATE ONE EYE AND MOUTH ALL
(*He turns to DARLING.*)
Bring the object of our hate
Wheel her
Wheel
(*In the silence, the wheeled box creaks along the floor and is parked by the bed. A pause.*)
Red
Head
(*Pause. The soldier trembles.*)
JULY: I hate redheads
TAXIS: Of course you do
JULY: Their
　　　Smell
　　　Their
　　　Accent
TAXIS: Yes
　　　And look at you
　　　The mirror will shriek
JULY: I've heard it
TAXIS: They have feelings too
　　　Pity the mirrors that must reflect your shattered gob
JULY: I WON'T DO IT
　　　(*Pause.*)
TAXIS: You won't
　　　(*Pause.*)
　　　You won't serve me
　　　(*Pause. The man bites his lip, shakes his head.*)
　　　And worse
　　　Worse even than refusing me
　　　YOU WILL NOT SERVE YOURSELF

REVENGE IS IT NOT A RIVER OF THE SOUL
COOL
YOUR SOUL
(*The soldier suffers. Again he shakes his head.*)
And you hate her
(*The soldier lifts his shoulders helplessly.*)
Yes
I know you do
(*Pause. TAXIS leans to the soldier and kisses his head. JULY
weeps.*)
I can't punish you
You're punished already
(*He walks away from the bed, stops.*)
Instead
I'll wash the enemy and feed her fruits from my own table
Dress her lavishly
And if her body's to my liking
Spread it over the royal bed
(*DARLING laughs.*)
Things you've not glimpsed in all your life of poverty
I'll bestow on her
She'll lie by pools indulgently this slit-eyed enemy while
you tramp roads and beg
(*He casts a glance at all the injured and walks out.*)

## 8: THE PHILOSOPHER'S PAVEMENT

*A noose and a chair. FOURTEEN sits in the chair.*

FOURTEEN: In my letter I say eight o'clock
Obviously he could not have come at seven this would
have created the erroneous impression that he a celebrated
philosopher was made frantic by mischievous threats from
hysterical and manipulative students
(*Pause.*)
On the other hand to wait until the clock struck eight
would reveal him to be a man of calculated vanity more
anxious to demonstrate his own magisterial superiority
than to save his student's life no
(*Pause.*)

He will neither ignore my letter nor will he hasten to my
rescue it will be a calculation of infinite subtlety befitting
such a mind as his a mind I think I can say I am through
years of study quite familiar with I say quite I don't
exaggerate quite quite familiar with
(*Pause.*)
Three minutes to the hour he'll appear
(*Pause.*)
Not a second before
(*Pause. He looks at his watch.*)
One minute to go
IS THAT THE DOOR
(*He rises half-out the chair.*)
You can't be sure no that's the blind woman taking her dog
out or
(*He rises again.*)
NO NEED TO SLAM IT
He doesn't slam he wouldn't slam not unless a draught
caught it and tugged it out his fingers the whore slams
is she a whore I've no idea I call her whore without the
slightest evidence so what I haven't any evidence the
whore slams doors
WHAT'S THAT
I do detest these mundane comings and goings so many
people on the stairs if I were not
(*Pause.*)
A suicide
(*Pause.*)
I'd move I'd find a silent place wet dark and surrounded
by a forest no one would ever come there he's late he's
been obstructed possibly an air raid someone suffered a
heart attack in front of him no that wouldn't delay him
not a minute he'd step over the twitching body I am his
favourite student am I not?
(*His shoulders slump with despair.*)
He's late
He's late it's
(*A clock chimes.*)

NOW THAT'S

(*He shakes his head violently.*)

THAT'S NOT ACCURATE

(*He stares at his own watch as the chimes tell the number eight. Pause.*)

It is accurate

(*Slowly FOURTEEN rises to his feet. He takes the noose and pulls it gently to test its strength. He prepares himself. He climbs onto the chair. He stands quite still. He is about to fling himself off the chair when MACHINIST enters the room, unhurriedly…*)

Three minutes past eight…

(*FOURTEEN is enraged.*)

THREE MINUTES PAST DID YOU WANT ME TO DIE

(*MACHINIST appears uninterested.*)

And now you have the moral advantage over me because it appears I delayed hanging myself in order that you could rescue me it appears my decision to die at eight o'clock was not made in good faith it appears I am a liar and a fraud whereas you as always you unfailingly have selected the very moment to secure the maximum advantage it's horrible it's uncanny I dislike you go away I want to die

(*A door slams.*)

THAT WHORE IRRITATES MY NERVES

(*Pause.*)

She's not a whore I don't know what she is

(*He rips the noose from his neck.*)

How can you die in a place like this it's impossible I'll do it later

(*He jumps off the chair, goes to undo the rope.*)

MACHINIST: Leave the rope

(*Pause.*)

FOURTEEN: Leave it?

MACHINIST: I might need it

(*Pause. A strange smile crosses FOURTEEN's face.*)

FOURTEEN: You?

You need a rope?

MACHINIST: Yes me why not me do you think you are the only one who suffers do you think you are the only one

who ever contemplated his own extinction yes me the
simple answer is so often the best one me yes why not me
let's do it together
(*They stare at one another. At last FOURTEEN smiles.*)
FOURTEEN: This is an exercise
Ha
This is a philosophic exercise and you
(*MACHINIST leaps out of the chair and grabs FOURTEEN by the throat.*)
MACHINIST: Yes
It is
It is an exercise in
(*FOURTEEN chokes.*)
TRIVIALITY
WHAT ELSE IS LIFE BUT
(*FOURTEEN struggles for his life.*)
TRIV – I – ALITY
(*He hurls FOURTEEN to the floor.*)
FOURTEEN: What are – you nearly – are you mad –
YOU NEARLY KILLED ME
(*He sobs. He nurses his throat.*)
MACHINIST: Forgive me I
(*He shakes his head.*)
Forgive me I
(*He sobs also.*)
FOURTEEN: (*Moved by MACHINIST's tears.*) No no
Shh
If anyone should ask forgiveness it must be me I
(*He laughs.*)
I asked to die didn't I? I asked and you
Ha
You obliged me
MACHINIST: Everyone I love I want to strangle
(*Pause. FOURTEEN looks at MACHINIST.*)
Explain that can you
(*Pause. FOURTEEN shrugs.*)
I want to have them lifeless in my arms
EXPLAIN THAT IF YOU CAN
(*He stares.*)

And stranger still
Oh this is strange
THEY WISH TO DIE
(*MACHINIST prepares to go.*)
I was late because I had walked to the house of my mistress
there were no trains again today and you know how I hate
bicycles I walked I had no appointment the door was open
she was not there for several days this door had been wide
open perhaps since my last visit leaves and litter had blown
in the door I immediately assumed that she was dead she
walked into the sea apparently she had mentioned this
before but whether it was suicide or whether she was under
the illusion she could swim to the other side I can't tell
nobody can a woman had witnessed it this woman had
failed to dissuade her I was paralysed for some minutes I
had your letter obviously I fully intended to be here before
the clock struck eight I chose the time most carefully three
minutes to the hour I know how scrupulous you are and
how you would not act prematurely but my calculation
was rendered futile by the shock of this woman's absence
I crawled over the floor I found one of her hairs only then
could I discover the resources to run here I ran I so rarely
run have you ever seen me run

FOURTEEN: Never

MACHINIST: I never do and to my horror I heard the clock
    chime as I staggered up your stairs
    (*He laughs, he shakes his head.*)
    This woman and I
    We had nothing in common
    Look
    Still between my fingers
    Her red hair
    (*He displays a single strand of hair. He walks slowly out.*)

# 9: A PAIR OF GLOVES

*A park. PRACTICE marches with a tray the length of a grove.*

PRACTICE: She asked for nothing
    The Old Queen

Nothing or a dish of onions

But you will starve I used to say a body can't subsist on
hate

HA HA HA HA

She laughed like that a strange laugh

HA HA HA HA

I took that to mean she found all the nourishment she
wanted

HA HA HA HA

In hatred

(*PRACTICE cannot help laughing himself. His laugh fades.*)

My son was killed last year how dare you sit in this park
(*Pause.*)

Not killed they hammered bullets in his eyes how dare you
how dare you
(*Pause.*)

And having tortured him they left his body in a field my
little boy my little little boy GET UP GET UP YOU THING OF
FILTH

(*TENNA, in dark glasses, stands, folds down her skirt.*
*PRACTICE is aware that TAXIS is nearby. He is at once*
*formal.*)

This is a dry white wine selected for its almond flavours
generous but also faintly cruel as if a goddess had plunged
a ring of platinum into the cask

(*He pours.*)

On leaving the cellar it was if anything too cool but
walking here has raised the temperature by one or two
degrees I walked under the trees I avoided sunlight

(*TAXIS takes the glass. He sips. He looks into the servant's eyes.*)

TAXIS: I don't like her either she has no hips

(*The servant is stiff with anxiety.*)

And where her eyes should be

Look

(*He removes the dark glasses from TENNA's face.*)

Slits

(*The servant looks from one to the other.*)

Her whole appearance confirms my feeling that all
redheads are degenerate what's more she's sterile many

men have slept with her but to no effect unfortunately I
love her
(*PRACTICE sways.*)
IS IT UNFORTUNATE
(*PRACTICE is agonized. He shrugs. He closes his eyes.*)
You say
(*PRACTICE is reluctant.*)
If it is unfortunate or not
(*A pause.*)

PRACTICE: Perhaps whilst making love to her
Desperate as these acts can be
And in this instance more desperate than usual given the
absence of a common language in which to communicate
your needs
A tragic accident might easily occur
She might
Like some kitten suffocated by an adoring child
Be discovered limp and lifeless in your arms
(*He looks at TAXIS.*)
A terrible grief
Your howling oh a legend in these parts I think we can
assume
Inconsolable for weeks
And her tomb
I can see it now
A pyramid beneath these trees where you might be
discovered in those brief interludes from the exacting
business of the state pale and statue-still
(*He pours a second glass of wine.*)
Profoundly beautiful a young man's grief I think
(*TAXIS takes the glass. He sips…*)

TAXIS: Tenna
This man thinks I should strangle you
(*TENNA laughs.*)
Yes
Yes
That's what he says
What's funny about it?
(*He looks at PRACTICE.*)

She finds it funny
Perhaps it is
Yes
It is funny
Lie down now I am giving you a baby
Down now
On the grass and naked
(*He thrusts the empty glass back on the tray. He taunts
PRACTICE.*)
Stay if you want to
(*TENNA is hesitant.*)
ON THE GRASS I SAID

PRACTICE: (*As TENNA obeys.*) She is a redhead

TAXIS: Yes and a strange odour clings to her

PRACTICE: A REDHEAD

TAXIS: Something in the diet I've heard they don't eat fish
smell that only potatoes
(*He tosses TENNA's shirt at PRACTICE.*)
Not unpleasant it reminds me of a church
SMELL I SAID
(*PRACTICE has allowed the shirt to drop to the ground.*)

PRACTICE: A PRINCE MUST GOVERN HIMSELF OR HE
CANNOT GOVERN OTHERS

TAXIS: Pick up the woman's shirt and breathe its odour
(*A pause of profound menace. TENNA watches, sitting on the
grass.*)
Breathe I said
(*A pause. PRACTICE shakes his head in defiance.*)

PRACTICE: Never in my life have I refused an order
(*His shoulders heave with despair.*)
But what an order
I WISH I WAS DEAD
You should not ask a
You should not ask
(*TAXIS goes to his servant and placing his hands on his shoulders
gently lowers him to the ground. The old man sits with the tray on
his knees weeping. TAXIS loosens his belt and going to TENNA,
copulates with her.*)

# 10: AN OVERGROWN GARDEN

*A thin king. A naked girl.*

DARLING: I am a gift
    (*Pause.*)
    And it was not easy for him much affection still remains
    between us laughter and memory we were children the old
    queen neglected him in ruined summerhouses we played
    kings and queens on frozen lakes we
    (*She swallows a sob.*)
    So making a gift of me was hard for him correctly he said a
    gift should hurt
    (*Pause.*)
    To give should hurt the giver
    (*Pause.*)
    So he says
    I came in a beautiful gown but someone stripped me of it
    (*Pause.*)
    Then other things occurred
    (*Pause.*)
    So I am a spoiled gift
    (*Pause.*)
    Sorry
CALLTOLD: (*Turning at last.*) The Old Queen I understood
    (*He looks at DARLING, critically.*)
    The only gifts she sent were poisonous
    Tricks
    Murder machines
    Girls who exploded when they were kissed
    I got to like the Old Queen
    Hatred is simple but this fluctuating prince
    (*He scrutinizes her.*)
    The kindness of certain individuals is worse than their
    cruelty and in what way do you constitute a gift a gift must
    please the recipient that is its first criterion surely not that
    it should pain the giver you see we are poles apart even in
    the way we approach the simple act of giving poles apart
    (*Pause.*)

DARLING: I'm sorry I don't please you

CALLTOLD: On the contrary your nakedness irritates my nerves

DARLING: Forgive me but my clothes were stolen

CALLTOLD: So far from placating us this so-called gift only stimulates more anger

DARLING: That was never his intention

CALLTOLD: Perhaps it is precisely his intention my dislike of girls is not a secret yet a girl is what he sends me

DARLING: He hoped however foolishly

CALLTOLD: You see I am angry now

DARLING: It was foolish possibly

CALLTOLD: Very foolish

DARLING: Foolish but he hoped that my appearance naked or in the gown

CALLTOLD: What gown?

DARLING: The gown I came in but which was stolen from me

CALLTOLD: (*Shouting to his staff.*) LOOK FOR A GOWN

DARLING: Would change your character

(*Pause. CALLTOLD smiles thinly.*)

He is

(*She shrugs.*)

Some sweet innocence clings to the prince and he is in love

(*She shrugs again.*)

This love

(*She looks for words.*)

You know how it is with lovers they

Ha

Want all the world to love like them

(*A long pause. CALLTOLD's intense scrutiny discomforts DARLING.*)

Don't hurt me

Don't hurt me I'm only a gift

(*A servant enters with an embroidered gown. CALLTOLD takes it and drapes it over DARLING's shoulders. He stops in mid-movement.*)

CALLTOLD: You see
I am not like other men I am completely indifferent to
your nakedness
DARLING: Yes
CALLTOLD: My flesh is not my master I do not run in the
shafts of instinct like a carriage horse I am not whipped
and bullied by desire I am not the idiot of my sex
DARLING: No
No I see you're not
(*Pause.*)
That is a magnificent achievement in a man who
(*She falters.*)
Surely cannot lack for
(*Pause.*)
Sensuality
(*Pause. CALLTOLD makes a slight gesture to his staff. Two
officers walk over, and take DARLING by the arm and wrist.
They lead her away. As they go NORRIS passes, pushing a double
pram.*)
NORRIS: Ha
(*She points contemptuously at DARLING.*)
CALLTOLD: Yes
NORRIS: Same old tricks
CALLTOLD: Same old tricks yes
NORRIS: God bless your majesty
CALLTOLD: And let Him bless you Mrs Norris
NORRIS: You'd never fall for that
CALLTOLD: Not I
NORRIS: And yet they persist
(*She stops. She points to the pram.*)
Two more for the army
(*She laughs.*)
WE CAN'T BE BEAT
(*She starts off again.*)
CALLTOLD: We can't and yet
(*She stops.*)
It's obvious we can't win
NORRIS: WIN
What's winning

(*She laughs and is about to continue.*)

CALLTOLD: Wait

(*She stops.*)

This war

This war do I take it you don't expect to win?

NORRIS: If it's not treason to say no no I don't no

(*She looks at CALLTOLD boldly. She laughs.*)

It's eighty years old

It's my grandmother the war

(*She laughs, then stops.*)

You talk of winning because you are the king

How could a king not talk of winning I talk only of not

losing for not losing I have given up eleven kids

(*CALLTOLD looks to the ground, humbled.*)

Eleven

Eleven and we have not lost

(*She grins.*)

CALLTOLD: Do you read the poets Mrs Norris?

NORRIS: I don't myself but someone does

(*She sets off. CALLTOLD is apparently alone. The wind blows.
Suddenly two cyclists appear, one of whom throws down his cycle
and attacks the king with a knife. The king overcomes his attacker
and kills him. The second cyclist, having turned, passes at full
speed and pedals back in the direction from which they came.
CALLTOLD lifts his hands. Horrified servants rush up and begin
wiping his hands. Some shots are heard. A violinist enters and
begins to play.*)

## 11: A SURGICAL DILEMMA

*TENNA lying on a bench. A violinist and an OBSTETRICIAN in
attendance.*

TAXIS: My mother oh the ugliness of my mother's soul it
     shrivelled at the sound of birds it stiffened at the music
     of a fountain all the peacocks she had hanged not only
     peacocks little larks and all the basins filled is she perfect
     the child has it her eyes or mine her slits of sky or my grey
     pools of melancholy which?

(*TENNA gasps.*)

DON'T HURT HER WITH YOUR CLUMSINESS

OBSTETRICIAN: I am not clumsy

TAXIS: You are not clumsy? Then why did she gasp?

OBSTETRICIAN: Not clumsy in the least but sometimes in
    pregnancy there is a tenderness which

    (*TENNA gasps.*)

TAXIS: SHE GASPED AGAIN

OBSTETRICIAN: She did but

TAXIS: Possibly you are not familiar with the underneath of
    red-haired women? I asked specifically has this surgeon
    experience of red-haired women yes they said he has
    travelled extensively in his career

    (*Pause.*)

OBSTETRICIAN: There is no discernible difference in
    the anatomical structure of red-haired individuals I can
    confirm from many years of

TAXIS: THEY ARE MORE DELICATE

    (*The violinist plays.*)

    They are more tender and their skins are thinner altogether
    thinner than our own as are the walls of their hearts oh yes
    you need not scowl at me I know I have touched her heart
    as I have touched her womb

    (*Pause.*)

    Continue now bearing this delicacy in mind

    (*With infinite caution the surgeon returns to his examination of
    TENNA.*)

    You are only the first of my child's many enemies

    (*The surgeon stops. Pause.*)

OBSTETRICIAN: Enemy? Me?

TAXIS: Oh yes she will wander all her life through forests of
    hatred if it is a she she will march down avenues of malice
    if it is a she her narrow eyes will search every smile for its
    hypocrisy it must be a she I insist you drag a she out of my
    darling's body God help you if it's a boy

    (*The surgeon is horrified.*)

OBSTETRICIAN: I'll do my best

TAXIS: YOU WILL BUT IS YOUR BEST SUFFICIENT?

    (*TENNA gasps.*)

Oh

My

Razor

Arse

Listen

(*He suffers TENNA's pain. He turns to the violinist.*)

Play

Play

(*The violinist plays.*)

OBSTETRICIAN: I think

(*He examines, his head on one side.*)

I think I can

(*TENNA gasps.*)

Yes

I think I can satisfy you

TAXIS: It's a she?

OBSTETRICIAN: Not a she exactly

(*TAXIS is perplexed.*)

TAXIS: Not exactly?

OBSTETRICIAN: Not a she but could be

TAXIS: (*Knitting his brows.*) COULD BE?

OBSTETRICIAN: Shh

(*TENNA cries out.*)

TAXIS: (*Whispering.*) Could be, how?

(*Pause. The surgeon looks at TAXIS...*)

OBSTETRICIAN: At the moment it is inclined towards the
masculine

(*Pause.*)

But

With some encouragement

(*TAXIS, with an irritated gesture, silences the violinist.*)

We might persuade it to be

(*He examines, his head on TENNA's belly. Suddenly he stands
abruptly.*)

I've done it before

Once only

A lovely girl a blonde blue-eyed skin like a peach small
hands small feet and loving oh

Unfortunately it's costly

(*He trembles.*)

TAXIS: Costly is it?

OBSTETRICIAN: Yes the expertize is so

Nobody else can do it

Only I

Unfortunately only I

Say fifty

TAXIS: Fifty what?

OBSTETRICIAN: Thousand

TAXIS: Fifty thousand what?

OBSTETRICIAN: Crowns

(*The surgeon bites his lip anxiously.*)

TAXIS: That's

(*TENNA gasps.*)

That's an army

OBSTETRICIAN: (*Faking ignorance.*) Is it?

(*TENNA gasps.*)

Maybe it's better than an army

(*He dares look TAXIS in the face.*)

Maybe a slit-eyed girl is

(*Suddenly TAXIS seizes the surgeon and forces him into a terrible headlock. He drags him in a struggling circuit of the bench on which TENNA lies gasping. The surgeon cries out in his despair. The violinist plays desperately...*)

## 12: BRICKS AND THEIR ADVENTURES

*The tower. Distant guns.*

FIRST LABOURER: (*Entering with a barrow of bricks.*) Oh

she's wild

She's so wild

(*He drops the handles.*)

Listen to her

(*He looks up to the sky, hands on hips.*)

Listen to her

(*He shakes his head. A SECOND LABOURER enters with a barrow also of bricks.*)

Bones all rattling

Skull and knuckles hammering the box

(*Both men look up.*)

She's right of course

Any fool can stop a war but can you start it up again?

SECOND LABOURER: Five minutes

FIRST LABOURER: (*Bemused.*) Listen to her

SECOND LABOURER: Five minutes to everlasting peace

(*He extends his wrist, examines his watch.*)

Four now

(*TENNA enters with a pram. Court officials and servants drift in behind. They collect at the cliff edge...they listen.*)

TENNA: Oh it's sad

(*She sobs. She fights her tears.*)

It is I don't know why it's sad

(*The gunfire increases in intensity. She turns to the others.*)

Aren't you sad?

(*Others sob. The sobbing is infectious. Soon the whole group is weeping. TENNA lifts her child from the pram and walks to the cliff edge. The SECOND LABOURER, eyes on his watch, shows three fingers to indicate the remaining minutes of the war. The increasing roar of the guns inhibits speech. With slow steps, TAXIS walks into the scene. The court and the labourers bow to him. He also stares over the sea. The SECOND LABOURER shows two minutes. TAXIS takes the child from TENNA and lifts it high over his head. The final roar of war is deafening. The labourers cover their ears. The SECOND LABOURER indicates one minute. The assembled courtiers reel and clutch one another. The SECOND LABOURER brings down his arm, a decisive gesture. The guns cease. A lurid silence, from which comes the solitary bawling of the child...*)

TAXIS: (*To the workmen.*) Haul down my mother's box

(*The workmen go to the ropes.*)

TENNA: Why is she crying?

THIS CHILD NEVER CRIED BEFORE

(*The court looks uncomfortable...*)

TAXIS: And the tower

The tower also must come down it is a thing of hate

Kiss me

TENNA: (*Hurrying to the child.*) Terrible sound

TAXIS: (*As TENNA removes the child from him.*) Kiss I said

TENNA: (*Ignoring him.*) This crying
STOP HER SOMEBODY
(*She appears helpless with the child, extending it to one person after another. They hesitate. TENNA hurries off…*)
FIRST LABOURER: (*Puzzled.*) Take the tower down?
TAXIS: Raze it, yes
FIRST LABOURER: But we–
(*He points to the wheelbarrows.*) We haven't topped it yet –
TAXIS: Top it then and when it's topped demolish it OH THE FUTILE JOURNEYS OF THE BRICKS they don't complain however why should you?
FIRST LABOURER: We
We
(*He turns to the SECOND LABOURER.*)
We're not complaining but
TAXIS: How swift you were to carry out my orders when the orders were sodden with hate but now when every one of my commands is wrapped in love you hesitate you hang back and scrutinize me from beneath dark eyelids as if I were a mad dog and might bite I do not bite do what I say we are building a bridge of one hundred spans
(*He turns to the court.*)
YES
AND SUCH AN EDIFICE WILL NOT BE CHEAP
(*The court stirs uneasily.*)
The bridge is love and like an imploring hand will cross the water to our neighbours trade and commerce painters poets and
(*He is coy.*)
PASSIONS
(*He smiles.*)
Will travel to and fro
(*He seems to recollect something.*)
I wasn't kissed
(*He puts a finger to his unkissed cheek.*)
Ha
I asked her and
Where is my

(*He looks for TENNA.*)

My darling where is she?

SATDY: (*Stepping forward.*) Some feel

Some wish

TAXIS: Did my darling go?

(*He looks.*)

SATDY: To build a bridge when all is spoiled here from the everlasting war whilst it might satisfy some

(*TAXIS turns to inspect SATDY.*)

sentimental

(*He shrinks under TAXIS' gaze.*)

Or

idealistic

(*He lifts a vague hand. He looks to the court for moral support.*)

COSTS TOO MUCH

(*SATDY hangs his head in desperation. TAXIS looks to the FIRST LABOURER, who this time only shrugs his shoulders and also looks at the ground. This inactivity is noted by TAXIS.*)

TAXIS: The stone

The brick

The timber

Of the warlike tower will provide much of the substance of the bridge

SATDY: Rather little

TAXIS: Rather little you say

SATDY: With respect

TAXIS: And for the rest some further exertion of the people will be required some adjustments to the tax

SATDY: MORE TAX

MORE TAX HE SAYS

(*A tense hiatus. TAXIS looks at SATDY with narrowed eyes. The courtiers shrink with fear.*)

TAXIS: (*With infinite patience.*) More tax but the soldiers and the sailors who even as we speak are marching home will

SATDY: Home yes

Home

Is

Where

They

Are

Marching

To

(*He looks boldly at TAXIS.*)

Burned home

Starving cattle in the woods

Dead wives

And children wild as pigs

The thatch has slipped off every roof

(*Pause.*)

HOME

YES

NOT

THIS

HOWEVER

(*With a swift bow, SATDY returns to the group of courtiers. They watch TAXIS as he absorbs and digests the situation.*)

TAXIS: Good advice

Oh

Good advice

A king is no king if he cannot heed advice let him plant his feet squarely in the racing river of opinion how cold it gets however it chills the bone and when in flood the torrent might sweep him to his death

I don't know

I don't know yet

I ASKED FOR A KISS WHAT HAPPENED TO HER?

(*The courtiers drift away in ones and twos…*)

# PART TWO: A BRIDGE

## 1: THE LOST PAINTINGS OF THE LOUVRE

*A field.*

FOURTEEN: I don't have to die
(*He laughs.*)
I DON'T HAVE TO DIE
(*He hugs himself.*)
Of course it was never certain that I would die it was
possible that no matter what the danger was that I was
exposed to still I should have come through uninjured
possibly without a scratch such things happen in wars
but so rarely as to be a negligible part of any equation no
far more likely I should have been severely injured look
around you look at the cripples hideous and instead of
limbs peculiar machines blind some of them I avert my
gaze the GROTESQUE DETRITUS OF HISTORY what are their
ruined bodies but the obscene testimony to a lie no wonder
they hide no wonder they pull down the blinds
(*He shudders.*)
HOW CLEAN MY LIMBS ARE AND UNSPOILED
(*He stretches his hands to the sun…*)
It's strange that no one loves me
(*He turns his hands.*)
Strange I don't love anybody else
(*He shrugs. He is aware of two slowly moving figures one of whom
weeps uncontrollably. The other, a pace behind, holds a sunshade
for the weeping man, who is CALLTOLD. FOURTEEN stares,
puzzled by the spectacle of this promenade. He recognizes the king
and accosts him.*)
Your Majesty
Thank you for the peace
(*CALLTOLD looks at FOURTEEN through red eyes.*)
Thank you for this undamaged body
(*CALLTOLD erupts in more tears, and continues his way.*)

## 2: THE COMEDY OF MOONLIGHT

*TENNA dining alone. PRACTICE in attendance.*

TENNA: SHH
> (*Pause. PRACTICE goes to the table, fills TENNA's glass, withdraws again.*)
> SHH I SAID
> (*Pause. TENNA giggles.*)
> OH THIS INCESSANT CHATTER
> (*Pause.*)
> Coughing
> Belching
> Farting
> SHH I SAID
> (*She plays with her fingers.*)
> I've nothing on under this dress
> (*Pause.*)
> AS USUAL
> (*She laughs.*)
> And the fabric is transparent clinging so thin it appears my body's wet
> (*Pause. She sips.*)
> It is wet
> (*Pause.*)
> I love you throw me across the table
> (*Pause.*)
> Send the cutlery flying
> Over the flagstones the cascade of knives and forks
> (*Pause.*)
> Broken glasses
> (*Pause.*)
> If you cut yourself so what if I do so what we are in love
> (*Pause.*)
> Blood and love
> (*She sips.*)
> They go together
> SHH
> (*She laughs.*)

I love you and I want you naked
(*PRACTICE sobs.*)
SHH
PRACTICE: Oh my poor master
TENNA: SHH
PRACTICE: I wish I were dead
(*He shakes his head bitterly.*)
TENNA: SHH I SAID
(*PRACTICE seals his lips.*)
You have no desire whatsoever to be dead if you wanted
to be dead you know perfectly well how to achieve it you
give me a baby
(*Pause. PRACTICE serves more wine, withdraws again.*)
The existing one
(*Pause.*)
Is…
(*Pause. She sips.*)
It would be a slow death if he caught us
Castration
Crucifixion
Disembowelling
Stuck on all the fences
Bits of me bits of you
LISTEN TO HER
And that's coming from the West wing
(*The faintest sound of a child's wailing.*)
KISS ME
KISS ME PLEASE
(*Pause. PRACTICE is still.*)
I'll say you kissed me anyway
I'll say you tore my dress
(*She rips the thin dress at the shoulder.*)
THAT WAS YOU
And bruised my shoulder
OW
(*She injures herself.*)
THAT HURT

*(She glares at the old man, who is horrified. TENNA smiles.*
*With a sweep of her hand she sends all the plates and cutlery off*
*the table.)*

MANIAC

*(PRACTICE is a picture of a dilemma. His hands rise and fall.*
*Suddenly TENNA launches herself onto the table and lies in a*
*state of abandon. She cries in a fictional act of love. She kicks off*
*a shoe. It flies over the floor. In the silence, the distant cries of the*
*child. Pause.)*

PRACTICE: This bridge

What a lot of time it takes what a lot of energy it consumes
the master's never here if he's not with the architects he's
poring over drawings with the engineers as for the bankers
they are distinctly uncooperative and the common man he
is oh forgive my scepticism he is not burdened by ideals

*(TENNA writhes in a parody of erotic love.)*

This bridge

What a monument to human vanity what a monument
to human pride and yet the master is relentless in pursuit
of it when did we last see him weeks months is it he's
never here if he's not with the architects he's poring over
drawings with the engineers

*(Pause.)*

This bridge

*(Pause.)*

Every stone brings our two peoples closer I'd better fetch a
broom

*(He does not go. He looks at TENNA.)*

The architects

*(Pause.)*

The engineers

*(Pause.)*

I'm sorry I ripped your dress I was inflamed and you
moved so swiftly I

*(Pause.)*

The architects

*(Pause.)*

The engineers

*(Pause. He bends to pick up the scattered items.)*

Before you came we did not use knives or forks
We were perfectly content with spoons
(*He replaces odd pieces on the table where TENNA squirms.*)
But now
Oh
I find it quite embarrassing to think we ate with spoons
(*He replaces others.*)
And this change in the tools brought changes also to our
diet
Ha
You'd think it would be the other way round
(*He kisses TENNA passionately on the mouth. They embrace.
TENNA sobs.*)

## 3: DUST AND ITS ADMIRERS

*A box of bones.*

THE BONES: We come and go
(*Pause.*)
And when the wind blows
Drift
To settle on the lips of babies
And on window sills
(*Pause.*)
Another snow
(*Pause.*)
Certainly we don't go
(*Pause. TAXIS enters with a hammer. He stands by the box.*)
TAXIS: I gave this a lot of thought
(*Pause.*)
I thought whatever my emotions with regard to you
AND THEY FLUCTUATE THEY DON'T KEEP STILL
However terrible the angers and resentments nothing
could be ended between us until you were decently buried
(*Pause.*)
I thought my mother needs a grave
(*Pause.*)
WAS SHE NOT A GREAT QUEEN?
WAS SHE NOT A LEGEND?

Well
Yes
If cruelty is legend
If violence is great
(*He shrugs.*)
That's opinion
LEAVE THAT TO THE ACADEMICS
(*He flings up the lid of the box.*)
But then I thought
(One thought came after another the way they do)
You
Abolished
Graves
Because of you millions are graveless
Yes
BY WHAT RIGHT COULD YOU BE BURIED HONOURABLY
They stank the dead
The murdered peasants
We threw their bits in swamps
(*He looks into the box. He lifts the hammer. He pulverizes the contents of the box, an orgy of violence. As he smashes, he coughs. Dust rises into the air.*)
VIOLENCE TO THE VIOLENT
AND
ALL
COLD
MOTHERS
LET
THEM
BE
(*He stops, hammer in air.*)
Was she cold?
Not always
No
Not always cold
Perhaps it was me?
I'm cold
Not always but quite frequently I
(*He ponders, fretfully.*)

HER SAVAGERY WAS POSSIBLY THE CONSEQUENCE OF
GIVING BIRTH TO ME
I disappointed her
I did not suck
And this terrible absence of intimacy caused her to be
A MONSTER
(*He is aghast, the hammer still suspended…*)

THE BONES: We come and go

TAXIS: You could not be buried for one very good reason
that your grave even were it situated under a power station
floor still might become a shrine a site of veneration to
those unruly elements who think of war as beautiful who
stir up hatreds and who run with flags and emblems
through our silent streets no it is with profound regret I
(*He smashes again.*)

THE BONES: We come and go

TAXIS: Must

Grind

You

Finer

Than

THE BONES: And when the wind blows

TAXIS: FINER

THAN

(*He stops, thoughtfully.*)

Pollen

My

Mama

(*The dust drifts on the air. TAXIS lets the hammer fall to the
ground. The two workmen are discovered observing him.*)

Chuck this box in some quarry

(*They bow.*)

How severe the discipline of love must be I discover in
certain individuals a peculiar reluctance to love it seems to
me they find hate easier the bridge is not a bridge you see
if only it were a bridge a bridge pure and simple I could
understand their hesitations what's wrong with boats they

say to me have we not always found boats satisfactory I
have to smile I shake my head the bridge is love I say
(*He smiles. The workmen pretend to smile.*)
If the workers run away I will punish them
(*Pause. The workmen look uncomfortable.*)
With death possibly
(*He shrugs.*)
How severe the discipline of love must be
(*He smiles. He goes out. The workmen look at the smashed box of
bones. They regard it with awe. The FIRST LABOURER reaches
out a hand. He delves. He pulls out a bone. The SECOND
LABOURER sifts the dust. The sound of a child crying. They
turn to see TENNA carrying her baby, a nurse pushing a pram
behind. TENNA stops. The workmen bow to TENNA.*)

FIRST LABOURER: She never stops crying

TENNA: She never does and it's a sound you cannot get used
to one of the nursemaids hanged herself and the other
three are deaf we chose them specially you hold her
(*The FIRST LABOURER is embarrassed.*)

FIRST LABOURER: Hold the king's child me?

TENNA: (*Extending the baby.*) You yes
(*The FIRST LABOURER hesitates.*)
Quick or I'll drop her

FIRST LABOURER: My hands are filthy

TENNA: QUICK I SAID
(*TENNA lets the child fall from her arms. The SECOND
LABOURER by a feat of alacrity swoops and catches the
baby before it hits the ground. The nurse, horrified, makes the
characteristic sounds of the deaf, and waves her arms.*)
Shut up
Shut up you
(*The deaf nursemaid controls her anxiety.*)

SECOND LABOURER: Peculiar

FIRST LABOURER: Look

SECOND LABOURER: Peculiar

FIRST LABOURER: (*Amused.*) She's licking you

SECOND LABOURER: She is too

FIRST LABOURER: (*Laughing out loud.*) She's licking him
clean

(*The LABOURERS are delighted.*)
SECOND LABOURER: Tickles
FIRST LABOURER: Funny little tongue
SECOND LABOURER: (*To TENNA, with pride and delight.*)
Tickling me…!

## 4: A DISLOYAL DOG

*A country road.*

MACHINIST: (*With a walking stick.*) Do not follow me
FOURTEEN: (*Running behind.*) I have to because I hate you
MACHINIST: You see how all the charms of peace and civil
reconstruction have no appeal for you go and make a
playground for orphans read to the blind you might even
meet a pretty woman with a similar inclination to lay the
bricks of paradise just leave me alone
FOURTEEN: I will not leave you alone you do not deserve to
be left alone
MACHINIST: I should have let you hang
FOURTEEN: YOU SHOULD HAVE YES AND BECAUSE
YOU DID NOT YOU HAVE A TERRIBLE AND ENDURING
RESPONSIBILITY FOR ME
(*MACHINIST stops.*)
Yes
I was ready to die rather than persevere with this absurd
struggle to make sense of my existence
MACHINIST: You were frightened of the army
FOURTEEN: It was a philosophical gesture
MACHINIST: It was cowardice
The sound of gunfire made you flinch
FOURTEEN: Perhaps it did so what should one like gunfire
should one anticipate with pleasure the disintegration of
one's limbs?
MACHINIST: It's history now your fear it's history now my
own indifference
(*He goes to set off.*)
FOURTEEN: PHILOSOPHY MUST MAKE US LOVE
(*MACHINIST stops.*)

MACHINIST: On the contrary it must make us more
discriminating about where we love if we choose to love at
all
I do not love you
You are the melancholy and undesired outcome of my
method
Nothing more
(*Pause. Tears fill FOURTEEN's eyes.*)
Oh don't cry
Oh
(*He lifts his hands.*)
I am not happy why do you follow me?
(*FOURTEEN shakes his head bitterly.*)
Now you have made me dishonest
I know perfectly well why you follow me I am the only
person who tells a truth your own instincts accord with but
listen
(*He goes back to FOURTEEN.*)
I do not think you possess the necessary
(*FOURTEEN sobs.*)
Yes forgive me the necessary resources for this painful truth
you must marry and live in a clean house yes
(*FOURTEEN wails.*)
Yes with a clean woman
(*FOURTEEN protests.*)
YES
YES
DON'T QUARREL WITH ME
(*FOURTEEN bites his lip.*)
And on long evenings let a little sadness sit on your brows
she'll get accustomed to it
(*MACHINIST shrugs.*)
It's not for everyone this
This
(*Pause.*)
Solitude
(*FOURTEEN recovers…*)
FOURTEEN: Oh

Sometimes when I listen to you I hear not the finest
sentiments of an agonized and searching mind
dropping like dew on a still pond but trombone notes
of a preposterous vanity SOLITUDE HE SAYS WITH THIS
MARTYR'S GAZE do you think you are the only one who's
lonely?
(*Pause.*)

MACHINIST: Let's stop this

FOURTEEN: Stop it yes

MACHINIST: Before it leads to even greater ugliness

FOURTEEN: Yes
    Yes

MACHINIST: You go in one direction

FOURTEEN: Certainly

MACHINIST: And I will take the opposite

FOURTEEN: Yes

MACHINIST: I shan't look back

FOURTEEN: Me neither

MACHINIST: Nor shall I wave

FOURTEEN: When did you ever wave?

MACHINIST: It is the style of parting most befitting a pupil
    and his master

FOURTEEN: Unsentimental and yet beautiful

MACHINIST: You choose

FOURTEEN: No you

MACHINIST: Thank you I will stay on the road I am already
    on

FOURTEEN: Good

MACHINIST: Goodbye

FOURTEEN: Goodbye to you
    (*MACHINIST walks.*)
    WE DIDN'T SHAKE HANDS

MACHINIST: (*Not stopping.*) It's insignificant
    (*MACHINIST walks off. FOURTEEN remains on the spot.
    He makes a move in the opposite direction to the one taken by
    MACHINIST, but is unconvinced by it. He hesitates, his foot in
    the air. He is aware he is being observed. He is uncomfortable.
    He pretends to relax. DARLING enters. She looks at
    FOURTEEN...*)

DARLING: You've separated, then?

    (*FOURTEEN is puzzled.*)

    The genius and you?

    You and the philosopher, it's over?

    DON'T GAWP I SHALL SMACK YOU

FOURTEEN: Yes

    He

    We

    (*He shrugs.*)

    For the time being anyway he

DARLING: Good I'll follow him

FOURTEEN: HE DOESN'T LIKE FOREIGNERS

    (*She stops.*)

    It's complicated for example during the War of Eighty
    Years' Duration he was ambiguous in his views sometimes
    it seemed as if he would oppose the war but he never
    actually

DARLING: I LOVE HIM

    (*FOURTEEN stares at her.*)

FOURTEEN: Love?

DARLING: Yes

    (*Pause.*)

FOURTEEN: Could you say exactly what the word love
    means to you? In our language it has all sorts of tones and
    cadences so many in fact it is better not to use the word at
    all

DARLING: I love him in any language

    (*She goes to leave.*)

FOURTEEN: I AM HIS FAVOURITE PUPIL IF YOU WANT TO
    SPEAK TO HIM YOU MUST ASK ME

    (*DARLING stops.*)

    Who are you anyway?

    (*DARLING looks at FOURTEEN darkly.*)

    You come here

    Everybody comes here

    Swarming over this new bridge as if

    And

    Throwing yourselves at our philosophers

He has to be alone
HE SAYS THE WAR WAS NO WORSE THAN THE PEACE
I don't agree but
(*She is about to go.*)
DO NOT VIOLATE HIS SOLITUDE
(*She stops.*)
We can't help noticing the manners on your side of the
bridge are quite different to our own we would not dream
of simply
(*DARLING slaps FOURTEEN with a sudden impatience. He is
shaken… She looks at him… She runs after MACHINIST.*)
WE WOULD WRITE A LETTER FIRST
(*FOURTEEN rocks to and fro with indecision, then he chases
after her.*)

## 5: THE COMPENSATIONS OF MYOPIA

*A chair. TENNA astride it naked.*

TENNA: BEFORE THE BRIDGE
How often do we say
BEFORE THE BRIDGE
BEFORE THE BRIDGE I WAS THE ONLY REDHEAD
I saw one in the kitchen yesterday
Slut
Slovenly
I had her sent away
Undress now
(*Pause. PRACTICE removes a pair of spectacles from his top
pocket and puts them on.*)
Always you put on your glasses is that because you cannot
see your buttons or to watch me watch your nakedness I
like you to fumble like a child you are nearly blind now
aren't you I am nothing but a smear of red to you don't
hurry never hurry every move is infinitely painful to me I
love you naked you are like a bird that fell out of the sky I
could cry

(*PRACTICE removes his clothing. TENNA is aroused but nearly still. Her mouth moves… At last PRACTICE stands naked before her, an old man but not without strength.*)

How hard that was for you at one time

PRACTICE: Yes

TENNA: You could not bear my scrutiny

PRACTICE: No

To be so desired made me feel ashamed

TENNA: (*Amused.*) Yes and your shame I don't know how the fact you were ashamed made you more desirable than if believing yourself desirable you felt entitled to it

Ha

(*She stares at him, adoringly. She bites her lip as she contemplates him. TAXIS wanders in, he sits, he joins his fingers thoughtfully.*)

TAXIS: Am I not seven times more beautiful than him?

I say seven

Fifty-seven times

The flesh is loose on every rib and on those poor knees it

oh

I CAN'T LOOK

(*Pause.*)

I can look

(*Pause. He looks.*)

If love were effortless we would not value it I said that

of the bridge we must SUFFER THE BRIDGE the bridge is

sacrifice this old man is my bridge and I suffer him

I suffer him as the seabed aches from the weight of the

bridge

HE CLAMPS ON MY JAW

HE CLAMPS ON MY HEAD

And he brought a sandwich to me at my mother's bed

The plate was blue with five red shields on it

Ha

(*He shakes his head.*)

I must

I must

ENDURE THE BRIDGE

Do you love me at all or to put it altogether differently

did you ever love me once you said a man had tried to

strangle you not once but many times and to avoid him
you had swum the sea ditch did you love him perhaps your
swimming was an act of love did you think of him when I
lay inside you
ADD STONES TO MY BRIDGE
(*TENNA does not remove her eyes from PRACTICE.*)
TENNA: Yes
TAXIS: Yes to what?
(*Pause. His fingers stretch, join together again.*)
I GO ON DON'T I?
WHY DO I GO ON?
(*He laughs.*)
Yes you do love me or yes you never did I'm in such a
state I
IT'S GOOD TO SUFFER
OH YES
(*TENNA goes to PRACTICE and folds him in a profound
embrace. PRACTICE himself is still.*)
Surely
It
Is
Good?
(*Pause. He forces himself to observe TENNA's passion. Suddenly
he jumps off the chair.*)
I think what makes this particularly difficult
(*He walks in a circle.*)
AND IT WOULD HAVE BEEN DIFFICULT IN ANY CASE
Let us admit it
Always difficult
What makes it especially punishing to me what causes me
some profound offence is
THIS MAN'S DECREPITUDE
I shudder to look at him why don't you shudder
surely shuddering is what anyone would experience
A TERRIBLE SHUDDERING
I must get on
I must
I must

(*He looks and looks…*)
get on
(*He does not move…*)

# 6: THE OPINION OF THE MEADOW

*A field of dead men. CALLTOLD on a stool weeping. NORRIS digs.*

NORRIS: You can weep too much
(*She plunges in her spade.*)
You can make a habit of it and I don't say you have
No
You're sensitive but all the same
CALLTOLD: I bury them
NORRIS: Yes
Yes
CALLTOLD: With my own hands I bury them
NORRIS: I'm not stopping you it's just that I am vastly better
than you are
CALLTOLD: Yes
NORRIS: At digging holes
CALLTOLD: You are I don't deny it
NORRIS: And I'm pregnant
CALLTOLD: You are remarkable in every way
NORRIS: I don't shirk my responsibilities I don't say sorry
I must lie down
CALLTOLD: I've never seen you lying down
NORRIS: I'll lie down when the dead are buried
(*She stops digging. Youths ride by on cycles, laughing and ringing bells. NORRIS shouts.*)
THIS COULD HAVE BEEN YOU
(*They jeer.*)
YES YOU HAPPY BASTARDS
I shouldn't swear
YOU CUNTS
CALLTOLD: Shh
NORRIS: I shouldn't swear
(*She stands with her hands on her hips.*)
These had bikes once

These had bells
(*She shakes her head.*)
Going to the bridge
Crossing the water to fuck the girls
CALLTOLD: Better surely than
(*He drags a body to the hole.*)
Crossing the water to
(*He cannot shift the body further.*)
Hack off their breasts?
(*NORRIS looks critically at CALLTOLD.*)
I can't move this
(*She declines to assist.*)
This
(*Pause.*)
Would you be so kind as to
NORRIS: They never did
(*Pause. CALLTOLD is uncomfortable.*)
Never did a boy of mine hack off a woman's breasts
(*Pause.*)
CALLTOLD: Not a boy of yours perhaps
NORRIS: No boy I knew of
(*Pause.*)
CALLTOLD: And yet in places far from here we know such
things did happen
In dark forests
In pale fields
I CAN'T MOVE THIS
(*They stare at one another.*)
NORRIS: No boy I said
(*The body held by CALLTOLD suddenly emits a terrible scream.
The dead leap up and applaud as MACHINIST walks in.*)

# 7: THE POETRY OF THE POLICE

*An assembly.*

MACHINIST: (*As the ecstasy recedes.*) Years since I spoke
(*Pause.*)
Years

(*Pause.*)
Years and I don't know how to
(*Pause.*)
It goes like every gift the gift of speech a pity
(*Pause.*)
And I would like to please you after all a philosopher is
no different from a dancer no different from a singer a
magician and I possess the means oh yes I have the tools
just as a plumber locks his spanner to a valve and twisting
it makes water spout so I can yes oh yes I can make you
spout in all the war years I was silent this filled you with a
desire to destroy me some of you set fire to my house
(*Pause.*)
And now you hate the peace
(*Pause.*)
Pity
(*Pause.*)
The end of pain is not the same as pleasure here is a
photograph of my house burning
(*He takes out a small, worn photograph.*)
I took it myself
(*He extends it.*)
Pass it round
(*Some go to take it, reluctantly.*)
Years since I spoke but silence how dangerous that is
(*He laughs. He shakes his head. The snapshot is passed from hand
to hand.*)

FIRST STUDENT: I apologize
I was not one of those who burned your house nevertheless
I hated you and helped create an atmosphere in which the
burning of your house was possible

SECOND STUDENT: I also
I was not one of those who burned your house but I was
gratified when others burned it I laughed I laughed when
pages of your books floated in the air I said what use were
those books anyway if they had not enabled you to speak?

THIRD STUDENT: I would like to apologize something in
me prevents it however

(*She bites her lip anxiously.*)
I did not burn your house but
(*She summons her powers.*)
I AM NOT AGAINST THE BURNING OF HOUSES
(*The audience stirs against her.*)
I'm not
I'm not
SOME HOUSES SHOULD BE BURNED SO SHOULD THEIR
OCCUPANTS
(*The audience is aghast. The STUDENT stares at MACHINIST.*)
It is the condition of a culture
YOU KNOW IT IS
And as our city fell in flames you knew it and that is why
you did not speak
(*She shudders. She covers her head with her hands. She experiences
a fit. She falls. She rolls. Those near her leap aside as her flailing
body travels from side to side. MACHINIST watches with a fixed
expression. Some of the students fetch buckets of water and fling
the contents over the THIRD STUDENT.*)
STUDENTS: House on fire…!

House on fire…!
(*A general laughter erupts…*)

## 8: A STREET PLAN OF TROY

*TENNA running on a wooden bridge. A CHILD follows. They pass
over. TAXIS in pursuit. He stops. He gasps for breath.*

TAXIS: The bridge
(*He inhales deeply.*)
The bridge is also
(*He straightens up.*)
THE FULCRUM OF DESERTION
(*He howls. PRACTICE enters, exhausted. He hangs his head. He
puts out a hand to comfort TAXIS.*)
PRACTICE: She swam one way
(*TAXIS howls.*)
She ran the other
TAXIS: WITH MY CHILD

PRACTICE: With your child yes
*(He recovers.)*
With your child but a king can always have another
whereas I let us admit it never will discover love like hers
again
*(Pause. TAXIS looks at PRACTICE.)*
TAXIS: Never
And rightly since you never were entitled to it
A HUSBAND COULD NOT HAVE GRANTED MORE COULD HE
SHOW ME SUCH A HUSBAND AS I'VE BEEN
PRACTICE: There isn't one
TAXIS: There isn't one and still she
PRACTICE: Still she
TAXIS: Still she yes still still
*(He chews his tongue.)*
The razor-eyed oh I am going to abuse her razor-arsed
DID YOU EVER KNOW WHAT SHE WAS THINKING I NEVER
DID
I looked into her eyes
These blue blue ribbons
WHAT
WENT
ON
IN
THERE?
PRACTICE: One never knew
TAXIS: Never and this concealed her ignorance I often
thought this room is empty and like any empty room when
the blinds are down you can only guess its emptiness she
echoed with absences a drum a tin a bucket rolling in the
wind
I AM GIVING WAY TO HATRED
I MUST NOT
STOP ME
Possibly this bridge should be demolished
Yes
Explosive charges placed beneath the central arch
SPARE SOME POOR LOVER HIS ORDEAL

(*He disciplines his rage.*)

In some battles we were locked like stags and hours went by heels in the mud and heads down whole weathers passed both sides were silent and each man thought I knew he thought how easy it would be to give way now I ache oh how I ache and in ten terrible minutes the world would go dark silent and lusciously dark the night birds crying and the clink of coffee cans so what if I were dead?

(*Pause.*)

It's the same with me and temper I could yield to it oh yes the ecstasy of letting loose my rage and I have this pain in my chest feel it

(*Pause.*)

Feel my pain

(*PRACTICE puts a hand inside TAXIS' open shirt.*)

Feel it?

PRACTICE: Iron

TAXIS: Iron thing yes

PRACTICE: And heavy

TAXIS: Heavy yes no wonder I could not catch my razor arse

(*He laughs. He pulls together his shirt.*)

Get out your map I'm visiting the cities and the farms already probably she regrets her spontaneity and like an angry child sent to her room waits for her father to open his arms

(*He starts to walk.*)

If necessary I'll apologize

PRACTICE: (*Puzzled.*) You? Why?

(*TAXIS proceeds over the bridge.*)

WHY SHOULD YOU APOLOGIZE?

(*PRACTICE shakes his head. He does not follow TAXIS. A distant sound of laughter on the bridge. PRACTICE chooses to return the way he came. His age tells. He rubs his knees. At this moment a group of jeering cyclists hurtle by. They thrust PRACTICE into the sea. Their bells ring as they pedal on…*)

# PART THREE: A TOWER

## 1: A CAT MOVES IN

*DARLING dead and naked on a kitchen table. Four others sit in chairs, heads in hands.*

FOURTEEN: (*At last.*) What have we agreed?
(*Pause. No one replies.*)
I will summarize what we have agreed
(*Pause.*)
We have agreed the death of an unknown woman is of significance from the universal point of view only in so far as it might infringe general rules of ethical behaviour but we are not happy with this undiscriminating moral obligation in the case of Professor Machinist and in any case he says this particular woman is not the woman he intended to kill but one who so to speak stood in for her and even then he is not certain if he wished to kill even this woman he only knows a woman was strangled in other words he acknowledges the act he does not admit to the intention I think bury her I think she is the stuff of philosophical enquiry not such a bad thing after all do we want the professor hanged I don't if he's to be hanged I'll do it I have as good reasons for hanging him as anyone I'm prepared to dig the grave and if this makes me an accomplice so be it it is an honour to be the accomplice of the greatest man of his or any generation who has a shovel?
(*He stands, he waits.*)
NORRIS: Machinist is peculiar
FOURTEEN: Yes
He is
He is peculiar
So what?
(*NORRIS shrugs.*)
You have a shovel don't you where do you keep your

NORRIS: I'm peculiar myself but I don't kill girls

FOURTEEN: I think if you were listening at all I have just established that what occurred could not possibly be understood as killing even if by the usual definition a killing did occur

NORRIS: A killing's a killing

FOURTEEN: Is it? Is it really? I have wasted my breath, Mrs Norris

NORRIS: She was some

(*She shrugs in her frustration.*)

She was some ordinary girl

THIRD STUDENT: AN ORDINARY GIRL IS DEAD SO WHAT SO WHAT ANOTHER ORDINARY GIRL

She was not ordinary she was a torturer she had done many things that ordinary people would call terrible I have a problem with this word ordinary I could torture people am I ordinary

(*NORRIS shakes her head. She looks for a word. She shakes her head again.*)

NORRIS: I like Machinist I have known him for years

(*She sobs. MACHINIST gets up, goes to her and wraps his arms about her.*)

Yes

Years and always he was nice to me

Brought flowers sometimes

The shovel's in the garden

Once he gave me an egg

An egg when eggs could not be had

You have the egg he said you're pregnant

I'm always pregnant I said

A woman should be

It's in the cabbages

(*FOURTEEN goes out to fetch the shovel. NORRIS gets up and follows him.*)

No not the cabbages the turnips

(*Pause. The THIRD STUDENT looks at MACHINIST.*)

THIRD STUDENT: You're not digging?

(*MACHINIST looks at the THIRD STUDENT.*)

You kill someone and you let other people dig the grave
(*She bursts out laughing. The laugh is bitter. She shakes her head.*)
Oh let them dig
They're good at it they have the expertise whereas you
whilst you are skilled in killing people are probably useless
with a spade an embarrassment we would all suffer acute
discomfort watching you why don't you fetch a deckchair
do you want a sunhat I can make you a cold drink ice
lemon we do so long to serve you why is that I do not
understand the way men make ladders of themselves
some cluster at the bottom some perch at the top you are a
murderer and look at us the bottom the top the bottom
(*She laughs falsely. MACHINIST declines to respond.*)
MY TURN TO DIG
(*The THIRD STUDENT hurries out. MACHINIST is still. He
is unperturbed by the appearance of the CHILD, who sees the
body on the table and goes to it, drawn, fascinated. The CHILD
looks at MACHINIST, sensing his relation with the body.
TENNA enters. She goes to a chair.*)
TENNA: When your face is black with bruises
And your little eyes shrink at the sight of daylight
let alone of men
You don't dream a king's desire
But it was then I was desired
Never more than then
He slapped me sometimes to rediscover it but kindly
Kind slaps don't bruise
(*TENNA looks at the body of DARLING.*)
She
Oh
She
The darker streams of pity she never guessed they are
black with sex I was adored for weeping and if I was in
pain he fucked and fucked me
Can we stay
I heard your new work was hated by the critics but not for
its content for its length
Seven volumes

Oh

I had them sent to me but you know I never much liked
reading so I stood them on the shelf they looked so oh
I ran my fingers over them oh SEVEN VOLUMES on this
occasion I thought the critics probably were right

I'm staying

Write seven more

AND SEVEN AFTER THAT

(*She throws back her head and laughs.*)

I like you Machinist you are always in the same place

(*Pause.*)

MACHINIST: Yes

The same place always

TENNA: We're tired

I'll put the child to bed

(*She gets up. FOURTEEN enters, sees her. His mouth falls.*)

Bed

(*She extends a hand to the CHILD.*)

Bed

(*Reluctantly the CHILD goes to her mother.*)

CHILD: She smells of us

TENNA: She's dead

CHILD: (*As she is led out.*) She smells of us

(*They leave. FOURTEEN gawps. He points vaguely in the
direction TENNA has taken.*)

FOURTEEN: I've seen that woman on a stamp

The stamps on letters from across the bridge

And magazines in several languages

She

I've seen that woman naked on a beach and

(*He lifts his hands in confusion.*)

She's a queen

ARE YOU FAMILIAR WITH HER I SAW SIGNS OF INTIMACY
THERE

(*He holds his head.*)

I'M TERRIBLY CONFUSED I'D BETTER DIG

(*He hurries away. He runs straight back in.*)

I'm entitled to some clarity

Is she
(*MACHINIST slaps FOURTEEN, who begins to cry.*)
Thank you
Thank you

## 2: A CONNOISSEUR OF RIDICULE

*A beach. A body comes ashore.*

NORRIS: After a battle oh this beach
  (*She stares as the body drifts one way and the other.*)
  Clogged
  Redheads blackheads mixed and these little bits which
  could have been from either
  (*She walks a little, impatiently.*)
  And now it's suicides oh what a beach redheads
  blackheads leaping off the bridge
  (*She walks back again.*)
  He's dithering
  He's dithering if it is a he
  (*She walks parallel to the shore, hands on hips.*)
  Can't make up his mind you see
  COQUETTISH ARE THE DROWNED
  First one way then the other and when you go to lift them
  out they sink
  Coquettish are the drowned I say
THIRD STUDENT: (*Plunging in.*) GOT HIM
  (*Cries from the water as FOURTEEN runs to assist.*)
FOURTEEN: NOT DEAD
  (*They hoist PRACTICE and bear him ashore…*)
THIRD STUDENT: (*As they pass.*) Not dead
PRACTICE: NOT DEAD BUT WISH I WAS
  (*He splutters. TENNA, holding the CHILD by the hand, comes
  down the beach. She sees PRACTICE but ignores him as he is
  carried by.*)
CHILD: He smells of us
TENNA: Salt water's what he smells of salt water weed and
  little fish
  (*The CHILD stares after the retreating party.*)

CHILD: He smells of us
  (*TENNA releases the child's hand petulantly.*)
TENNA: She says nothing she does nothing I give her toys
  I take her to circuses no words no tears no laughter
NORRIS: Have a baby
TENNA: I DON'T REQUIRE A BABY I HAVE HAD ONE
NORRIS: (*Mocking.*) ONE

    ONE BABY

    SHE'S HAD ONE

    One's no baby razor hips
  (*NORRIS turns to walk away when FOURTEEN accosts her
  and starts to strangle her. TENNA is astonished, unable to
  intervene. The CHILD, a few yards away, watches with one
  finger in her mouth. Despite her greater weight, NORRIS cannot
  throw off FOURTEEN. She sinks to the ground. FOURTEEN
  nurses his wrists.*)

FOURTEEN: A queen cannot be spoken to as if she were an
  infant on the contrary in the presence of a queen it is we
  who are the infants I am now much closer even than I was
  to the great Machinist and also I dare hope a little closer to
  you how I would have liked to serve our people in a war
  the war was wonderful but only memory now so because I
  must dedicate myself to something I dedicate myself to you
  (*He looks modestly at the ground.*)
  Poor Mrs Norris but to talk to you like that a rage rose in
  me a purple rage and yet I was absolutely in control
  (*He smiles.*)
  Machinist he understands that rage and that control
  (*He lifts his hands in wonder.*)
  THE ENTIRE WORLD HE UNDERSTANDS
  (*He grins.*)
  Don't you think?
  (*He goes, discreetly… TENNA is uneasy. She extends her hand to
  the child but the child ignores her.*)
TENNA: Hand

    Hand
  (*The CHILD sits on the ground. TENNA's hand falls. She weeps
  bitterly.*)

MACHINIST: (*Entering, and looking at the body.*) The world
    without Mrs Norris
    (*He looks at TENNA.*)
    Already I feel it is a less kind place
TENNA: She wasn't kind
MACHINIST: She wasn't kind but kindness clung to her
    rather like a spider's web that in a night-time garden
    catches on your face you pluck you squirm but it can't
    be shaken off Mrs Norris found kindness irritating how
    beautiful that is
TENNA: Machinist I ran ten miles to be with you
MACHINIST: Reluctant kindness oh
TENNA: Ran ten and walked a hundred
MACHINIST: It is the only kindness I believe
    (*They look at one another. They are drawn into a long kiss. The
    CHILD watches. TAXIS walks into the scene. He also watches.*)
CHILD: A smell like us…!
    (*She turns, sees her father. He puts his finger to his lips…*)
TAXIS: Murderers
    Yes murderers I think more than any other class
    adore the bridge
    One wrote to me to say so
    He killed in one language and confessed it in another
    I feel the same
    I feel the same permission now
    (*MACHINIST separates from TENNA.*)
    Hurting and returning
    Hurting here
    Returning there
    I'm dining with the king at seven they baked a cake with
    seven spans and iced it very pretty I expect only the two of
    us too much cake for two we'll have a small piece each the
    rest is for the hospitals
    (*Pause.*)
    How I would love to say to him
    (*Pause.*)
    TO BOAST
    (*Pause.*)

I have my redhead queen again

(*TAXIS goes to his daughter and draws her to his side…*)

MACHINIST: How will you eat the cake?

With a fork?

Or with a spoon?

(*TAXIS removes a spoon from his top pocket. MACHINIST smiles.*)

TAXIS: Tenna

Let me boast

Let me boast we two are reconciled

(*He waits.*)

I THINK THE BRIDGE IS GREATER THAN WE ARE

(*He seizes TENNA and fixes her in a cruel hold. He twists her head.*)

These eyes

These eyes fit into spoons

(*Pause.*)

TENNA: (*Horrified.*) Seven volumes

SEVEN VOLUMES TALK FOR ME

(*TAXIS fits the spoon over TENNA's right eye and stays…*)

MACHINIST: During the War of Eighty Years Duration

I was urged to speak first urged then threatened and it would have served me to speak I would have been adored for speaking no matter what I said but I had a feeling too terrible to utter that to speak was wrong that speech was not the thing as if some god had placed an ice-cold finger on my lips and I feel it now I feel his finger and I love your eyes

(*Pause.*)

TAXIS: The philosopher

Even his desire cannot make him lie

Or

Has

He

Ceased

Desiring?

MACHINIST: (*His eyes cast down.*) Never have I ceased

desiring

I desire even now
My desire for the woman you are threatening has been the
agony of my life
(*He laughs suddenly, strangely.*)
BUT NOT THE ONLY AGONY
NO
NOT THE ONLY ONE
(*He doubles up, smacks his thigh, closes his eyes. In the pause he
hears TENNA laugh…*)

TAXIS: I am the husband of this woman

MACHINIST: So you are

TAXIS: I DON'T SAY KING I DON'T SAY KING AND QUEEN STUFF

MACHINIST: You don't no

TAXIS: HUSBAND
HUSBAND
DO YOU KNOW THE WORD?

MACHINIST: Yes
Yes
I think so
(*He shrugs.*)
And to dispute its meaning
(*He looks up at last.*)
There isn't time

TENNA: Do dispute it
Do
(*MACHINIST shakes his head.*)
Oh do you want me blind?

MACHINIST: I don't
I don't
My Razor Eyes
(*Pause.*)
At least I do not think I do
(*TAXIS lets out a derisory cry.*)

TAXIS: Philosopher you have no heart
No heart only the dried-up stream of curiosity

MACHINIST: I HAVE A HEART
I HAVE A HEART
AND IT PUMPS BLOOD LIKE YOU LIKE YOU LIKE YOU

(*He crushes his head in his hands.*)
PITIFUL BRIDGEMAKER YOU ARE THE BLIND ONE YOU
(*Pause. TAXIS suddenly flings the spoon at MACHINIST.*)
TAXIS: Eat your dinner with that
MACHINIST: (*Catching.*) Thank you
(*He looks at it.*)
That is the proper purpose of a spoon presumably
(*He puts it in his pocket. He stops.*)
Or not?
(*He takes it out again.*)
Possibly
(*He examines it.*)
It was conceived
Ha
It's obvious
Conceived as a tool for blinding women
Yes
Only later did an inspired individual see its potentiality as
an aid to eating
(*He smiles.*)
SAME WITH FORKS I GUARANTEE
(*For a long time TAXIS inspects MACHINIST, half-
contemptuous, half-amazed. MACHINIST allows this critical
gaze to travel over him. Then he extends a hand to TENNA. She
goes to him, kisses him. A wave of cyclists pours over the stage,
noisy and coarse.*)

## 3: CONTRA CONTRACEPTION

*The CHILD alone. She wears dark glasses and sits under a black
umbrella. The sea rises and falls. PRACTICE, deeply decayed,
approaches with a milkshake on a tray. As he comes near he collapses,
the tray flies out of his hands, the glass breaks. For some time he lies
still, then he struggles to lift himself. He kneels on the stones.*

PRACTICE: (*At last.*) It's you I'm sorry for
(*Pause.*)
I'm not sorry for myself
(*Pause.*)

You never play
(*Pause.*)
You never talk
(*Pause.*)
CHILD: I will play
I will talk
PRACTICE: (*climbing to his feet.*) It's you I feel sorry for
(*He collects up the tray and staggers out.*)
CHILD: MILK – SHAKE
PRACTICE: (*Off.*) Yes…
CHILD: STRAW – BERRY
PRACTICE: Yes.…
CHILD: MILK – SHAKE
(*She is alone. The cyclists pour by. They jeer at the spectacle of the CHILD, who covers her ears. When they have gone FOURTEEN appears. He watches her.*)
FOURTEEN: Don't talk
(*Pause.*)
Don't play
(*Pause.*)
And when your body says so show it to me
(*The CHILD stares ahead.*)
Let me lay siege to you
(*PRACTICE appears with a tray and milkshake. He staggers over the stones.*)
Let me be your enemy
(*PRACTICE falls. The tray flies out of his hands. He lies quite still. The jeering cyclists return, and pass. FOURTEEN walks away. The CHILD is alone.*)

13 OBJECTS
Studies in Servitude

# 13 Objects

**1. A Lonely Spade**
*A Spade*

**2. Cruel Cup Kind Saucer**
*A Cup and Saucer*

**3. Tin**
*A Medal*

**4. Navy Blue**
*A Pair of Shoes*

**5. The Talk of a Toy**
*A Rattle*

**6. Cracked Lens**
*A Camera*

**7. Not to Escape Now**
*A Ring*

**8. The Investor's Chronicle**
*A Painting*

**9. Poet Ash**
*An Urn*

**10. Blind Prejudice**
*A Pair of Spectacles*

**11. South of That Place Near**
*A Postcard*

**12. The Hermit's War with God**
*A Bucket of Water*

**13. Listen. I'll Beat You**
*A Drum*

# A LONELY SPADE

*A spade in the ground. Two PRISONERS attending. An OFFICER enters.*

OFFICER: Dig now
    Dig
    Dig
    (*The PRISONERS exchange looks.*)
    Dig now
    (*They hesitate over the spade.*)
    The one showing the less enthusiasm for digging will occupy the grave
    (*The PRISONERS reach simultaneously for the spade.*)
    However
    (*They stop.*)
    From what I say you are not entitled to deduce that the digger of the grave will not himself be buried
    (*Pause.*)
    Not in this grave perhaps
    And possibly not today
    But another grave
    And another day
    (*Pause.*)
    Dig
    Dig
    (*The PRISONERS simultaneously go to grab the spade. They stop. One asserts his superior will. He digs.*)
    Scum
    (*The digger stops.*)
    Scum
    Scum to dig your comrade's grave
    (*Pause. The FIRST PRISONER frowns.*)
    How I hoped that you would say
    Tilting your chin and drawing back your shoulders say
    I will not stoop to dig
    The spade shall not be lifted from the clay
    Not by me
    The lonely spade

(*The OFFICER addresses the SECOND PRISONER.*)
So now you dig
You dig his grave
Dig
Dig I say
(*The SECOND PRISONER seizes the spade and digs.*)
Dignity when it appears when it makes one of its rare
appearances comes only as an intimate of death it is part
of death's retinue we cannot speak of dignity without
speaking of death it is not to be discovered on the football
field the dance floor or lurking in the opera house it is
not a passenger on trams or the habitué of cafés lunching
laughing or seducing boys no it shuns all places but
the sites of death and there even it walks on silent soles
discriminating where discrimination seems a fatuous
refinement refinement at the grave but that is the mouth
of terrible equivalence surely there we are if anywhere the
same?
(*He snorts.*)
On the contrary
The
Grave
Is
The
Apotheosis
Of
Distinction
Scum
(*The digger digs. The other stands stock still.*)
How few possess the subtlety of mind the gravity of
character the cultural profundity to grasp the opportunities
for perfection that cluster at the edge of our extinction
time's short obviously but let us not be spoiled by time let
us not be robbed of this singular beauty which certainly
evaded us elsewhere by the mundane disciplines of time
what are we clerks what are we bus drivers two minutes
remaining but what what quality of minutes stop and you
stand in the hole

(*He looks at the FIRST PRISONER.*)
The hole
The hole
Step in as if it were your lover's room
(*Pause. The FIRST PRISONER hesitates.*)
Your mother's bed
Her womb
Step in with some oh some semblance of demeanour
(*Pause. The FIRST PRISONER goes to obey.*)
No
(*The FIRST PRISONER stops.*)
Far from regarding death as the abyss I am now persuaded
all men resolutely forbid themselves the briefest
contemplation of its sublime character possibly he who
first described it in these terms was not himself perched
on the rim the abyss may be a metaphor belonging to the
bedroom or the library perhaps it speaks to him who is so
far removed from it it is no more apposite than the verdict
of a wrecked lover studying the photograph of the woman
who destroyed him
(*He looks to the SECOND PRISONER.*)
You try
You demonstrate this quality I am struggling to elucidate
(*The SECOND PRISONER frowns. He thrusts the spade into
the ground. He prepares to step into the grave. He lifts his eyes to
the OFFICER.*)
Oh be the one
Be the one who takes leave of himself in such a way it
haunts my memory
(*The SECOND PRISONER steps into the grave. He folds his
hands in front of him.*)
Yes
Yes
(*Pause.*)
Yes and yet
Oh
This is
Oh
Forgive me

Forgive me and my cynical character
See this cynicism if you can as no more than the shelter of
a delicate and always disappointed soul
I think you have a strategy
Yes
And far from sharing with me your preparation for an
exquisite death you think I will
Oh dear
You think I will be gratified and give you back today
Tomorrow you think
Tomorrow he will make me die
Today's my present if I try
(*The SECOND PRISONER lifts his hands bitterly.*)
Scum
Scum
Lie on your back and watch the sky
(*The SECOND PRISONER is aghast.*)
Lie
Lie
(*The OFFICER makes the slightest threat. The SECOND*
*PRISONER lies in the grave.*)
You
(*He gestures to the FIRST PRISONER.*)
Take the spade and bury him
Yes
Bury him alive
(*The FIRST PRISONER begins to shovel earth on the SECOND*
*PRISONER. The OFFICER kneels by the grave.*)
The world is nothing but the sum of your perceptions
Always I have been convinced of this
Since childhood
Yes
The greatest moments of awareness are granted us prior to
thought
Later
Absurd it is not
We are obliged to retrieve them by the exertions of the
intellect
(*He turns wildly to the FIRST PRISONER.*)

Don't cover his face
Don't deprive him of the sky
(*Pause.*)
In view of this
This fact about the world that I have just described
It cannot be said that death
Death insofar as you are experiencing it
In any way diminishes us
The contrary
The contrary must be the case
The world is in death also
(*He turns angrily to the FIRST PRISONER.*)
Dirt
Dirt on his face
(*The FIRST PRISONER is still with horror.*)
Perhaps you should occupy the hole
Perhaps the hole is more appropriate to you
(*Pause. The OFFICER returns to his theme.*)
This death
Far from being the extinction of perception
Is itself perception
(*He stands up swiftly.*)
Oh
It is so hard to say
It is so hard to enter the territory of this
It calls for a new language
It calls for poetry
But poetry is sometimes obfuscation let us admit it
Let us admit the poet often hides in the metaphor as a shy
creature takes to the woods
It dreads the light
It dreads exposure
No
We must struggle with the language that we possess
we must employ the inadequate knowing full well its
inadequacy
Stop

(*The FIRST PRISONER stops shovelling. The OFFICER looks at him. A pause of intense pain and frustration. The FIRST PRISONER casts down the spade, childlike and defiant.*)

Pick up the spade

(*Pause.*)

Pick up the spade which you threw down

(*Pause.*)

Scum

Scum

(*The FIRST PRISONER glares at the OFFICER, and with a gesture of contempt throws back his chin. The OFFICER bursts out laughing.*)

You

(*He cannot speak for laughing.*)

You

(*He shakes his head.*)

Oh

When scum discovers dignity we

Really

We can only laugh

Dig your own hole now and bury the embarrassment that you have caused not only to yourself but me

Smother it swiftly

Please

(*He walks a little. The FIRST PRISONER is resolute.*)

Oh come on

(*The FIRST PRISONER is about to capitulate when the voice of the SECOND PRISONER comes from the hole, singing an elegy. The OFFICER seems inclined to listen. His stillness is a measure of his emotion. Suddenly he interrupts the SECOND PRISONER.*)

No

No

Shut up

Shut up

I'll fill your mouth with dirt

Shut up you

(*The voice ceases.*)

He
Oh
The calculation
The manipulation
Never
Never
Is a man sincere
(*He addresses the FIRST PRISONER.*)
That
If I interpret him correctly
That
Is scum's attempt to make me like some vessel like some
bronze urn
The repository of his memory
He thinks I'll dream his singing
He thinks on summer evenings in my senile years I'll hear
that voice come floating over fields
Or in the night awake
Oh
The buried prisoner
Oh
So
He
Thinks
(*He half-spits contempt.*)
No
I promise him the absolute obscurity he so fears
Yet
Yet
Believe me I am susceptible
I am
But not alas
To imitation
Everything you two scum do is derivative
And that's a pity
That's a profound pity for in many ways you can't be
blamed
The reproduction of things is oh
Oh

Universal now and like some gnawing sea undermines
even my sense of the immaculate
(*He strolls, stops.*)
How
How
How can we achieve in moments replete with stale and
sordid imitation the authentic gesture?
How invent new and untarnished forms in which to enter
death?
It's
All
Contaminated
Now
(*As if by mutual agreement the OFFICER and the FIRST
PRISONER turn to one another, an innocence communicates
itself. The FIRST PRISONER flings himself at the OFFICER's
feet and kisses his hand. A look of dismay passes over the
OFFICER's features. He holds the FIRST PRISONER's head by
one hand, affectionate, discreet.*)
We all
We all want it to be right
Yes
And how could you know that I also wish to die properly?
Dig now
Dig
(*The FIRST PRISONER retrieves the spade and works with a
religious conviction.*)
Stop
(*The FIRST PRISONER looks up. Pause.*)
Assure me now
Assure me with a single motion of your head that you have
abandoned every futile hope of further life
(*The FIRST PRISONER nods once.*)
In no crevice of your imagination does there lurk some
desperate hope I may relent?
Assure me
(*The FIRST PRISONER nods again. Pause.*)
It's good
Oh

It's good
(*The OFFICER also nods. The FIRST PRISONER offers
the OFFICER the spade. For a moment the OFFICER seems
confused. Then a smile passes over his features.*)
Yes
Yes
Someone must bury you
(*He goes to take the spade, stops… He looks at the FIRST
PRISONER, the outstretched arm, the expression of utter
renunciation. He contemplates him.*)
Scum
Oh
Scum
How beautiful you are today
(*The FIRST PRISONER cannot hold the spade longer. It falls
from his grasp.*)
Run
Run
(*The FIRST PRISONER's eyes lift, close with an agonized
disbelief.*)
Run
(*He takes to his heels. The OFFICER watches him. He then turns
and walks away. The SECOND PRISONER calls from the grave
in which he lies.*)
SECOND PRISONER: Hey
Hey
Hey
Hey
•

## CRUEL CUP KIND SAUCER

*A tin table and chairs. A seated woman.*

WOMAN: Shame's a moment
(*Pause.*)
Long in my case
(*Pause.*)
A long shame but I fight it
I fight it knowing I need not be ashamed

263

I fight
And fight it
This particularly unnecessary shame
(*Pause.*)
Every day we came here and sometimes he was late and
sometimes it was me if I was late he did not seem much
troubled by it whereas his lateness produced in me a small
low pain a gathering fear not of his failing to appear he did
he always did appear but of public opinion public opinion
is the enemy
(*She laughs.*)
I could not lift my eyes
(*She laughs again. A waiter deposits a coffee on the table. He
retires.*)
Whereas
Alone as I am now
I dare them to pity me
(*Pause.*)
In the first place obviously my inclination was to flee to
shun the place to make outlandish detours passing down
unsavoury alleys even I confess it to move house yes I
contemplated moving to a different district ha and I adore
my house my dear my loyal house I would have quit in
order not to pass by here this mood lasted a few weeks
(*She takes the coffee cup and sips.*)
A few terrible weeks when every instinct
And not only instinct
Every exertion of discrimination combined to steer my
footsteps round this place
A café
Only a café
A café with green tables
A small green painted café distinguished by what
What exactly
Nothing
But
My
Struggle
With

Myself
(*She sips again.*)
And they don't like it they really do not like a remnant of
a shattered love affair to wash up on their tables to cling
to their chairs when love is wrecked they much prefer you
to sink with the baggage whereas they smiled at one time
whereas they applauded you for the charm of your passion
suddenly they're cold they think you are an omen they
look at you as a sick man might focus on a crow
(*Pause.*)
Am I a crow?
(*She calls to the waiter.*)
Am I a crow?
He smiles
He carves a smile into his face
I don't doubt he would much prefer me to be dead
Oh yes
I'm bad for business
And wishing people dead
Oh
I do it all the time
We all do
Yes
I defy a single man or woman to state they never wished
another dead
I defy
I do defy
If he came here if he turned up at the same hour as I do if
he retained the habit of our passionate encounters despite
my failing to appear they would be oh so very oh so utterly
newspaper sir the usual sir cold wind today sir oh yes it
would be normality itself perfect perfect normality
(*Pause.*)
But me
(*Pause.*)
When was I last offered a newspaper?
(*She taps the empty coffee cup with the spoon to attract the
attention of the waiter.*)
How terrifying how nauseating how fatal is

(*Pause.*)
The shameless one
(*She suddenly grabs the empty cup and examines it.*)
He
Drank
From
This
(*The waiter delivers a second coffee and goes to take the saucer of the first.*)
No
(*The waiter withdraws.*)
Or was this the single cup which by the law of coincidence never once in all our history came near his lips?
(*She replaces it on the saucer.*)
Whereas this
(*She tips out the coffee on the floor.*)
This certainly must have
Oh certainly he drank from this
(*She bangs it down.*)
It's not mystical it's arithmetic
There are sixty cups and sixty saucers at the counter
Stacked
I counted them
I was not the only customer though I came early still two others had preceded me
I counted fifty-eight
Two on the tables
Sixty therefore
And allowing for breakages and the replacements of the breakages one must deduce that for a considerable length of time to come the coffee cups in this establishment will bear the intimate traces of his lips
Not all of them
We submit to the law of coincidences
But
Most
(*She is very still.*)
Yes

Have
Him
Indelibly
Around
The
Rim
(*Pause. She lets the cup fall to the ground. It shatters.*)
One less
Oh
Sorry
(*She makes a face in the direction of the waiter.*)
The gnawing prospect of a world in which a few a handful
a solitary example possible of these relics remains after
my own demise poses a dilemma it is not as if he were a
man of much celebrity notorious or popular a singer or a
demagogue no he concealed his qualities from all but me
so
(*The waiter brings a third coffee, places it down on the table,
retrieves the broken pieces of the second cup and goes.*)
It is reasonable to assume that in say
I pluck a figure randomly
Five years
(*She lifts the new cup.*)
Most will have been removed from circulation and not
only because they are broken chips will condemn them
and one must not conceal from oneself that in a culture
so susceptible as this to fashion the whole lot might be
swept away I might arrive here on a somewhat ordinary
morning ordinary in most regards at least and find the
entire stock replaced I have seen such things they do not
consult the customer why should they possibly they live
under the illusion we are as charmed by innovation as they
themselves are I should rummage in the dustbins but oh
but
(*She shakes her head.*)
And were this solitary cup to escape destruction
Without me
How could its history be
I'm crying

I'm crying and
(*She lifts the saucer and shields her face from the world.*)
Ha
Ashamed to cry
However hard I fight with shame
Ha
(*She removes the saucer to expose herself.*)
Crying
Me
(*The waiter comes back and stands by her. She shakes her head. The tears roll down. He offers her a clean handkerchief...*)
•

# TIN

*A soldier enters holding a medal.*

SOLDIER: For bravery
(*Pause.*)
He pinned it to my chest
He smelled of perfume
He had a small cut from a razor
His fingers fumbled
His eyes met mine
But not for long
The King
(*He tosses the medal to the ground and is about to stride off.*)
OLD WOMAN: Dropped your medal
(*The SOLDIER stops. The OLD WOMAN enters, points.*)
Dropped it son
(*Pause. The SOLDIER looks at the medal.*)
SOLDIER: Dropped it?
Didn't drop it no
(*He starts to go.*)
OLD WOMAN: Wear your medal son
(*Pause.*)
SOLDIER: You wear it
OLD WOMAN: (*Rebuking him.*) WEAR YOUR MEDAL
(*Pause.*)

SOLDIER: Old woman you might get a dinner for that medal

OLD WOMAN: Weren't you brave then?

SOLDIER: I was brave the war was stupid the king's a ninny and the medal's tin

OLD WOMAN: WEAR THE TIN THEN

(*He shakes his head.*)

Wear the beautiful tin

(*He goes out. The OLD WOMAN bends and retrieves the medal. A MAN enters, passing.*)

Hey

(*He stops.*)

Were you in the war?

MAN: Never

OLD WOMAN: Never in the war? How was that?

MAN: I hid in a hole

OLD WOMAN: Clever

MAN: War is for idiots

(*He starts to go out.*)

OLD WOMAN: Wear this medal

(*He comes back, examines the medal.*)

MAN: For bravery it says

OLD WOMAN: Wear it for cleverness instead

(*He goes out. The OLD WOMAN looks swiftly about her. A SECOND MAN passes.*)

Wear this medal

(*The SECOND MAN stops.*)

It's not heavy

(*He looks at her.*)

It's tin

SECOND MAN: (*Recognizing it.*) It's the medal for bravery

OLD WOMAN: That's right it is

SECOND MAN: I was not brave mother on the contrary I fled

(*He starts to go.*)

OLD WOMAN: (*Frustrated.*) CONFESS TO YOUR PILLOW BUT MARCH IN THE STREET

(*Piqued, the SECOND MAN returns.*)

SECOND MAN: And what good would it do me to wear a strong man's medal when I myself am weak?

OLD WOMAN: Don't you like women? Wear that and they'll beg you into their beds

SECOND MAN: (*Going out.*) And their husbands will thrash me

OLD WOMAN: YOU DESERVE TO BE THRASHED
(*She seethes. An OLD MAN observes her.*)

OLD MAN: I'll wear it
(*Pause.*)

OLD WOMAN: You? How can you wear it?

OLD MAN: Got a chest

OLD WOMAN: Little chest

OLD MAN: (*Going to her.*) Pin it then pin it to my little chest
(*She looks at the OLD MAN with contempt.*)
PIN IT I SAID

OLD WOMAN: Pin it to you? But then bravery will look grey and toothless bravery will have a stoop better a dog runs with it brave animal we say lithe limbed if necessary a dog
(*A dog barks. She calls offstage.*)
Lend us your dog
(*She holds out the medal.*)

SOLDIER: (*Returning.*) I was thinking

OLD WOMAN: Too late it belongs to a dog

SOLDIER: The war was certainly stupid

OLD WOMAN: A criminal wore it and was taken for an honest man

SOLDIER: The king is a ninny

OLD WOMAN: A coward wore it what a hero they said all the women naked just like that
(*She clicks her fingers.*)

SOLDIER: And the medal is tin

OLD WOMAN: (*Calling.*) DOG
DOG

SOLDIER: All the same what I did the action I performed and which looked at objectively was certainly beyond the call of duty
(*The OLD WOMAN whistles the dog.*)

That I daresay cannot be diminished that can't be
tarnished by considerations of politics or morality let alone
aesthetic judgements as to the relative values of silver or tin

OLD WOMAN: (*Clapping her knees.*) HERE

HERE BOY HERE

SOLDIER: So I'm wearing it

(*He extends a hand to the OLD WOMAN.*)

And any man who mocks me let him watch out for his
teeth

(*The OLD WOMAN ceases calling the dog. She goes to the
SOLDIER and is about to pin the medal on his chest. He stops
her with a hand.*)

The thing I did

The bravery

I did not think I shall have a medal doing this

OLD WOMAN: No son

SOLDIER: No

(*Pause.*)

Pin it

(*She pins it to his chest.*)

Good

Now walk behind me

OLD WOMAN: Yes

(*The dog barks with excitement. They walk out.*)

•

# NAVY BLUE

*A discarded pair of women's shoes. A courting couple, slow.*

WOMAN: (*Pointing.*) Old shoe…!

MAN: Two

WOMAN: Two shoes…!

(*They look about them.*)

MAN: Two shoes

Two shoes in the meadow

Two shoes by the stream

Immediately you think

So this place after all is frequently visited this place far
from being secluded is the destination of oh thousands

possibly thinking to escape the asphyxiating odour of
the crowd we fetch up precisely where the crowd itself is
lapping lapping like the lip of the sea rather worn shoes
she did not clean them often
(*He picks up one shoe.*)
Possibly never
Possibly from the day of their purchase they were never
cleaned
And sitting here
Or lying here
Her body recumbent for a lover she chose once they had
fallen not to step into them again
But went home barefoot
Or he
Yes
He carried her in stockinged feet through fields and over
fences
Strong
Supremely strong
Or if not strong
Inspired
Yes
A frail man inspired
(*He contemplates the shoe… He looks at the WOMAN. He closes
his eyes. He kisses the shoe, longingly. The WOMAN observes
him.*)
WOMAN: Or perhaps she's dead
(*Pause.*)
Perhaps if you explored the undergrowth items of her
clothing might be discovered
Her skirt on thorns
Her pants in thistle
And protruding from the reeds
Her
Beckoning
Hand
These secluded places make men murder possibly because
in failing to be paradise they only make us horribly

ashamed for seeking paradise at all the poverty of things oh
it mocks us the trodden over used up and soiled character
of everything it could produce a rage a murderous rage
cheap shoes I notice
(*She is holding the second shoe.*)
She wasn't wealthy
(*Pause. The man retains the shoe.*)
Or was wealthy
Was
Wealthy
And
Preferred
Cheap
Shoes
(*Pause.*)
Or did not so much prefer them as concluded that to buy
shoes of a higher quality would neither satisfy her nor
make much impression on others
(*Pause.*)
A wealthy woman but not stylish
(*Pause.*)
A wealthy woman without friends
(*Pause.*)
Or simply a poor woman I don't know
(*She laughs. The laugh fades. She discards the shoe.*)
Her shoe
Her empty shoes
Her empty and uncleaned shoes
MAN: (*Retrieving the second shoe.*) I'm in love with her
(*Pause.*)
Painfully
(*Pause.*)
And I came here to make love to you
(*Pause.*)
I love her for her idleness I love her precisely for the
reason that she never cleaned her shoes the very reason
one might adopt a critical attitude towards her serves in my
case to

(*Pause.*)
And not only in my case
(*Pause.*)
To arouse me and then this gesture this ecstatic gesture
tossing them to either side you recollect they were some
yards apart the distance describes so eloquently her
passion her spontaneity I think if they had been placed
neatly and together I should not feel so
(*He shrugs.*)
So
(*He shrugs again.*)
And I don't require to know much more I think if more
of her belongings could be discovered lying as you say in
reeds or thickets still I shouldn't
(*Pause.*)
No
(*Pause.*)
No that isn't true I would I would certainly try of course
I would try certainly I'd
(*He chuckles, and stops.*)
The world
It's all collisions
It's all encounters
It's all accidents
How terrible I shall never see her
Never
Never
She left this beautiful suggestion
This
Equivalent of breath
Or perfume on a draught
The traces of a stranger obviously more perfect than the
stranger is herself
I'm not stupid
I know
I know

Probably the shoes should be left to rot rain-soddened sun
bleached and bitten by the nocturnal fox slowly the soil
would swallow them however I
(*His eyes meet hers.*)
WOMAN: Don't take them home
MAN: No?
WOMAN: Let them lie where she discarded them
(*Pause.*)
Let others suffer as you have
Let others writhe with curiosity
(*Pause.*)
MAN: I
  I
  I don't think I can do that
WOMAN: It's what she wanted
MAN: Is it?
WOMAN: Yes
  Oh yes
  We all do that
MAN: We all?
WOMAN: We all do that
MAN: What?
WOMAN: Fling bits drape bits scatter relics yes we do
(*Pause.*)
MAN: You too?
WOMAN: All of us
(*Pause.*)
MAN: All of you?
  Knowing that passing men will certainly
WOMAN: Knowing that obviously
  And how frustrated we would be if one like you one more
  susceptible than others seized the item for himself made
  himself sole possessor
MAN: But that is what
  Oh
  Is that not the perfect act?
(*He is puzzled.*)
  She left the shoes for me

275

Her ignorance of my identity is the essence of
(*Pause.*)
What do you discard?
What do you drape?
(*The WOMAN is silent. Pause.*)
So
(*He shrugs.*)
Ha
(*He frowns.*)
I never knew
(*He fathoms, his hand searches. He expostulates.*)
Excellent
Oh
Excellent
And were you traced
Were you discovered
His forensic passion abolishing your anonymity

WOMAN: Catastrophe

MAN: Yes
Catastrophe
(*He laughs with pleasure.*)
How vastly superior this is to the tedium of knowledge
And how immune we are to disappointment and the flat
notes of familiarity
She is forever perfect to me
I'll keep one
And the other
(*He flings it aside.*)
Will fascinate another
(*He wanders a few paces.*)
Navy
She likes navy blue
(*He starts to wander off.*)

WOMAN: Or not

MAN: Or not
Or not
Yes
One of the reasons possibly for my encountering the shoes

WOMAN: Is her dislike of navy blue
MAN: Exactly
    You see
    She is a mystery
    She retains forever an incorruptible distinction
    (*He stops.*)
    Whereas
    Whereas you
    (*He seems to grapple with himself. He cries out. The WOMAN runs to him. She clasps him in her arms, as he flails. He becomes less wild as she comforts him.*)
WOMAN: The world's all right
    The world's all right
    (*He moans.*)
    The world's all right
    (*He moans.*)

    •

## THE TALK OF A TOY

*A child's rattle is flung onto the stage. Some voices.*

FIRST WOMAN: Oh
    Oh
    She
    Little
SECOND WOMAN: Little
FIRST WOMAN: Such
    A
SECOND WOMAN: Little
FIRST WOMAN: Little
SECOND WOMAN: Miss
    (*A QUEEN enters.*)
QUEEN: My rattle
    My rattle
    Pick it up
    (*Pause.*)
    My rattle
    (*Pause.*)
    On the floor my rattle

Pick it up
(*Pause.*)
Or die
Whoever fails to find my rattle dies
(*Pause.*)
Very well
(*Pause.*)
Die
(*Pause.*)
It's there
It's right beneath your eyes
I sometimes think frustrating me is a pleasure to you
the extraordinary lengths you go to simply to avoid
obeying my instructions when obedience itself would
cost you nothing obedience is quick whereas recalcitrance
takes hours think about it life's short life's short
bring it bring it quick
(*Pause.*)
I see
(*Pause.*)
I see
(*Pause.*)
Or do I?
(*Pause.*)
I may not see but I do sense what your game is you are
hoping I will fly into a rage this rage will entitle you to
punish me and why do you want to punish me because
you do oh yes I know how much you want to punish me
because I'm perfect and the perfect oh the perfect
(*Pause.*)
Horrifies you
(*Pause.*)
The perfect fills you with a burning shame
(*Pause.*)
Fetch it
(*Pause.*)
My rattle
(*Pause.*)

Fetch the awful instrument of my authority
(*She thrusts out a hand. Pause. She withdraws it.*)
I've been extravagant
I've shaken it when strictly speaking I did not require to
Yes
Yes
I've even shaken it from boredom
Arbitrarily
Purely for effect
No more of that
From now on I shake it rarely
This rare shaking will cause you to recognize the profound
significance attaching to it
Oh
This
Rare
Shaking
(*She thrusts out a hand. Pause. She withdraws it.*)
For example
(*Pause.*)
Death it might mean death it might mean whoever hears it
is condemned to death swiftly and without the possibility
of argument dragged out dragged down dragged through
the halls the corridors the stairs skull bumping spine
bruising deep into damp dark where the drowning out of
earshot where the strangling never a note the stamping out
of brains is
(*Pause.*)
A leaf blowing over the tiles
(*Pause.*)
It might mean that
(*Her hand goes out. An attendant, dressed in black, enters,
retrieves the rattle and gives it to her, bows, and walks away.
She leaves her hand in the air.*)
I wonder why I did not die
(*Pause.*)
Some infants do
(*Pause.*)
Some pay a visit to the world

Open their eyes
And find it unsatisfactory
(*She smiles…*)
Such refinement
Such discernment
Such a capacity for dissent
This place offends us from our first breath
(*She shakes the rattle violently. Black clad figures rush across the
stage in all directions, doing her bidding. A pause. She holds the
rattle poised.*)
How silly speech is
How silly when all it really means is
(*She waits. She rattles violently. Again the stage erupts in running
figures. She laughs, staccato. Silence returns.*)
As an infant
Struggling to speak
The rattle seemed a poor and primitive substitute for the
perfect articulation of a mood or thought a temper or a
loneliness
Wooden and approximate
But with the acquisition of the thing called speech I
And did I not read books
Oh
Books
And
Dictionaries
Did I not scour libraries
I did
I did
I crawled shelves long to gather one new word I tracked it
by its spoor its scent I trapped I hunted it
(*Pause.*)
Now
It's
(*She ponders. She rattles violently. The servants race in all
directions. She laughs. The laugh outlasts the rattle…*)
Obvious to me speech is

(*She throws down the rattle. She pouts. She points to the discarded rattle. No one appears. She stamps. She clicks her fingers. Still no one attends on her. Her face expresses the ambiguity of her crisis. She reaches for something in her clothes. She exposes a second rattle. She shakes this. The attendant enters and picks up the first. He gives it into her empty hand. Now she shakes both. The stage fills with running figures.*)

•

# CRACKED LENS

*A youth with a camera.*

YOUTH: I am an idealist
    (*Pause.*)
    Oh
    Such
    Impossible
    Such
    Unattainable
    Such
    (*Pause.*)
By idealist I mean this that the very simplest encounters with the world pose for me agonizing dilemmas for example I will identify one only I will not fatigue you with a plethora of pains one is sufficient I was given a camera my father who is generous as well as loving as a gift provided me with this it wasn't my birthday it wasn't Christmas either he simply saw this camera in a window and thought it beautiful and because he thought it beautiful purchased it not for himself but for me little did he realize this innocent desire to give a little pleasure to his son would only add to my what my what what shall I call it the melancholy burden of my dreams you see I do not know how to employ a camera obviously I understand its functions I understand its purpose but
    (*Pause.*)
I cannot help resenting the generosity of my father he bestows gifts without the slightest apprehension of the pain they cause

(*Pause.*)
Not to everyone
(*Pause.*)
To idealists
(*Pause.*)
To an idealist a gift is oh
(*Pause.*)
As your trembling fingers unwrap the gift oh
(*Pause.*)
Another
Yet
Another
Door
To
Pains
(*Pause.*)
It's rather ancient
(*Pause.*)
He loves the old the old has charm for him rather
absurdly he bestows significance on an object simply
for its antiquity that isn't idealism that is sentimentality
from his sentimentality I took only the finest elements
the mechanism is infuriating and arcane but that is not
the problem I have mastered the mechanism no the
mechanism is not the problem if only it were no I have
nimble fingers such nimble
(*Pause.*)
It is the world that is the problem
(*Pause.*)
It is the world's unworthiness
(*Pause.*)
I have to ask myself each time I lift the camera to my eye
and I have done this a number of times now I am not
indulging an hypothesis does this this spectacle appearing
in the lens does this constitute sufficient
(*Pause. He agonizes.*)
And the answer's no
Always
Always

No
No
Always
I regret to say
(*Pause.*)
After all a camera is not looking
Oh
The fools who
The idiots who
I hate to condemn but so many think the camera is an eye
they do I have heard them say so I have seen it written it
is quite the opposite to an eye the furlongs of film mankind
has wasted thinking the camera is an eye
Ha
(*He shakes his head.*)
It's a prison
It's a tomb
It's a torture chamber
(*Pause.*)
AND HE GIVES IT TO ME MASQUERADING AS A GIFT
I saw a girl
The girl seeing I possessed a camera offered to be naked
In a park this was an ornamental park with swans with
grottoes fountains and the like seeing I had a camera
started to undress I don't criticise people see a camera they
want to strip they cannot help themselves and grinning all
the time as if nakedness were funny of course she knew her
beauty had a term she knew her loveliness was finite and
wanted it preserved by anyone she didn't care she knew
even the passing hour swept her on towards decay I don't
criticize and these pitiful poses plucked out of magazines I
wept
(*Pause.*)
Not unusual
(*Pause.*)
My weeping
(*Pause.*)
I am an idealist I said my tears are of a special sort but to
remove your clothes and find oh to remove your clothes

and discover that your nakedness stimulates not rage but
tears oh oh
(*Pause.*)
She was profoundly disconcerted
(*Pause. He lifts the camera slowly to his eye. He looks into the
lens. He suddenly removes it from his eye again.*)
And the thing's old so old it must have in its time been
used for
(*He shrugs.*)
I dread to contemplate the banal subject matter it has been
focused on if one could wash a camera I would wash it
yes or fumigate it holidays babies in prams unreturning
soldiers football teams some pitiful pornography the
uncleanliness of it appals me if he was buying me a camera
why not a new one how thoughtless he can be my father
how shallow what a saucer of authentic imagination that
man has he cannot help it I suppose I forgive him I said so
in a letter I did not say thank you for the present I said I
forgive you he was baffled he looked strangely days on end
HOW HARD HE HAS MADE IT FOR ME
HOW HARD
(*Pause.*)
This could drive me to suicide
This
This
FOCUS ON THE WORLD
(*Pause.*)
On the other hand it might be argued
I'll argue it now
I will
I'll argue it
That my father's misguided generosity has in fact contrived
to concentrate my mind has in fact put a term to that
fatuous speculation that characterizes idealistic youth and
licenses it to wander with an open mind through cultures
landscapes women museums laundries and god knows
what attempting to discern whether life is valueless or
infinitely beautiful no the camera does this
Oh

What
A
Terrible
Instrument
It
Is
It obliges me to say this object in the lens this woman in
the lens this life within the lens is
(*Pause.*)
A miracle
(*Pause.*)
Or
Not…
(*A GIRL enters.*)
I argued it
(*She looks at him.*)
I argued that my father had unconsciously shortened my
life
(*Pause.*)
I argued that he had
How sad for him
Poor man
(*Pause.*)
Killed me
DON'T UNDRESS YOU'RE NOT A MIRACLE
Someone tried that yesterday
Yes
Like you
Same thing exactly
Erroneously believed herself so perfect no camera
could resist
Mine can
Mine does
NOTHING I HAVE SEEN IN THAT SAD SQUARE DESERVED
ETERNAL TESTIMONY NO
(*Pause.*)
Decay on your own
Decline elsewhere

I'm throwing this into a lake which is to dignify it more
than it deserves are there not a million cameras ten million
yes ten million instruments of terror my flinging it into a
lake is purely symbolical therefore it has served its purpose
oddly served its purpose without ever being used not a
single photograph taken by me not once have I depressed
the shutter or wound on the film and having flung in the
camera I should fling myself
Oh yes
It's logical
The world has failed me
It's logical to drown

GIRL: I'll take you

(*Long pause.*)

YOUTH: Take me?

(*Pause.*)

Take me to the water's edge?
Thank you I prefer to march alone I think an idealist
contemplating suicide can dispense with conversation of
the sort you might

GIRL: Take your photograph

(*Pause.*)

YOUTH: TRAP

TRAP

(*He laughs. He shakes his head.*)

Clever and

Subtle and

I admire your cleverness your subtlety if I were not a
suicide I should like to know you better

TRAP

OH BRILLIANT TRAP

You think a ruthless idealist such as I am can be seduced
by one thing only

HIS OWN IMAGE

Brilliant

Subtle

You think me susceptible to the temptation of finding one
thing only in the world worthy of contemplation

MYSELF

Oh subtle brilliant clever girl
Take it then
I'll pose
I'll pose
And die
Will that gratify you
Print two
One for my father
One for you
Say to your children I never knew this man he did
however leave an indelible impression on me
(*He extends the camera to the GIRL. She hesitates, then collects it.*
*She holds it to her eye.*)
How strange I
(*She lets the camera fall a little.*)
How strange I feel uncomfortable
(*He shrugs.*)
I
Silly
Please carry on
(*She lifts it again.*)
No
No
I'm
Look my feet are shifting
Far from posing I am acutely embarrassed
Ha
It's
(*She presses the shutter. He is still with horror.*)
I wasn't ready
GIRL: No I pressed it by mistake
YOUTH: I was nowhere near ready
GIRL: I'll take another one
YOUTH: Will you will you take another one but the one you
  have just taken what of that it's in the camera it's wound on
  it's there it's why did you do that
GIRL: I made a mistake I
YOUTH: But you're clever
GIRL: I'm clever but

YOUTH: Clever girls don't make mistakes

GIRL: I did

I did make a mistake then

(*Pause.*)

YOUTH: I believe you

Obviously my nervousness communicated itself to you

Rip the film out of the camera

GIRL: Rip

YOUTH: Rip it out

(*Pause.*)

I cannot possibly take my leave of the world so long as that absurd relic of my existence remains behind my whole demeanour suggests reluctance I was staring at the ground my toes were crossed even the way my hands were held they will say he gave himself unwillingly to death the photograph will be exploited by those who propagate the idea of the world's magnificence I know I have studied the misuse of photography give me the camera give it to me

(*He extends a hand.*)

My father will be haunted by it

My poor father

GIVE ME THE FILM AND KEEP THE CAMERA

(*The GIRL smiles.*)

Oh

Oh

You subtle and I won't go on you brilliant and

I won't go on

You think so long as such an image of me lingers in the world I shan't destroy myself oh you

SAVAGE PHILANTHROPIST

If I were not determined on my suicide I would marry you

You

You

We were made for one another

Years of struggle years of silence years of everything

(*He extends a hand violently.*)

THE FILM

THE FILM

THANK YOU

(*Suddenly she photographs the YOUTH. He is shocked and still.*)
That
(*He closes his eyes.*)
That is worse
My hand extended like that
My poor father
Such a sentimentalist he will surely read that gesture as a
plea
YOU ARE HEARTLESS AND I MUST HAVE THAT FILM
(*He makes a threatening move towards her. She steps back. Pause.*)
How unfortunate
How very unfortunate and irritating
You are mischievous
(*The GIRL laughs. The YOUTH shakes his head.*)
I who am so serious has collided with
That is the only way to put it
Collided with
Someone who takes refuge in mischief
We all have our ways
We all have our methods
Any stratagem to blind us to the melancholy spectacle of
life which photography has only served to emphasize
I'll have the film now
(*The GIRL begins to sob. The YOUTH looks at the ground.*)
Mischief followed by grief
Yes
They go hand in hand
(*She wails. He stares at the ground.*)
Shh
Shh
(*He makes a clumsy, indistinct gesture of pity.*)
Shh
(*She stifles her sobs. She extends the camera to him. He is
indecisive, then dashes and seizes it from her. He tears the film out
of the back and triumphantly displays it.*)
There
There
Was anything more eloquent than
SPOILED FILM

He was
And then he wasn't
(*He laughs. He is thoughtful.*)
Show it to my father
He will search the dark for me
His eyes will ache
Red-eyed
My father
From peering at the film
(*He extends the dangling film to the GIRL. She hesitates.*)
My absence
Take my absence to him please
(*The GIRL dithers, then runs away…*)
I really must stop attempting to recruit bewildered and
uncomprehending individuals to my cause it is a weakness
of mine and I suspect a weakness in all idealists so severe
is the climate of our solitude we attempt to alleviate it
by trailing samples of our agonized perceptions before
strangers strangers whose brutal indifference only serves to
deepen our
(*He calls after her.*)
HAVE THE CAMERA IF YOU WANT
There I go again
No
It's an instinct but must a man be tethered to his instincts
(*He calls again.*)
IT'S A FREE GIFT
All gifts are free
Why did I say that why did I say the gift was free perhaps
unconsciously I recognized an element in giving which
implies reciprocation yes by a slip of the tongue I was
exposed to an unpalatable truth a truth concealed in all
ostensibly selfless acts oh she isn't stupid I said did I not
say this girl is far from stupid on the contrary she
(*Pause. He holds his head in a spasm of pain. He sways, the
film hanging from his hand… He lets it fall to the floor… He
chuckles…*)
How perfect is the camera without film
(*He lifts the camera to his eye. He presses the shutter.*)

How entirely me
(*He photographs again, another subject, arbitrarily.*)
My father knew presumably
The camera without film
(*He takes another subject.*)
Is
Me
•

## NOT TO ESCAPE NOW

*A MAN holds a wedding ring. A WOMAN enters.*

MAN: I own you put this on
WOMAN: (*Scoffing.*) Own me?
MAN: Put this on
WOMAN: OWN?

OWN

ME?

MAN: Put on the ring
WOMAN: I will put on the ring I would not have asked for a
ring if I did not intend to wear it
MAN: You are owned the ring says
WOMAN: You are loved the ring says
MAN: You were loved without the ring the ring is not to do
with love extend your finger
WOMAN: I betrayed you not once but many times
MAN: You will not betray me again
WOMAN: Certainly the ring will discourage me
MAN: And others seeing it will be discouraged also
WOMAN: They will see that I have loved a man and possibly
still love him
MAN: They will think twice therefore
WOMAN: They will think twice certainly
(*She extends her finger. He looks at her hand. He swiftly and
passionately kisses it.*)
How you love me
(*Pause. He withdraws his lips at last.*)
MAN: I love you and I would chain you to a wall

WOMAN: Yes
    Your possession of me is
    (*She shrugs.*)
    Terrible
MAN: Yes and what is more terrible is your reluctance to be
    possessed
    (*Pause. Her finger is still extended.*)
WOMAN: Put on the ring then
    (*He slips the ring on her finger. At the same time he slaps her
    violently across her face. She cries out. She staggers…*)
MAN: The ring has a chain
    (*She studies him.*)
    Not to escape now
    (*He goes to leave.*)
    Oh my loved bitch not to escape
    (*He goes. The WOMAN examines her finger and the ring. A
    YOUTH enters. He stares at her.*)
YOUTH: Married?
WOMAN: Married yes
    (*Pause. He is about to walk on, but stops.*)
YOUTH: The hand with the ring
WOMAN: The left
YOUTH: The left hand yes
    (*He undoes his shirt a little.*)
    Place this hand on my chest
    (*The WOMAN laughs. The YOUTH also for a moment…*)
    And after my chest use this hand with the ring to fondle
    my arse
    (*She looks at him.*)
    Let it glide let it climb let it travel my dark
    (*Pause. They stare.*)
    This hand with the ring
    (*The WOMAN is ambivalent. Then with decision she walks
    to him and kissing him, handles his body as he proposed. She
    suddenly lurches away from him. The YOUTH laughs and
    departs. The WOMAN examines her left hand in silence.*)
MAN: (*Returning.*) A youth came by
    (*She looks up at him.*)

I was going to the city he was coming from it we
exchanged a look how dangerous that can be it can
be death as the distance grew between us I thought of
this look the look it seemed to me was both charm and
malice I knew at once this look would be flung in your
direction how will she fend off such a look I wondered and
wondering I fretted I retraced my steps of course the ring
chains you you are chained by the ring still I fretted absurd
did he pass you did he look?
(*The WOMAN looks at the MAN.*)
WOMAN: I love you
MAN: I did not ask you if you loved me
WOMAN: I love you so much
  (*Pause.*)
MAN: Yes
  Yes
WOMAN: My darling
MAN: Yes
  Yes
  Your eyes are wet
WOMAN: Wet because I love you
MAN: Mine also
  (*He bites his lip, smiling. He wipes his eyes with the back of his
  hand.*)
  Did the youth pass?
WOMAN: Yes
MAN: And the ring?
  Perhaps it was enough to show the ring?
  Seeing it he thought this woman is owned but I am telling
  you you tell me what occurred
  (*The WOMAN is silent.*)
  You removed the ring
WOMAN: I love you
MAN: You love me but you removed the ring you saw the
  youth and casually oh I've seen it done one hand covering
  the other or behind your back swiftly slid it off your finger
  I've seen it done I ALSO HAVE BEEN A SEDUCER show me
  the ring show me show

(*The WOMAN extends her hand. The MAN kisses her fingers.*)

Warm ring

(*He sobs, half-enraged, half-abject.*)

WOMAN: I did not remove the ring

MAN: You did not

My darling

(*He looks up at her.*)

When you are an old woman and alone gaze at the ring
sometimes

WOMAN: I shall

MAN: And when your daughter marries let her wear it as a
bride

WOMAN: Yes

Yes

Now go to the city and if you pass a man do not retrace
your steps or

MAN: (*Laughing.*) I shall never reach the city at all

(*The MAN goes out. The WOMAN is pained, taut, she goes to call
him back, but stops. The YOUTH insinuates himself.*)

YOUTH: Deceive him again

(*The WOMAN looks at him.*)

DECEIVE HIM AGAIN

(*She hurries to the YOUTH and embraces him. She suffers. She is
ecstatic, she tears free, she is distraut.*)

WOMAN: THE RING

OH THE RING

YOUTH: Naked now

Naked now but for the ring

(*She hesitates, aroused, suspicious.*)

I STEAL YOU

I STEAL YOU

NAKED I SAID NAKED BUT FOR THE RING

(*The WOMAN goes to strip the clothes from herself but stops in
mid-movement.*)

WOMAN: Not stolen

Not stolen surely if I

YOUTH: (*A paroxysm of impatience.*) NAKED I SAID

(*Pause. She is quite still, a hand at a button.*)

WOMAN: What wills to be stolen cannot be thieved
YOUTH: UNDRESSED

OH

UNDRESSED

(*The YOUTH goes to tear away her clothing. The MAN hurries in and seizing the YOUTH, strangles him and lowers him to the floor. The WOMAN watches, a hand still at a button.*)
MAN: I knew this I knew this

(*He is glad, excited.*)

I was crossing a bridge and your words came back to me wonderful words I ran back I sprinted is he dead my running oh my running what wonderful words is he dead
WOMAN: Who cares if he's dead
MAN: DO NOT RETRACE YOUR STEPS YOU SAID

My darling I did retrace them

(*He offers a hand.*)
WOMAN: (*Looking at the body of the YOUTH.*) Take off your ring

(*She looks at the MAN.*)

That's what he said
MAN: You did not
WOMAN: I did not
MAN: And will not?
WOMAN: And will not

TAKE OFF YOUR RING

Never

Never

I shouted this never

(*She laughs.*)
MAN: I heard it
WOMAN: You heard it?
MAN: NEVER

NEVER YOU SAID

(*She kisses him swiftly, passionately.*)

•

# THE INVESTOR'S CHRONICLE

*A rich MAN holds a portrait by Holbein.*

MAN: I'm burning it
　(*Pause.*)
　I think
　I try to be honest
　I think
　Even as I bid for it
　As I lifted my fingers off my knee
　(I love those auctioneers they see the slightest movement
　it might have been a nod but I just lift my fingers off my
　knee)
　I knew it would be burned by me
　Yes
　The blood rushed to my face
　My heart beat quicker and this wasn't nerves this wasn't
　the anxiety of bidding in a public place the thrill of the
　accumulating figures
　(This went in tens of thousands incidentally)
　It was my terrible desire rising
　It was my animal leaning on its chain
　(*Pause.*)
　They were all
　Oh it was pitiful
　All after it the thin curators the dribbling collectors even
　yes an actor in dark glasses I don't know his name a
　million women wet themselves for him an American
　I don't know his name he sat stone still he was acting
　probably he never stops I left him far behind I left him at a
　million and a half he got up silently and silently he left he
　had no curiosity he had to make a film a million and a half
　so much for his love of art I smiled I particularly resent the
　proximity of actors actors belong in restaurants I permitted
　myself one thin smile
　(*Pause.*)
　Holbein
　(*Pause.*)

Holbein
(*Pause.*)
1553
(*Pause.*)
And it isn't as if I don't know art
Oh
The
Contrary
(*Pause. He takes out a hip flask, unscrews the top and sprinkles whisky over the painting.*)
Holbein is my favourite
Twenty years I waited for him
AND THE PUBLICITY
I won't quote
BILLIONAIRE RECLUSE
That's me
PAYS FOUR-POINT-FIVE MILLION FOR
Oh these figures get me down what do they know about art it's arithmetic to them the more noughts on the end the more appreciative they are
CONNOISSEURS MY
(*He takes out a cigarette lighter.*)
ANUS
(*Pause. He ignites a flame.*)
Holbein
(*Pause.*)
1553 they say I've got my doubts he was in Ghent in 1553 and yet the subject is an Englishwoman of course he could have travelled or so might she but 1554 is more accurate in my opinion but let the experts always let the experts let them let them I say
(*He is about to put the flame to the picture but stops.*)
And the frame's nice
The frame is pear inlaid with ivory
Which won't burn obviously
The ivory
Only the pear
The ivory
(*Pause.*)

I'll kick that into the flower bed
(*Pause, then he lets the flame snuff out.*)
I hate them all
I hate
I hate them all
(*Pause.*)
Not Holbein
Oh no
Not him
THOUGH HIM I MIGHT HAVE IF WE'D MET
I don't rule it out
A snob he was no doubt
He might have peered at me down his long nose he might
have revealed under those heavy eyelids a contempt for
me
(*Pause.*)
I hate them all but
(*Pause.*)
And I try to be honest
I do try
(*Pause.*)
That is not the reason I am burning it
I'M NOT A SCHOOLBOY
WHAT DO YOU TAKE ME FOR SOME SNOTTY VANDAL
SPRAYING HIS NAME ACROSS A BROTHEL WALL
I AM A BILLIONAIRE
(*Pause.*)
It said so in the papers
(*Pause.*)
I am burning
Not
A
Painting
No
Oh
No
I am burning all the human filth who make this painting no
longer a painting at all
(*Pause.*)

Of course it's personal it's private it's all to do with my
warped and tragically misshapen character my mother
my father my sordid history etcetera I was a criminal I
have done time beat up women on the Riviera shall I go
on my violent my anti-social etcetera shall I go on but
notwithstanding or
(*Pause.*)
Because
(*Pause.*)
Of such things I
Oh dear the whisky has evaporated
(*He drops the painting on the floor and stamps on it.*)
Painting
(*He shakes his head.*)
Once it was
Once
Once
(*Pause. He looks down at the splintered panel.*)
Then it became a mirror to an actor's
(He would have got it if not me)
An actor's vanity
A banknote
Or
Some
Thing
On
A
Wall
For parties of infants to gawp at
I DID HOLBEIN A FAVOUR
(*He jumps on the panel again.*)
I saved his soul
And mine
I saved that too
Really I am suffused with a sense of my
What is it
Yes
Religion
I am

Don't laugh
PECULIARLY ETHICAL
(*He drives his heel into the ruin on the floor.*)
And one must persevere because these connoisseurs these
dealers these museum curators in their Italian suits their
costly haircuts and spectacle frames they will oh give them
half a chance they will
(*He stamps now.*)
Restore it
They are so good at sticking bits together
Matchsticks
Fragments smaller than your thumb
More forensic than the police
Demonic
Leave a square inch and they create the thing
again
NO WONDER
IT'S GOT SIX NOUGHTS HANGING OFF THE END
(*He laughs now, kicking bits in every direction.*)
OR MORE
TEN NOUGHTS SOON IT NEVER STOPS
(*He grows tired. Pause. He looks up.*)
Rain
That helps
The acid in it
Eats through paint
Crows peck
Holbein
Just the thing to line your nest
(*Pause.*)
I am only a little mischievous
(*Pause.*)
This small amount of mischief enables me to carry through
an action which for most men would remain a thought
A trapped and strangled thought
So in the world of ethics a little mischief is a blessed thing
IT IS A SIGN OF MORAL HEALTH THAT ONE MAN ONLY ONE
ONE IS SUFFICIENT ONE CAN PERFORM AN ACT OF SUCH
DIGNITY LUTHER LUTHER

Holbein knew him possibly
LUTHER WAS SUCH A ONE
Mischief and Luther
Ha
Mischief and me
We the haters of idolatry
And unlike Luther I don't have my portrait painted
I don't say
POSTERITY REQUIRES MY PROFILE
GAZE UPON MY MUG YOU UNBORN MILLIONS
I'm rich
But vain
Oh I don't think so no I don't think vanity is among
my many
(*He stops.*)
HOW TERRIBLE TO HAVE TO DO SUCH
And already
Yes
Already the regrets come flocking in like starlings
in the Autumn
MIND THE SHIT
(*He covers his head in his hands.*)
MIND THE SCREECHING
The whirling cloud of persecution
GUILTY
GUILTY
OF IRREVERENCE
(*He ceases his antics.*)
No
We must love Man
Man we must admire
Since there's only Man
(*Pause.*)
I'll burn myself
Why not
Yes
Auto-da-fe
Private obviously
No witnesses

Puff of smoke behind the stables
Oh he's burning leaves they'll say
He's burning rubbish
My charred remains a subject of endless curiosity
BILLIONAIRE TORCHES HIMSELF
Headlines in the papers
And underneath in smaller lettering
Holbein missing
No
Not Holbein
Isn't he a footballer
OLD MASTER MISSING
And the price of course
Those six noughts again
Oh I can't wait
And I deserve it I deserve to fry and choke my fingers
wrapped around what what exactly a bible no a postcard
reproduction of a masterpiece any one will do
EXPIRING HERETIC
Subject for a painting in itself
I'm
I'm
IN
ECSTASY
(*He folds himself in his arms, shudders.*)
As
All
The
Martyrs
Were
(*He stops.*)
And I'm a martyr oh I am I am a martyr four-point-five I
paid for that a martyr yes I could have fed the starving of
the globe I could have swum their gratitude the garlands
of philanthropy perfumed round my neck but did I no I
have how infuriating for you all I've principles a lout with
principles what an excruciating paradox and now it's
(*He stops. He stoops, picks up a fragment of the panel.*)
My animal leaning on its chain

My great dark hound of malice
What a heart he has
(*Pause.*)
Lonely of course
(*He puts the fragment in his handkerchief and goes out.*)
•

# POET ASH

*Three louts see an urn.*

FIRST: The church door opened
SECOND: Not a church
FIRST: Not a church he says
SECOND: A chapel
FIRST: The chapel door opened
THIRD: We pushed it
FIRST: We pushed it and it opened
THIRD: Silly someone
FIRST: Silly not to lock it yes
SECOND: But had it been locked
THIRD: Still we would have opened it
FIRST: Not so silly therefore
    (*They perambulate, and stop.*)
    Funny chapel
SECOND: Nothing in it
THIRD: Not nothing
SECOND: Not a lot in it
FIRST: This would explain the absence of the lock
SECOND: To some extent
FIRST: To some extent it would explain the absence of the
    lock but not entirely since we have come across locked
    doors behind which
THIRD: When we broke the lock
FIRST: We found nothing only space
THIRD: Yet this space was locked
SECOND: And therefore beautiful
FIRST: True
THIRD: Beautiful space
    (*Pause.*)

In this instance whilst there is much space there
is also
(*Pause.*)
What is that?
(*They stare fixedly.*)
Read
Someone
Read
The
Plaque
(*Pause.*)
SECOND: Laxon
His
Mortal
Remains
It
Says
FIRST: Laxon
THIRD: Kick it
FIRST: Laxon
SECOND: Another nobody
THIRD: Kick it I said
FIRST: A nobody who has a chapel
SECOND: Families could live in here
FIRST: The poor where are their chapels?
SECOND: A fridge there
THIRD: I'm kicking it
FIRST: A shower unit
SECOND: Make it cosy get a lock
THIRD: Shall I or not?
(*Pause. They look at one another.*)
Kick his ash?
(*They hesitate.*)
SAY SOMEONE
(*FIRST and SECOND shrug indifferently.*)
Saved
His
Ash

FIRST: Laxon was a poet a poet and a nobody by kicking his
ash we would only align ourselves with critical opinion
which is not our way is it if anything we should unearth
Laxon and learn one of his awful sonnets bawling it
in town squares at night let us rather kick the ash of
Shakespeare Dryden or somebody somebody not nobody
I have a soft spot for these nobodies in urns some of whom
SOME OF THE NOBODIES were unjustly eliminated not all of
course most nobodies are rightly regarded with contempt
Laxon we can't say whether Laxon deserves obscurity or
not can we we cannot say
(*Pause.*)

THIRD: My passion for kicking things

SECOND: Not only yours

THIRD: Not only mine kicking we have in common

SECOND: It unites us

THIRD: It does but my kicking is independent of my moral
attitudes if I have moral attitudes

FIRST: I'm not sure that you do

THIRD: I'm not sure that I do I kick spontaneously I kick for
pleasure

FIRST: Yes

THIRD: So when I kick the ashes of this poet over the floor
am I saying I think he is a bad poet not at all I am not
saying anything
(*Pause.*)

FIRST: Yes
(*Pause.*)
Yes I think that is the case with you
(*Pause.*)
And I am not protecting the ashes of this probably bad
poet from your spontaneity kick on I was being whimsical
Laxon what a stupid name kick by all means
(*Pause.*)

THIRD: Can't now
(*Pause.*)

FIRST: Can't now?
(*SECOND laughs.*)

THIRD: Can't
    (*He shrugs.*)
SECOND: Gone you see
    The spontaneity
    Gone
FIRST: How often has this crucial hesitation saved Laxon's
    ashes from a rude dispersal obviously no one can remain
    in a state of excitement over Laxon for very long his very
    insignificance ensures the preservation of his memory
    (*He starts to leave.*)
    Come back tomorrow possibly
SECOND: We won't
FIRST: (*Going out.*) No we won't probably
THIRD: (*Marching out.*) Leave the door open
SECOND: Leave it yes
THIRD: (*Calling.*) Wind and rain
SECOND: Wind and rain
    (*He goes out.*)
    •

# BLIND PREJUDICE

*An OLD WOMAN seated. An OPTICIAN enters with a pair of spectacles.*

OPTICIAN: Do you want to see?
OLD WOMAN: I want to see I want to eat I want to walk
OPTICIAN: I don't do teeth I don't do legs
OLD WOMAN: You do eyes
OPTICIAN: Eyes yes
OLD WOMAN: Start with the eyes then
    With eyes I'll find my way to the legman
    And with legs to the dentist
OPTICIAN: Yes
    (*Pause.*)
    But do you really want to see?
    (*Pause.*)
    Always I ask this always I remind my clients of the
    consequences it's only fair it's only honourable so many

opticians nowadays simply prescribe they dish out
spectacles like sweets they fling sight at everyone it isn't
proper this profligacy sight is precious try these
(*He balances the spectacles on the OLD WOMAN's nose. He
stands back.*)
These came from a murderer
(*Pause. The OLD WOMAN strains her vision.*)
Not a vicious one he suffocated a sick child
(*Pause.*)
Still technically a murderer
(*Pause.*)
Let us call him a bus driver who happened to become a
murderer
(*Pause.*)
For he was a bus driver that was unambiguous

OLD WOMAN: Can't see a thing
(*She twitches her nose.*)
Can't see a thing and why should I have second hand
things just because I'm old I am sick of being thrust to the
back of the queue remove them please and fetch another
pair

OPTICIAN: These are the ones

OLD WOMAN: How can they be they were made for a
murderer

OPTICIAN: They were but all the same they are perfectly
suited to your needs

OLD WOMAN: I can't see anything

OPTICIAN: So you say

OLD WOMAN: I don't say I'm certain

OPTICIAN: You are a difficult woman and full of prejudices
I now wish I had never mentioned the fact of these
spectacles having originated with a murderer if I had kept
that to myself you would now be thanking me profusely
for restoring your sight take them off give them back stay
blind it's nothing to me if you collide with lamp posts he
was a bus driver he paid his taxes he voted at elections and
the murder he committed was committed out of love out
of compassion you are privileged to be the owner of his
spectacles and all you do is

OLD WOMAN: Shh

OPTICIAN: Mutter grumble and

OLD WOMAN: Shh

OPTICIAN: Pretend they are not suitable examine your
conscience examine it though it's probably as decayed as
all the rest of you give them back
(*He extends his hand. Pause.*)

OLD WOMAN: Perhaps they
(*Pause.*)
I don't know they
(*Pause.*)
If I

OPTICIAN: Go on

OLD WOMAN: (*Straining.*) Half close my eyes

OPTICIAN: Yes

OLD WOMAN: I
I

OPTICIAN: Good

OLD WOMAN: Can just make out the

OPTICIAN: Good
Good

OLD WOMAN: Vaguely

OPTICIAN: (*Urging her on.*) Fight
Fight
Your
Prejudice

OLD WOMAN: (*Triumphantly.*) Yes
Yes
They'll do

OPTICIAN: (*Offended.*) Do?
Do?

OLD WOMAN: Thank you I am entirely satisfied with these
my life's transformed

OPTICIAN: Excellent
And now I must confess a prejudice of my own which
is that with regard to the aged I sometimes doubt their
rationality their intellectual flexibility their willingness to
entertain a new idea how wrong that is in your case forgive
me please

(*The OLD WOMAN laughs.*)
Forgive me I said
(*Pause.*)
OLD WOMAN: I do
I do forgive you
Now I must be
(*She tries to get off the chair but falters.*)
Oh
I nearly fell
I
I so nearly
(*Pause.*)
Perhaps if I moved them further down my nose
The spectacles
I might
The floor seems all
(*Pause.*)
Ha
Getting used to them
(*She starts off again.*)
Oh
I
Oh
Swimming
Swimming all the
Thank you
Goodbye
(*She lurches.*)
OH
OH
(*She steadies herself.*)
OH I CAN'T SEE A THING AND
(*She flings away the spectacles.*)
FUCK ALL MURDERERS
(*The spectacles slide across the floor. The OPTICIAN gazes at them…*)
Off to the dentist now
Off to the maker of new legs
(*She goes out. The OPTICIAN picks up the discarded spectacles.*)

OPTICIAN: You
> Only
> See
> (*He puts on the spectacles.*)
> What
> You
> Require
> To
> See
> AND YOU WANT VISION YOU WANT ALL LIFE UNDER YOUR
> GAZE GLUTTON THE PLAINS OF AFRICA THE TROPICS STUFF
> IT IN OLD MONASTERIES THE MOUNTAINS OF TIBET GREED
> GREED SHOVEL IT THROUGH THE SOCKETS PAINTING AND
> PORNOGRAPHY
> How perfect
> Only the shade and the glow of the sun
> (*Reaching his hands before him the OPTICIAN departs.*)
> •

## SOUTH OF THAT PLACE NEAR

*A WOMAN holding a postcard.*

WOMAN: The post office
> The trickery of the post office
> The trickery and malevolence of the post office
> The trickery malevolence and criminal mismanagement of
> the post office
> Is legendary is it not
> THEY DELIBERATELY CONCEAL THE ORIGINS OF LETTERS
> How can they in an age of such sophisticated and sensitive
> machinery contrive to
> SMUDGE THE CANCELLATION MARK
> It's deliberate
> Oh yes
> It's human intervention
> Some clerk read this some sorter I don't know some minor
> I don't know some operative at the very lowest levels
> read it bored perhaps thought oh a postcard I'll read that
> stopped the machine oh yes they can be stopped trod on a

button stopped it paused and read squinting short-sighted
put his glasses on read my read his the few untidy words
and thought I'll smudge I'll cause the name of this place
to be rendered utterly illegible not just difficult but utterly
oh utterly he must have smiled he must have known
and smiled at my inevitable frustration laughing loud
triumphant smudging card from nowhere
JOIN ME
JOIN ME
SAYS MY LOVE
(*Pause.*)
Picture of a mountain and a cable car and underneath
the legend the mountain and the cable car as if it wasn't
obvious but I don't criticize I keep my passionate
resentment for those who most deserve it
HOW MANY MOUNTAINS
SNOW-CAPPED MOUNTAINS
HOW MANY SNOW-CAPPED MOUNTAINS HAVE A CABLE CAR
And it's antique
The card
Typically he sent an antique card black and white or grey
to be precise no brilliant colour splashed with names of
the resorts no discreet ever discreet the mountain and the
cable car the stamp is Swiss that helps ha a Swiss mountain
with a cable car ha and even if the mountain has not
changed the cable car certainly has
JOIN ME
JOIN ME
Oh I want to
Oh I so want
(*She aches. She bites her lip.*)
He might have written such and such a place
(*Pause.*)
He might have but he's hasty passionate and so on
probably he thought the name was there in black and
white but being passionate and hasty did not check I'm the
same we are alike so very much alike he was inspired look
the handwriting inspired and steeply sloping to the right
HE'S WAITING AND I HAVEN'T COME

(*Pause.*)

No the guilty party in all this is the anonymous and paltry
clerk who knew my heart would break

A MURDERER OF THE EMOTIONS

Imagine his diseased and wretched life his poverty his
obscurity no wonder he plucked it off the moving line
of letters like a hawk swooping his talons sharp to spoil
another's happiness why didn't he simply burn it no
obviously he anticipated the breaking of my heart and
smiled

THE MOUNTAIN AND THE CABLE CAR

WHICH MOUNTAIN LAUGH ON YOU

WHICH CABLE CAR OH LAUGH YOU VILE

(*She is stopped by a thought.*)

Or

(*Pause.*)

Or

(*Pause. She suddenly drops the card to the floor.*)

The infantile behaviour of this clerk his pernicious
instincts his wormlike triumphs are nothing but the shrill
cries issued by grinding machinery the machinery of
an individual's fate yes why not why not regard it from
another point of view an altogether different

(*She snatches it off the floor.*)

Thank God the identity of this mundane holiday resort
shall be forever illegible to me what kind of man pricking
an atlas with a pin would settle for such a

JOIN ME

JOIN ME

Where

There

Ha

Contemptible imagination am I to be seduced by this
what this what

HEALTH RESORT

And there are Baltic cities clinging to the sea whose spires
pierce the mists and Syracusan colonies where lizards flirt
between the brows of fallen statuary Zeus Apollo Pan

A HEALTH RESORT

*(A snort of contempt. She seems to shudder faintly. Pause…)*
The postman spared me
Imagine my years of disappointment is anything
worse than a woman who has yielded up her life to an
unsatisfactory man I should have looked with such dead
eyes as he announced some fatuous initiative some futile
holiday I've seen it oh I've seen these women grey with
shame
OH NEVER ME THAT DIM LABOUR
*(She tears the card across. She is still.)*
Certainly I should have been there
In clean clothes
Certainly
My little bag patient as a spaniel on the rack
Certainly have been on the train
My hat
This way and that in the mirror pluck and tuck my hair
Oh
Certainly
*(Pause. She extends one half of the card before her and turns it…)*
Santa Maria
*(Pause. Her hand remains outstretched.)*
How clear it is the word black under black when sunlight
strikes it some things cannot be obscured the police know
that under the ink another ink I'm so
Oh so
RELIEVED
To know I do not have to go
No obligation even though I know the place I should have
run to even one hour ago
SANTA MARIA
The mountain and the cable car
Sit alone then
Meet every train
And looking down the platform see me never there
A dying dream
Your heart shrinks
Hurts
YOUR HEART HURTS WITH MY ABSENCE

A Pernod
Another Pernod
Darling
How hard those streets lean on your nerves
The sarcastic sun
The
Unconsoling
Earth
Sheds
On
Your
Shoes
•

# THE HERMIT'S WAR WITH GOD

*TWO POOR MEN carry a brimming bucket of water between them.
They put down the bucket and wait. A THIRD POOR MAN enters,
stares at the bucket, and with a desperate move, flings himself down
beside the bucket and drinks deeply and desperately. Satiated at last,
he lies on his back, shielding his eyes with the back of a hand. The
carriers go to remove the bucket.*

STILPO: No
　　*(The MEN stop, hands to the bucket handle.)*
FIRST/SECOND POOR: No?
　　*(They look at one another.)*
FIRST POOR: Master we are emptying the bucket
　　*(They go to lift it.)*
STILPO: Leave the bucket
SECOND POOR: Leave the bucket? But it's got water in
STILPO: LEAVE IT WITH THE WATER IN
　　*(The POOR MEN are troubled, thoughtful. Pause.)*
SECOND POOR: Forgive us Master but is it not the case that
　　if we leave the bucket full of water it will be impossible for
　　you to resist drinking it?
　　*(The THIRD POOR MAN struggles to a sitting position and
　　looks critically at the carriers.)*
　　Better surely to contemplate the empty bucket as you have
　　in the past?

(*His look reduces the SECOND MAN to a state of shame.*)

We will leave the bucket full

(*They go to leave.*)

STILPO: I hold God in a terrible embrace

SECOND POOR: Yes

STILPO: As He holds me

SECOND POOR: Yes

STILPO: I shall not drink the water

SECOND POOR: No

STILPO: Obviously this will be worse for me

SECOND POOR: Much worse

STILPO: But because it is much worse my victory over God will be much greater

SECOND POOR: Certainly

(*Pause.*)

Master may I say that should God overcome you and compel you to drink the water we would not I am certain I speak for both of us when I say this we would not even for one second experience the slightest diminution in our bottomless regard for you

FIRST POOR: Not for one second

SECOND POOR: In our eyes you have exceeded every

STILPO: Your eyes?

(*Pause.*)

What are your eyes to me?

(*Pause.*)

SECOND POOR: Forgive me my eyes are nothing to you shall we leave the bucket here or

(*He falters.*)

We'll leave it here

(*He turns to go.*)

STILPO: It can be done

(*They look at STILPO.*)

If I did not know I could live without water I should not attempt to live without water

(*They nod gravely.*)

This knowledge does not protect me from the humiliating urge to drink which overcomes me at regular intervals but

you will have noticed these intervals are growing greater
my struggle is reaching its climax leave the bucket where
it is I can observe it with the same detachment I might
contemplate a rock a skull a feather observe me from the
hillside in the normal way but you will not I promise you
see me make the signal for water again not again in this life
(*The TWO MEN bow to STILPO and withdraw. STILPO sits
cross-legged beside the bucket. He looks at it. After some little time,
the SECOND POOR MAN rushes in.*)

SECOND POOR: This can't work
    This won't work
    You are the greatest philosopher who ever lived
    I am ignorant and a pig
    But this won't work
    I love you
    Let a pig advise you
    (*STILPO is perfectly silent. The SECOND POOR MAN
    withdraws, humiliated… His sobs are heard distantly. STILPO
    moves, but only to stretch a limb. The FIRST POOR MAN enters,
    arms akimbo.*)

FIRST POOR: I've followed you for five years
    Some have followed you for ten
    When we go into a new city people say you are the
    followers of Stilpo Stilpo the Great and they lay down mats
    for us to lie on they feed us their best dinners and frankly
    sometimes we can steal their wives that is the scale of your
    reputation which we poor mundane idiots we share a little
    of and I have to say that reputation is rotting like an apple
    no worse than that a fish a stinking carcass of a haddock
    people say Stilpo is insane not insane we say but frankly
    no one believes us may I be frank you may be Stilpo but
    Stilpo seduced us with his brilliance Stilpo is more than
    Stilpo he is also us
    (*The FIRST POOR MAN puts his fingertips together. STILPO is
    silent.*)
    And this silence is that a proper way to treat the public
    frankly I

*(He chews his tongue. He runs out. A pause. STILPO moves, but only to stretch a limb. Someone tosses a pebble. Then another. After a while, a third stone lands. STILPO ignores these provocations. The pebbles form a little landscape around him.)*

STILPO: The heat

(I refused a parasol)

The lack of water

(Despite its proximity)

The entirely predictable treachery of my erstwhile friends

Will certainly cause me to hallucinate

This phase of hallucination will be God's final try

And I will treat it with the same contempt I treated

all His other tries

I submit to nothing

I refuse His discipline

*(A PALE GIRL enters. She stands before him.)*

Precisely as I anticipated

Odd

I correctly judged the hour when my mind would

falter

Some little turbulence in my vision some strange

rhythm in my breath

PALE GIRL: Kiss me

STILPO: My lips are cracked and because I pursued girls in my youth it does not follow I will pursue them now on the contrary my first successful mutiny against God was ridding myself of the urge to kiss just as I gaze into this bucket so I gazed into the open thighs of girls I triumphed then and I will triumph now do not attempt to drag me back to the territory of earlier campaigns please

*(Pause. At last he shifts a limb.)*

PALE GIRL: If you won't drink water drink my milk

*(Pause.)*

STILPO: That is precisely the sort of cleverness I have come to expect from God and like all His cleverness it does not stand examination does He seriously believe I would suffer the ordeal of liberating myself from a dependence on water only to submit to a dependence on a woman's milk how poor He is more and more I see the poverty of Him the wretched quality of His ideas keep your milk for your infant I shall cease hallucinating in a while it is only a phase

(*Pause.*)

PALE GIRL: I have loved you for years

STILPO: Have you I have never seen you before now please go the effect of this conversation is to increase my thirst as He well knows you are His agent obviously I shan't speak again

(*Pause.*)

PALE GIRL: And when you die I will hold you it is my mission

(*STILPO ignores her.*)

Let them ridicule you I don't care

(*Pause.*)

Your fetid breath I'll inhale to the last gasp

(*Pause.*)

And lifting your thin body onto a cart I'll drag you through jeering crowds to a silent grove a place no one can find you and make your grave with my bare hands among the tree roots you will nourish a towering elm a spreading elm a king of trees

(*Pause.*)

Or

(*Pause.*)

Or

(*Pause.*)

I'll sacrifice my infant on an altar I never loved its father it was a brutal and pitiful act of concupiscence a sordid transaction in an alleyway do you need to know more so if you die so will this child it means nothing to me girls are always cutting babies' throats but I won't cut his throat the water you decline to drink I'll drown him in

(*Pause. At last STILPO moves a limb.*)

You see how everything can be made into its opposite what could be more innocuous benign and beautiful yes beautiful than a bucket of clean water and yet

STILPO: Shh

PALE GIRL: Here I am proposing to find an altogether
different use for it the beautiful becomes hideous the
life-giving is suddenly

STILPO: Shh

PALE GIRL: I mean it

I mean it

(*Pause.*)

STILPO: If you have no regard for this infant why should I
have you see it is a weakness of God and further evidence
of His fathomless vanity that having bestowed life upon
His creatures He dares presume our everlasting gratitude
will ensure we cling to it value it in others shudder at the
spectacle of death and so on drown your child by all means
babies are plentiful now I'm thirsty from arguing but that
only brings the crisis nearer I'm desperate for a drink but
that was inevitable

I stare

I stare the bucket in the face

BURN SUN

BURN

(*He gazes fixedly into the water. A pause elapses. The PALE
GIRL is desperate.*)

PALE GIRL: It's true God sent me

I'm His agent

Flirt He said

Show your pants blackmail him anything

BUT MAKE HIM DRINK

He's frightened of you

He thinks you might just conquer thirst

So do I

He thinks it's you or Him

So do I

ANOTHER GOD A BETTER ONE BORN BESIDE THE BUCKET

I'll drink if you don't mind I'm not a god I admit

I have these rather ordinary needs

(*She goes to stoop and drink.*)

STILPO: Fetch your own

(*She stops.*)

PALE GIRL: Fetch my own but you don't want it
    (*Pause.*)
STILPO: I like it before me
PALE GIRL: I don't want all of it
STILPO: There is a stream a hundred yards away go to the
    stream
PALE GIRL: I can't I'm ill
STILPO: Crawl
PALE GIRL: I won't crawl
    (*She draws up her knees and sits crossly. Pause.*)
    How unkind you are I could stop loving you so easily
    (*STILPO ignores her.*)
    Unfortunately my devotion is such that no matter how
    cruel you are still I
    (*STILPO emits a pained cry. His hands grasp the sides of the
    bucket. The PALE GIRL watches, a hand in her mouth…*)
    Drink…
DO
DRINK…
    (*He ignores her.*)
    I know how you got like this you find life unsatisfactory
    since you were a boy things always seemed less much less
    than they might have been even beauty failed to move
    you forests sunsets rivers falling over cliffs nice but not
    nice enough and someone had to bear responsibility for
    this someone needed to be blamed for such a string of
    disappointments as your life has been who else but God
    since He created everything and this penetrating gaze of
    yours has I know for certain has made God ashamed why
    don't you leave it there THE SHAME OF GOD is adequate
    surely that must satisfy your rage
    (*Pause, then STILPO emits another cry.*)
    GOD SENDS HIS APOLOGIES TO YOU
    (*Pause. STILPO collapses beside the bucket and is still. Flies
    murmur. The PALE GIRL dips her fingers in the water, plays
    like a child.*)
    Die then
    (*Pause. The TWO POOR MEN enter, mournfully. They stare at
    the body of STILPO.*)

FIRST POOR: Great was Stilpo

SECOND POOR: Stilpo did not drink

FIRST POOR: A bucketful of water and still he

(*Pause. The same idea occurs to both of them. Their hands reach for the handle and stop.*)

SECOND POOR: Not any old water

(*They smile.*)

FIRST/SECOND POOR: THE WATER STILPO DID NOT DRINK

(*They carry it out between them, religiously. The PALE GIRL hesitates then runs after them calling.*)

PALE GIRL: I loved him

I loved him

•

# LISTEN I'LL BEAT YOU

*A drum, violently beaten by a man. A WOMAN appears, armed.*

WOMAN: Noise you can keep it

(*The man glares.*)

DRUMMER: Noise?

Noise?

WOMAN: I bought this house

Is it silent I said

Silent he said what is silence not silent no I don't make
false claims but the noise he promised came only from the
throats of birds wind in the grasses etcetera get that fucking
thing away from here you itinerant trouble

(*The man glares.*)

DRUMMER: Trouble?

Trouble me?

WOMAN: The world is small and getting smaller obviously
I kept this in mind this shrinking character of the world
and did not ask more than I seemed entitled to some have
cars with seven doors some have kitchens higher than
cathedrals I don't criticize I asked only for one room silent
as a pool and now you appear and rape the air

DRUMMER: (*Glaring.*) Rape?

Rape me?

WOMAN: And I don't beg I don't plead straightaway I reach
for the gun this reaching for the gun was never my desire I
much preferred to ask but asking I never failed to observe
always left a thin smile on the face of my antagonist here's
the gun off you go now I will hole the drum and if you
thrash the holed skin you next
(*Pause. The man seems patient.*)

DRUMMER: I bring you my ecstasy and you recoil
(*He shakes his head.*)
I bring you the passion of my life and you shrink
(*He shrugs.*)
I pity those like you who have no blood left in their veins

WOMAN: I'll be bloodless I am drawing back the mechanism

DRUMMER: You oppress your spirit

WOMAN: What are you the spirit I am now aiming

DRUMMER: (*Indignant.*) I WANDER THE WORLD

WOMAN: Wander it quietly

DRUMMER: (*Snatching the drum.*) I'LL GO
(*He starts to move.*)
I'll go
Poor woman
Poor pale woman in fear of her soul

WOMAN: Others will welcome you quick now

DRUMMER: Yes
Oh yes
(*He stops and turns.*)
WHY THIS
OH
WHY THIS GNARLED AND ARID SILENCE IT ENRAGES ME
(*He glares at her.*)

WOMAN: (*Aiming the gun again.*) Swift or

DRUMMER: I LIBERATE YOUR PASSIONS I UNTIE YOUR
KNOTTED LIFE

WOMAN: SWIFT
SWIFT
(*He trembles, hesitates, runs. Alone, the WOMAN lowers the gun.*)
The grasses again
The birdsong oh
(*She listens.*)

The grasses again
The birdsong oh
(*She listens. Her fingers twitch. She taps her palm.*)
DRUMMER
DRUMMER
DRUMMER COME
(*Pause.*)
The grasses again
The birdsong oh
(*The DRUMMER is discovered passing silently. He stops.*)
DRUMMER: Plead
Plead for my noise
Plead for my trouble
Plead for my raping of the air
(*The WOMAN bites her lip in her anxiety. She shakes her head
bitterly.*)
WOMAN: The grasses
The
(*He taps the drumskin with one finger.*)
The bird and
Oh
The bird
THE BIRD
(*He taps louder. She shudders, covering her ears but her efforts
are in vain. She grins at the DRUMMER who delights in her
capitulation, beating now with his hand and then, pulling the
sticks from his belt, creating a crescendo of noise. The WOMAN
falls to the ground, oddly mobile. The man stops. She is still.*)
DRUMMER: I'll help myself to dinner
(*He goes to the house.*)
Is there beer?
(*She nods. He goes in.*)
WOMAN: (*After some moments.*) DRUMMER
DRUMMER
DRUM
(*In the silence, only birds are audible. The WOMAN sits up and
crossly bangs the floor with her fists.*)
DRUMMER DRUM

DRUMMER: (*Appearing, chewing.*) Up now
> And wiggle your arse
> (*He laughs, beating the drum. The WOMAN shakes and shudders in her ecstasy. Suddenly he stops. She freezes also. The DRUMMER goes to the house.*)
> I saw cake
> I saw tea
> (*The birds are heard in the silence. The WOMAN sobs and then bangs the floor with her hand.*)

WOMAN: DRUMMER DRUM
> (*He does not appear.*)
> DRUMMER
> DRUMMER DRUM
> (*He appears. She grins.*)

DRUMMER: Take off your skirt now I'm entering you

WOMAN: (*Hesitating.*) The birds they
> (*She shrugs.*)
> The birds

DRUMMER: I entertain the birds
> (*He unbuckles his belt. She recoils. He taps the drum. Her resistance collapses. She laughs.*)

WOMAN: Over the drum
> Over the drum lay me
> (*She turns the drum on its side and drapes her body across it, anticipating his act. He waits, stimulating her desire. Then with a cruel gesture, brings down his belt over her buttocks. The WOMAN gasps. After this single cut he sits. The birds sing.*)
> Surprises I will get accustomed to
> Anticipating pleasure I will welcome pain
> And
> The
> Reverse
> Quite
> Possibly
> Yes
> Surely
> The
> Reverse

I DON'T FEEL ABSURD

How wonderful no matter what occurs I never sense I am
absurd the very idea of discriminating between the absurd
and the unabsurd seems fatuous primitive old fashioned
so what if my arse is in the air so what so what no these
notions of embarrassment belong to the dark ages fuck me
now

(*The DRUMMER gets up and delaying for a moment, thrashes
her again. The WOMAN cries out, then laughs.*)

I used a coarse word perhaps the coarse word caused
offence but standing words in order approving some
words but incriminating others seems to me a relic of a
suffocating social system I have broken free of and whose
rules I now

DRUMMER: A whisky and I'm leaving did I see a whisky?
(*Pause.*)

WOMAN: Leaving?

DRUMMER: A whisky something in a bottle something
women use to smother pain brandy then a brandy and I'm
leaving
(*Pause.*)

WOMAN: I don't agree
(*Pause.*)

DRUMMER: Agree with what?
What don't you agree with?

WOMAN: My drummer leaving

DRUMMER: The drummer leaves it is the way of drummers

WOMAN: Pity

DRUMMER: The very act of drumming makes him leave

WOMAN: Pity
Pity again

DRUMMER: He marches
He wears out his shoes
And love he passes through the gates of like a field

WOMAN: I have shown you my arse
I
Who have never shown her arse
Not even to the sun
Have shown my arse to you

DRUMMER: A fine arse and I smacked it

WOMAN: This was the drum

DRUMMER: What else but the drum?

    A whisky and I must go

WOMAN: The drum is coercive but so is the gun

DRUMMER: Adieu I say

    To you and your arse

WOMAN: (*Rising.*) Here is your grave

    Look

    One day we say the drummer came and met his fate

    Under the turf the drummer

    His sticks protrude for a winter then decay or the birds by their incessant perching topple them

    IT WOULD HAVE BEEN ANOTHER IF NOT ME

    ANOTHER FARM

    ANOTHER HOVEL BY THE ROAD

    (*He looks at her levelled gun.*)

DRUMMER: I open doors but don't go through them

    It is a vocation opening doors

    (*The WOMAN is unmoved.*)

    Be grateful for my leaning on your door and I shan't stay for the whisky

    (*He plucks up the drum. There is a shot. The DRUMMER falls in a clatter of percussion. In the returning silence, the birdsong. The WOMAN is still…*)

WOMAN: If you can't keep the drummer you can keep the drum

    (*Pause.*)

    Unbeaten though

    Undrummed the drum

    •